Liberated Publishing
Presents:

Treva R. Gordon

50 MAGNIFICENT Men

Magnificent Men
Telling Our Stories &
Sharing Our Faith
will help motivate and
inspire every Man to WIN

Foreword Written by
Wess Morgan

LiberatedPublishing.com

Liberated Publishing Inc.
1860 Wilma Rudolph Blvd
Clarksville, TN 37040

ISBN: 978-0-9895732-9-0

First Printing: May 2015

Foreword by
Wess Morgan

> And I sought for a man among them that should
> make up the hedge, and stand in the gap before me
> for the land, that I should not destroy it: but I found
> none. Ezekial 22:30 King James Version (KJV)

God is always searching for a man. But the question is, what is God's definition of a true man? Many of us have different definitions of what a man is. Is it someone who has great sex appeal? Is it someone who has great influence or a large platform? Is he an arrogant man or one who thinks too highly of himself? Let's see what God really searches for.

Ezekial 22:30 shows God was in search of a man. The Hebrew word for man in this scripture is "iysh." "Iysh" is translated to mean "champion." God is searching for a champion!

A champion is someone who has first mastered his survival instincts. He is a warrior, a fighter, a man who doesn't know the meaning of giving up. He is one who does battle for another's rights or honor. He continues to fight and exist in spite of difficult circumstances or situations. You can't be a champion or a leader unless you've become a survivor. I know what it is to survive. It's getting up and moving forward every time you fall down.

Psalms 37:23-24 says, "The steps of a [good] man are directed *and* established by the Lord when he delights in his way [and he busies himself with his every step]. Though he falls, he shall not be utterly cast down, for the Lord grasps his hand in support *and* upholds him. Amplified Bible (AMP). There will be times that you fall, but rest assured the Lord is grasping your hand, upholding you, and encouraging you to continue to fight for survival.

As you read about these Magnificent Men, you will find a common thread that connects them . . . a survival instinct. You will find that some of the same obstacles, challenges, struggles that you are facing or have faced, these men have dealt with also. Life's challenges can often make us feel isolated and sometimes we ARE isolated. For the scripture says, "many are called, but few are chosen." Matthew 22:14 King James Version (KJV) Are you the individual that runs when it comes to a fight? Or are you the one who is a champion whom God has called and set aside to be an example of a Magnificent Man?

Born in Mississippi, but raised in Tennessee by an extremely musical family—his parents Joseph and Yolanda, both pastors, sang in and out of church—Wess knew at a young age that music and God was destined to be an integral part of his life.

It could be his powerful, soulful voice, or his refreshing delivery that makes inspirational artist Wess Morgan such a thrill to bear witness to. Or maybe it's because he has walked on a rough path—one that might have made another falter—that makes his music so moving, so unique, and so unforgettable. But one thing is for certain, Wess, by the grace of God, has proven that he is strong, resilient, and one of the most talented and anointed gospel / inspirational artists of this generation.

The road hasn't been easy, but because of his unwavering love of God, Wess is certainly on the right path. "God put something special in me and He was going to get it out of me regardless. I love my time before audiences because I know what God has put inside of me is life changing. That's why I love being on stage, because I see the people being blessed and there's nothing that can compare to it."

Contact: office@wessmorgan.com

Introduction by
Robert E. Gordon

What is the meaning of Magnificent? Magnificent is doing grand things; admirable in action; displaying great power or opulence, especially in building, way of living, and munificence (Webster's Dictionary). No doubt, Jesus was the first Magnificent Man. No one else can ever take His place, but as men we can set the example for others.

Men play a very important role in the home, work place, community, and in the church. It takes strong and determined Men to accomplish things that God has called us to do. When you hear of the word Magnificent being used, it should demonstrate honor. You should feel confident to accept what God has called you to do.

As a father, I will say to other men who are fathers to never take this title lightly. As Magnificent Men, you are more than just a father. You are a leader of your home. Your children are watching your every move. When you think they're not listening, think again. I remember my own father speaking great things to me. He helped me get on the right track and I'm thankful for it.

What does it take to be a Magnificent Man? I ask this question, but in saying, to not look at the appearance of a man. That can be misleading. But focus on the heart, a man's heart tells you a lot about him. A Magnificent Man loves and puts God first, and God has to come before his friends. He also has to love his wife and children. A Magnificent Man can never neglect his family. A

Magnificent Man must accept what God has called for him to do. You hear men say all the time that they are waiting on God, but in reality, God is waiting on us.

A Magnificent Man shows respect to others. In order to respect something, one must consider it worthy of high regard. This is the attitude that men should have towards others.

A Magnificent Man protects others. To protect is to shield someone from exposure, injury, or destruction. A man who respects others will act to protect not just himself, but others as well, from various forms of exposure and injury.

A Magnificent Man takes responsibility of any matter. Many would rather talk about their rights than their obligations and duties, but there has never been a greater need for men who are willing to take responsibility for their actions. Magnificent Men don't use excuses about being caught up in the moment and not being able to resist temptation.

I would like to share stories about men in the Bible who were Magnificent, although some had shortcomings.

When we read of Moses, we remember events showing a Godly man and others that show a man who struggled with failure in certain areas. Even though he sometimes failed, Moses was a man consistently in tune with God's plan. He loved the people of Israel who God called him to lead. Moses claimed to not be a great speaker yet he was able to lead the Israelites for forty years out of Egypt.

When Moses led Israel out of Egypt, one of the young men who quickly rose to recognition was Joshua. He was chosen as one of the twelve spies to enter the land that God had promised to Israel. Most of the spies returned with negative reports but Joshua reported wonderful things. Joshua was an obedient follower. He was also known as a strong leader of Israel as they conquered the land that God had given.

Many times in the Bible, David is recognized as a man who followed God and was sensitive to the leadership of God in his life. We first learn about who David would become when God rejected Saul's reign and said that he would give the kingdom to a neighbor of Saul's who was a better man. When God said this to Saul, David was only a boy at the time and between the ages eight and twelve. God knew that David would grow up to be a man in tune with God's heart and plan for Israel. We cherish many of the Psalms that David wrote in the midst of troubles. David trusted God and knew that his strength came from Him enabling him to lean on God during times of trouble.

I pray everyone will enjoy these chapters written by Magnificent Men. Every author has his own story about how God was the reason he survived. I encourage every author and everyone who reads this book to stay in the race and trust God. Every day is not the same, but everyday God is awesome. Thanks for taking the time to read this book. God bless.

Robert E. Gordon
Business Owner, Author, Motivational Speaker
www.gordonpublishingnow.com

Table of Contents

MAGNIFICENT
MEN

Dedication

This book is dedicated to anyone in life with a dream. Just believe that you can do it, and God will give you the strength to climb. Special thanks to our military who serve, and to every father, husband, brother, and more. God is good.

Phil. 4:13

Adolph A. Dagan

He raises the poor from the dust and lifts the needy from the garbage pile. He seats them with noblemen and gives them a throne of honor. For the foundations of the earth are the Lord's; He has set the world on them. 1 Samuel 1:8

My name is Adolph A. Y. Dagan. I was born and raised in Togo, West Africa. I am a U.S Army Retired Veteran, a Minister, a High School French Teacher, and Founder of the Dagan Foundation and Action Bethesda. I am married to Kafui Malé Dagan and we have three children: Gédéon Mawugnon Dagan (6), Deborah Délagnon Dagan (4) and Michaela Makafui Dagan (1).

I have been passionate about education since the age of 5 when I was unable to walk to school because it was so far from my village. At the age of 7, I was finally able to go to school, but also lost my father. Despite the loss, I did well at the elementary school. In Togo, before one can enter the middle school called College (French system), one must pass an exam commonly called BEPC (Diplôme d'Étude du Premier Degré). I passed it easily, but I could not attend the middle school because my mother was old and a widow. She could not afford to send me to the middle school that was more than twenty miles from us.

The first day of school in September of 1987, it was a day I will never forget. While my friends and other students were at school, I was working on a farm. I was singing and crying. When we returned home, my mother's friend told her that I was so smart and needed to be in school. He loaned her 1, 200 F CFA ($2.00) for my tuition, and she agreed to pay him back after she sold cotton in February of 1988. My mother bought me some notebooks, pens, and pencils. A week later, I moved to the village where I could attend the middle school. I still didn't have the entire tuition fee, but some of my friends allowed me to share their dorm room.

In the middle of the school year, my roommates dropped out, because they did not do well in the classroom. I did not know where I would stay, because I could not afford the rent that was 700 f CFA (USD 1.00), a month. My mother took me to her half-brother of my sister's husband who lived in that village. Thanks unto God, he allowed me to stay with him. In the 9th grade, I fell ill in the middle of the school year, and I could no longer stay in the classroom. I went back home to my village.

The following year, my big brother Christophe took me to Atakpamé where he was a mechanic apprentice. Thanks to him, I finished the middle school and passed my BEPC (Brevet d'Étude du Premier Cycle). I had to overcome another hurdle despite having made a good grade to finally be admitted at Lycée de Notsé (high school). I am thankful to a superintendant (inspecteur) in Atakpamé who was once a principal of that high school. I moved to Notsé without knowing where I would stay. After a few months of school, the general strike began in Togo and schools were closed. All the students returned to their villages for the remainder of the year.

The following year, I decided to move into Bénin, a neighboring country, at East of Togo. It was tough over there because food was scarce. In Bénin, we registered as refugees. We had received some corn from the United Nations every month. At the end of the year, I returned to Togo and struggled until I received my high school diploma in 1997.

Upon completing high school, I registered in the University of Lomé (formerly University of Bénin). My goal was to become a medical doctor in order to treat the sick, or a lawyer, so I could help and advocate for the less fortunate. I eventually chose law school (Faculté de Droit) because unless your parent is a doctor, or you are very smart, it is difficult to become a doctor. At law school, I passed my first year. In the second year, I passed my written exams. As some classes are reserved for oral exams, we took those oral exams, and one teacher failed me and three other students. The experience was devastating; I prayed and cried out to God that night. When I fell asleep, I dreamed that I went to the United States of America.

When I awoke in the morning, I did not believe that dream, because I didn't know anyone who could help me get to America. I forgot that I serve the almighty God who works miracles and wonders. "What is impossible with man is possible with God" Luke 18:27. I began to have regular dreams that I was in the USA. I saw many places in America in my dreams while I was in Togo. I saw Black Hawk College (Moline, IL), I saw some hospitals in Moline, and I saw soldiers in the Army Combat Uniform (ACU). I did not know what these things meant. However, God was talking to me about what He was about to do in my life. You know, God is not far from us. He is very close to us and He is still talking to us. When we are in good relationship with God, He will talk to us, He will direct us.

I ended up having to drop out of law school, because I could no longer afford it. Fortunately, I was hired as a Biology and Mathematics teacher in a private middle school in Lomé. During every school break, I used to go to a prayer camp in order to fast and pray. Fasting and praying became a part of my life. I was looking for God every day. Besides prayers, I set rules for myself. I knew that holiness is a key to getting closer to God. I controlled my attitudes and refused to pursue women, while at the same time, I prayed that God would give me a good wife who would help me to perform His work. With each day, my faith grew stronger.

One night, I dreamed that two of my friends and I were next to a river where I saw some very thin branches. One of my friends walked on the river and crossed it. I asked him how he could cross it; he came back and encouraged me to cross it. I walked on those little branches and crossed the river. When I woke up, I understood that God was about to take me to somewhere but I had an obstacle blocking the way. Before the dream, we had been applying for the Diversity Immigrant Visa Program (DV Program). This program is administered by the Department of State. Every year, more than 50,000 visas are available and applicants from countries with low numbers of immigrants in USA are drawn at random and the lottery winners will immigrate to the United States through the consular processing. I continued to fast and pray every day and night.

In June 2003, a pastor from the Assembly of God, some other people and I, were gathered in the pastor's house every night and prayed for seven nights. At the end of the week, I kept praying in my house asking God to restore every blessing that the enemy blocked or engulfed in the mud. It was a Saturday, June 28, 2003 around 2:00 pm in Togo, while playing a game with friends; a friend photographer came to me with one of his friends. They showed a paper on which there was my picture. They said that some people were looking for me for a long time, because I won the lottery visa and the response got into their box, because a mistake was made about my address.

On the following day which was a Sunday, we went to the person who had the package. We opened the package, and we found out that the deadline of my paperwork had passed except

4

one paper that was "Supplementary Registration." It would expire the following day, which was Monday, June 30, 2003. The task of completing the paperwork in French and English to send to the United States on the same day seemed impossible given the limited technology available in Togo.

My friends told me not to do anything about it, because it was too late. I was trying to go to the American Embassy that Monday morning to see how they could help me, but the security guards did not let me in. They told me there was nothing that could be done about it. I knew that my God could do something about it. I went to the person who helped people complete the paperwork. He told me that it was too late, and he told me to go back home. When I tried to insist, he yelled at me and people laughed at me. They thought I was stupid, but I was not. I was just a man of faith. I knew after that I sent the package; I would go to fast and pray for many days and my God would perform a miracle for me. I asked the translator if he could do all of my paperwork the same day so I could mail my package back to the USA that same Monday. Usually, it took him two weeks or more to finish the paperwork. He had many customers. He accepted to take 10,000 f CFA (around USD 20.00) to do it. His team worked hard to finish everything the same Monday, so I could mail it.

For me, if the package arrived to the USA, God would make them accept it because of the date of shipping. By the time they finished, the post office was closed. The translator said that he would give me the fax number, so I could fax the package to them, but he could not find it. I still had faith that something would happen. Fortunately, one of the translator's employees said that he would send me somewhere, and they would scan my paperwork and send it to the USA by attaching the files. I went to the technology center, and they did it. It was my first time to hear about those two or three words such as "scan" and "attached files." It was about 6:30 pm in Togo and 1:30 pm in the United States. Thank God that the time in Togo is hours ahead of the USA.

The following week was our first week of my summer break. On Monday, June 7, 2003, I went to fast and pray to my Heavenly Father, God Almighty. On the first night of my fasting and praying, I dreamed about the response back from the United States, and I had to apply for the visa through the consulate. After my days of fasting and praying, I went back home and kept praying. God did exactly what He showed me in the dream. Yes, God is good and faithful. The next obstacle that I encountered was that I needed money for a passport, medical exams, visa interview, airplane ticket, luggage, and some cash in pockets for the trip. Through intensive fasting and prayers, God helped find money to accomplish all those things. I got my visa, and I came to this great country, the United States of America.

I came to Moline, Illinois. Thank God, I found job in manufacturing. I worked hard and paid back those who loaned me money in Togo for my medical exams, visa fees, airfares, and more. While working, I enrolled in Black Hawk College to learn English. I experienced difficulties commuting via the bus system, because I did not know how to count money to pay the driver. After my first day of class, I dropped out. I then went to the mall and bought an English –French dictionary, and English books coupled with CDs. While my friends who were placed in the lower levels went to school in the morning, I played my CDs and read my books and used my bilingual dictionary.

After a year, my English was better, even better than many of my friends who were attending school. I bought a car after I obtained a driver's license. After a year of English school, I decided to enlist in the U.S. Army. I took my first ASVAB (Army Service Vocational Aptitude Battery) test and failed. My recruiter told me to stay in school to learn English for a year before taking it again. I came back home and prayed hard. When a person comes to the USA, no matter your degree in your country, many things are new for you. Division, decimal measurement units and so on are different from the ones in many other countries. I studied a lot. Just after three weeks, I told my recruiter that I was ready to take another test. He accepted my offer, and I passed it by more than double digits of my previous score.

I went to Basic Training in Fort Jackson, SC and AIT (Advanced Individual Training) in Fort Lee, VA. It was not easy for me at all, but God helped me through. I was assigned to Fort Campbell, KY. I faced many challenges there. As soon as I got to Fort Campbell, I enrolled in the American Military University where I received my Bachelor's Degree in International Relations with Peacekeeping in 2010. After my medical retirement from the Army in 2009, I worked as an assistant teacher at Fort Campbell Schools where I found out that I could be a teacher in the USA. I went back to school at Austin Peay State University, where I later graduated with my Master of Arts in Teaching in 2014. I also received a Certificate of Ministry at Berean School of the Bible, a Global University School in February 2014. I become a high school French teacher in the Clarksville Montgomery County School System (CMCSS), in Tennessee. A dream that came true!

Before I came here, I founded "Les Elus de Dieu" (The chosen of God) dedicated in helping underprivileged children. Here, I became a big financial supporter of the organization and started to spread the Word of God. In 2007, I went back to Togo and Les Elus de Dieu then later changed the name to Action Bethesda. I established two elementary schools to help children for free education: Elementary School of Daganhoé and Elementary School of Bokohoé in 2007. In May 2012, I launched the Dagan Foundation in the USA. In partnership with Action Bethesda, the Dagan Foundation is promoting education, providing clean water, spreading the Word of God through evangelistic crusades and more. Through the Dagan Foundation and Action Bethesda, five churches are planted for the Assembly of God in Togo, and more than a thousand souls have been saved, and more than a thousand children have been sent to schools.

This is the photo I took in June 2014 with some students of Daganhoé Elementary School, the first school I established in 2007 in Togo for disadvantaged children.

I did not choose where to be born or parents to be born unto. No matter where I was born, no matter the conditions of my parents, because I received Jesus, my love for God, and obeyed Him, He was able to change my life and honor me. In the Mighty Name of Jesus, all of my dreams are becoming true. Amen!

Contact: adolphdagan@yahoo.com
www.daganfoundation.org
daganfoundation@yahoo.com
www.facebook.com/DaganFoundation
www.twitter.com/DaganFoundation

Alexander M. Young

And David enquired at the LORD, saying, Shall I pursue after this troop? shall I overtake them? And he answered him, Pursue: for thou shalt surely overtake them, and without fail recover all. 1 Samuel 30:8

I would like to formally introduce you to Minister Alexander Young. I am a man after God's own heart and I love Him from the inside out! I was born and raised in Chicago, Illinois and was reared by my mother Tanya R. Algee, who is the strongest, most independent woman I know. I was raised to go to church and was taught many Christian principles, especially that of "sparing the rod, spoils the child." I was definitely not spared the rod as I can share many stories of being disciplined as a child for misbehavior, but that's a different story. I grew up on the south side of Chicago, which is one of the most dangerous areas in Illinois. Dealing with the pressures of violence, poverty, and other attributes that make growing up difficult, it helped me to realize at a young age that I wanted to make a difference not only in my life but in the community.

One of the most important sayings I was taught growing up is that "everybody is not going to like you." From the 1st to 6th grade I had lots of friends. We shared so many great times together in and out of school, but that all changed when my family relocated to Dolton, IL, the south suburbs area. From 7th grade and until I graduated high school, my circle of friends was small. I was the underdog of the crew. The friends I did have were popular, but I wasn't. Other students would take advantage of my kind and tender heartedness, even some that I hung around with, and some would try to bully me. Seeing how I always made excellent grades in my classes, the others didn't take to kindly to my success. Talk about being different, there was even a time when I dated a lady whom I thought really liked me, but that turned out to be a fluke. She stopped talking to me after a week because I did not wear name brand clothing and I replied with a message to her friend "tell her to buy my clothes for me". After I graduated in the year 2000, I said to myself, what is next?

I went to a community college for 2 years. During that period of schooling, I was unsure about what I wanted to do, until something in my heart said to sign up for the Army. I began my military career approximately twelve years ago and I received even more discipline in my life in terms of developing me into a strong man of valor. I gained profound knowledge of submitting to leadership and following commands from those who had authority over my life. Romans 13:1 states, "Let everyone be subject to the governing authorities, for there is no authority except that which God has established. The authorities that exist have been established by God." The knowledge I gained while in the military prepared me and helped shape me into the man I am today.

While in the military, I began to encounter various adversities which forced me to grow while increasing my faith and trust in God. My biggest adversities in the military for me were serving in Iraq 3 times (OIF I, II and III). As a Human Resources Specialist in the Army, while operating in hostile areas where my life was in danger every second, I had to learn how to adapt and utilize my basic combat skills to survive. Meaning, I had to think like an infantryman, but trust the person to my left and right. I have seen the action, been in action, and felt the pain of action. What I mean by "felt the pain of action" is how I responded emotionally when I had to kill. Being shot at is very different from a gang shooting or being in a vehicle after hitting a bomb, and losing friends in combat. The most rewarding experience in the military was when I got promoted from a Specialist to a Sergeant. Having the experience of being a leader in the Army helped me to gain more knowledge of how to lead and mentor Soldiers. I am proud to say that I had a great leader who mentored and shaped me as a Soldier, and molded me into a leader. "Great leaders develop leaders," thank you Jerry Addy.

The Christian foundation that was instilled in me as a child allowed me to stay grounded despite the many challenges and heartaches of a military career. Although I enjoyed my career in the military, it was abruptly ended by some unforeseen circumstances. These circumstances caused me much discomfort for 4 years until God showed up and out and changed the circumstances. The main circumstance where God had His hand over my life is when I decided to leave the mess I put myself in. I was a knuckle head for a moment, but after discerning God's voice telling me to "LET GO", I decided enough was enough. I didn't care about nothing else but my faith in God. I liken myself to the apostle Paul, when the Lord isolated me and stripped me down so He could work on me. I lived in a shelter where I had no freedom to go to school, talk on the phone, use a computer, or even go to church. After being there for a few months, I was connected to someone who saw the need for me to continue my education and for me to be able to see my children and go to church on a regular basis like I always have. I left the shelter and was entered into a Homeless Veteran Program called "Buffalo Valley" which is ran by the Veteran Affairs. I had more freedom to do what I needed to do. The most unique and important factor is that I was led by the Spirit not knowing that I would run into that one who would believe in me, whom would help me to believe in myself even more and is my current Spiritual Father,

Bishop Anthony L. Alfred. It was awkward at first, because It seemed like God was telling me something, but I didn't know what it was, as if I already knew. I just couldn't put my finger on it, but I didn't know that he had chosen and called me to be a Preacher. I accepted the call into ministry and I love to preach with passion and excitement that is evident. The Holy Spirit has free reign to use me as an earthly vessel. I truly trust and believe the steps of a righteous man are ordered by the Lord, so whatever trials and situations come my way I know God is still in control.

Perhaps the most significant event that really helped me to grow and mature even more was when God placed a special woman in my life who truly loved me and was there for me. Patricia Denise Curtis was a very sweet and loving woman who took that step to unite as one with God and me. Though we were engaged, our plans changed when she was called home to Glory on Feb 21, 2014. I've experienced pain in my life, but not like this. What helped me bear and endure through the pain and sorrow was that I kept in my heart "Jesus You're the Center of my Joy". Pat engraved a love legacy in my heart and I said that I will carry it and live it. Before she went home, our forever words to each other were "I Love You."

I am an anointed man of God that sings on the praise team and is a praise dancer in my church. I am very proud to be a Minister under Bishop Anthony L Alfred, and also happy to be a member of Family of Faith Outreach Ministries. Community Chapel on Ft. Campbell is where I started, but I had to spread my wings and fly, and it will always be my home away from home church. I currently attend college full time and am also part of a virtual prayer ministry known as Spirit of Life Ministries. I minister to everyone I come in contact with, inside and outside the church, men, women, and children. I am able to relate to them in ways that encourage and uplift them in their journey through life.

I am a very humorous and outgoing person that brings a smile and/or laughter to those fortunate to be in my presence in person or over the telephone. Even on days when I am stressed or worried, I always have a kind word of encouragement to speak to others. I truly want to shine like a beacon of light to many, so that God may continue to elevate me for His GLORY!

I truly give thanks to God for who He is and everything He has done for and in me. I thank Him for my three lovely children: Alex Jr., Jonathan, and Omarion. I thank the people who pushed me and help me through my circumstances. I never thought that I'd be in this place.

Often there are times where we ask God, why me? We even ask ourselves why? We each have a divine purpose in life. Some might say that you are not going to make it, will not succeed, but let me tell you that your victory dinner is ready and your doubters, haters, and frienemies are invited. (**Thou preparest a table before me in the presence of my enemies** Psalms 23:5).

Everything that was stripped and taken from you, You are going to get it back, but You have to **"DO SOMETHING ABOUT IT."**

Contact: alexmyoung55@gmail.com

Ambassador Dr. Bobby Jones

Photo Credit: Scott Cameron
EchoPark JDI Entertainment (EPJ)

National TV and Radio, Recording Artist, Pioneer
"When the student is ready, the teacher will appear."
–Maya Angelou

Introduction

I worked unyieldingly to bring my love for gospel music to the world. It could be said that I am a simple country boy that loves the Lord, my family, my friends, my fans, and my supporters. I have a tremendous love for gospel music, television, radio, and stage. I'm committed to uniting a part of this world in peace and love and will always do whatever I can to contribute to the betterment of humanity.

I was born on September 18, 1938, in Henry, TN. Henry, TN is a little country town that has about 150 people, outside of another country town, Paris, TN.   I come from a rural poor background; but that never stopped me from achieving my dreams and goals since a young age.

I was determined that there was more in life for me. I was bright and focused even as a young teenager. I completed high school at the age of 15.   I went on to earn my Bachelors of Science degree and my Masters in Education. Both of those were earned at Tennessee State University in Nashville, TN. I hold two Doctorate degrees. I earned my first Doctorate in Education at Vanderbilt University; my second at Tennessee State University.

It makes me feel really good to know that I from a situation growing up in a small community where opportunities for direct social engagements were not there.   When I go back there and look around and see what's going on, I say thank You Lord for letting me move out into the world.

God's Plan

In the beginning, I hadn't the slightest idea that I would become what God has assigned me to become in the field of religion; especially Christianity.   I was planning to remain a school teacher or at the very least remain in the field of education. I was blessed to teach on many different levels. From 1959 to 1965, I taught elementary school in St. Louis, Missouri. I moved back to Tennessee and taught at the elementary level for Nashville Metropolitan Schools from 1966 to 1968. I have also had the opportunity to be an instructor for two different Universities. I began teaching at the University level in 1974 at Tennessee State University in their Reading Department. It was at this time that I helped develop the idea for the Black Expo in Nashville, TN.

The Black Expo was an activity held in cities across the country which focuses on the contributions African Americans have made to their communities. During this, I introduced the

16

pilot for what has become Bobby Jones Gospel to WSM-TV. Not only did I create the show, but **once** WSM-TV picked it up, I co-produced and hosted it. That first run ran from 1976 to 1982. Concurrently, I created, produced, and hosted **Bobby Jones' World**, a public service talk show from 1978 to 1984. From there I was blessed to have the chances to be in movies and plays. I even wrote and performed in the black gospel opera, *Make a Joyful Noise,* which aired on PBS in 1980. I was able to make connections across the music and television world, recording a duet with country star Barbara Mandrell and appearing alongside country star, Ronnie Milsap, in 1983 on his television special, *In Celebration*.

In 1984 I received not only my first Dove Award, but also a Grammy, and an NAACP Image Award. Over the years I earned many honors and awards including a presidential commendation from President George A. Bush for, "revolutionizing the gospel music industry" and "exposing numerous gospel music artists to the world." My career and ministry has turned into something I could not have ever imagined.

I never knew if I was going to do another season or not, but I always had a feeling that I was coming back to do it again. My program is in its 34th season at B.E.T. This is the love of my life. I stopped my other profession to do this, and the results have been immeasurable.

I get asked what I think about the older gospel vs. the newer gospel and even hip hop. My take on hip hop and any genre of music is this. I am fine with it if it relates to Christianity and is about the meaning derived from the words. We can't judge that so we have to accept whatever God puts out there. If he puts it out there then go get it.

It amazes me how God changed my plans. Becoming an Ambassador to not one but two nations was probably my biggest surprise of all. People don't realize that being an Ambassador is an official position that I was appointed to in the governments of those nations. I let people know that it's not just a title that I gave myself. I was appointed to a three-year term. I assumed my responsibilities as the Ambassador of Dominica in January 2007 and the Bahamas, 2013.

According to an official Dominica government document signed by Prime Minister Roosevelt Skerrit, I am authorized to negotiate on Dominica's behalf (in the procurement and financing of projects with the potential for carrying forward the economic and infrastructural development program of the government of Dominica). I was recommended for the job after meeting with several of Dominica's cabinet members and discussing the need for increased tourism and economic growth in the small country. Moreover, Dominica's government officials were particularly impressed with my charitable work in the United States with the American Heart Association, the Diabetes Association and the Lupus Foundation. You never know what God has in store for you. Never give up. Just be obedient and follow His help. I'm going to continue working on what I am doing now until I can no longer do it. I'm going to thank God for longevity in the field that I'm in. I love what I do. There is nothing that I would rather do other than what I'm doing today.

I have my own signature and so should everyone. Try to develop yourself, understand business procedures. Get different ideas and concepts about how people do things. You have got to be you. You have to play on your own concepts and work to develop ideas, then use those. We do learn from each other. We can observe and see different things that happen. You might want to bring that into your process. But it has to fit your goals and not theirs. You have to do things that please you and not necessarily everyone that is trying to tell you what to do. I have been in television about forty years. My procedures were mine. But listen carefully, I always sought advice from people that had gone on before me. I always observed, I always put myself in places with people and things that do what I do to learn from them even if they are not gospel. I'm in gospel, but television is television.

Some of the principles are the same. This is my first advice for anyone reading, do what you do. Allow God to order your steps. If it is not of God, you may get off track by seeing other things in life that you think you may want. If God gives you the desire, HE will give you what to say and do. Go for it.

FAMILY

I am left to carry on the banner in the memory of my whole family. My mother, father, sister and brother have all passed away. I am fortunate to have had the family that I had. Things were not always perfect, but my young life prepared me for the life that I have now. I love and appreciate my family.

My Career

My career has been about so much more than promoting me. It is a ministry that gives others a platform to propel into their ministries. As gospel artists, we are not in competition. We all should have one goal and that is to advance God's Kingdom. I have had the great fortune to work with so many artists but to name a few, Albertina Walker, Sally Martin, Patti LaBelle, James Fortune, Vickie Winans, Faith Evans, Kirk Franklin, John P. Kee, Yolanda Adams, Shirley Caesar, Hezekiah Walker, Tye Tribbett, and more. I have been truly blessed.

I am thankful for all of my accomplishments. I want to continue inspiring people to discover their passion. What is it that you want to do? I am having a blast at the age that I am now. It is important not to take yourself too seriously. Here are some of the things I have done since I left Henry County, Tennessee.

TELEVISION:
- Black Entertainment Television: "Bobby Jones Gospel," highest rated show on the network 1980 to current
- Black Entertainment Television:" Video Gospel," second highest rated show on the network for eighteen years, 1986 to current, producer and host

- The Word Television Network: "Bobby Jones Gospel Classics," and "Bobby Jones Presents" 2001 to 2010, producer and host
- The Gospel Music Channel: "Gospel Vignettes" 2006, host
- The BET Gospel Network: "Let's Talk Church" 2002 to current, producer and host
- The Gospel Music Channel, "Bobby Jones Next Generation", 2008 to current, host

AWARDS:

- The Gabriel Award: *"Make A Joyful Noise"* First Gospel Opera 1980
- The International Film Festival Award: *"Make A Joyful Noise"* 1980
- The Grammy: "I'm So Glad I'm Standing Here Today" 1983
- The Dove Award: "I'm So Glad I'm Standing Here Today" 1983
- The Stellar Award: "Outstanding Achievement Award" 1996, "The James Cleveland Award" 1998.
- "The Living Legend Award" 2005
- The Thomas A. Dorsey Award: "Father of Gospel Music" 1987
- Tom Joyner: "Hardest Working Man Award" 2003
- The Full Gospel Baptist Convention: "Trailblazer Award" 2003
- Congressman Al Edwards: "Unsung Hero Award" 2003
- Congresswoman Sheila Jackson Lee: Outstanding Service Award 2003
- President Bush Citation: "Revolutionized the Gospel Music Industry" 2001

BOOKS:

- Touched By God 1998
- Make A Joyful Noise: My Twenty Five Years in Gospel Music 2000

MOVIE AND STAGE PLAYS

- *Movie: Sister, Sister* by Maya Angelou
- *Stage Play, Musical Joyful Noel* by Walter Rutledge
- *Movie: Dirty Laundry* by Maurice Jamal

DISCOGRAPHY

- "Sooner or Later" 1978
- "There's Hope for This World" 1979
- "Caught Up" 1980
- "Soul Set Free" 1982
- "Come Together" 1984
- "Tin Gladje" 1985
- "I'll Never Forget" 1989
- "Another Time" 1990
- "Bring It To Jesus" 1995
- "Just Churchin" 1998
- "Live in Perusia" 2004
- "Faith Unscripted" 2007
- "The Ambassador" 2007
- " Rejoice With Me" 2014

Contact: Bjones1938@aol.com

Magnificent Man

"King" Antonio French

I am Antonio Leon French, also known as "King Antonio," which is the name I am known by as a Gospel Rapper and Evangelist. I chose to start going by "King Antonio" after looking up the meaning of my name. I found out that my first name Antonio means "worthy of praise." At first glance that perplexed me, because there is only One who is worthy of praise, and that is Jesus Christ. Later, it was revealed to me that Christ is worthy of the praise from me. I also found out that my middle name Leon means "kinglike," which I also understand better now because I'm made in the image of Christ who is the King of Kings!

From an early age, it was evident that I had a gift to rap. I was rapping in the elementary school hallways and making beats on cafeteria tables and tabletops. I even joined the school band and played drums. It was an insatiable passion for me even back then.

At eight years old, I can remember having a "Teddy Ruxpin" toy in one hand and a recorder in the other. I would use "Teddy Ruxpin" to play beats and rap to them instead of listening to the children's book cassettes that came with the toy. This passion for rap continued into my teens. I would freestyle rap wherever an audience was available including parks and parking lots. Even back then, an audience that appreciated my gift was never hard to find.

Though I had "rap swag," I consider myself to have been a weird "ugly duckling" up until the seventh grade. I was very insecure and socially awkward. After inheriting several brothers through my mother's relationship with a man, the game started to change for me. My brothers were everything I wasn't, and it wasn't long before they took me under their wings. They were known in the streets and got attention from the ladies. At one point, I was able to ditch riding the school bus because they started driving me to school. I felt like I was living! The fun of it all had me hypnotized. The atmosphere was captivating. It felt good.

I found out later that this new life had a downside. I began to feel that as long as I had money, I was ok, I was good, and robbery became my method of getting it. A life of crime afforded me many luxuries, but I had no idea that these luxuries would come at the cost of my freedom. By the age of seventeen, I was incarcerated for the first time for two counts of aggravated robbery. I was initially facing twenty-eight years but was offered a ten-year sentence for a guilty plea of which I served four years. I can look back and see that what I did was wrong, but at that time I couldn't see any other way. I didn't feel there were any other options.

One good thing that came from my four-year incarceration was that it gave me time to perfect my craft as a rapper. I learned different ways to rap and finally began to put some stuff down on paper. By the time I was released, I had hundreds of pages of songs written down.

Incarceration did change me in some ways but not in every way. When I got out, I refused to go back to certain things out of fear being incarcerated again, but I did go back to the same crowd and in many ways the same life. Not only that, but within the first year after my release, I stepped into the role of a father to a child that wasn't even mine. Shortly after that, my first biological child was born. I knew I needed a plan to take care of my sons, so I enrolled in ITT Tech to try to find a better way to provide. I went to school during the day and worked at night. It was hard, and I was scraping by, so I made a decision to supplement my income by "hustling weed" on the side. I quickly saw that my side "hustle" was bringing in more money than my hard work. Realizing that eventually influenced me to quit school and my job. I then did whatever I had to do in order to maintain the lifestyle I wanted for me and my sons. The following years came with radical changes and difficult challenges. The time was coming when the price and the pain of it all would push me into making some major life choices and necessary changes.

Outside of visiting the chapel in prison and a few Easter visits with my grandma, I did not grow up in church or spend any time there. After being invited to church over and over again by a friend, I finally accepted the invitation and made a visit. When I arrived, I went directly to the back and took a seat. I came in high off marijuana and wasn't paying any real attention to the pastor's message. There was a lot going on in the room that night that distracted me from what he was saying, until the moment that he made a statement that changed the direction of my life forever. That moment will never be forgotten. He said, "give it all to God now or die." Those words resonated in my mind and my spirit. I had a lot going on in my life at that time, and the craziness of it all was at an all-time high. I was tired of it, and I believe God used that pastor to speak directly to me. I knew I had to listen and respond if I wanted to live.

That day, I went to the altar and surrendered my life to Christ. I was baptized shortly after, and my life as a "Christian" began. Though this was the beginning of my relationship with

Christ, it was not the end of my connection with the world. It took many years for me start experiencing freedom from my worldly ways. I loved God, but I also enjoyed the pleasures of the world that I had become accustom too. I would do things that I knew I shouldn't do, and though I did feel convicted about it, I wasn't persuaded. I wanted to serve God and still "do me."

There were times when I ended up in situations that could have landed me back in the penitentiary. I seriously lacked discipline in my Christian walk, and it was only pain that pressured me into a place of prayer and repentance over the course of time. It had taken about seven years of mediocrity before I was willing to move from a place of conviction to a place of application.

When I finally did get to that place of maturity, it led to a lot of breakthroughs in my life. One of those was developing a new passion for my rap. I finally realized that I had more than a gift, but it was truly a calling. It was a gift that could be used for God to express Himself through me and help other people.

My passion for music played a major part in my transition into doing the work of ministry. The thought of being involved in ministry never crossed my mind. I still remember the 1st time I wrote a gospel song. Doing that changed my life forever. It helped me fully realize my God-given purpose as a Gospel Rapper. The day I wrote my first gospel song has a story of its own. I was sitting in a recording studio about a week after I got saved watching some other artists recording a song, and it was a gospel song. They needed one more person to write to the song, and I happened to be the only one there. I was a bit arrogant back then, and I knew I had the skills to write a dope verse for any song, so I wrote a verse for them. I recited the verse once, then twice, and the 3rd time I recited the verse, tears began to fall from my eyes. That verse had God all over it. He directed me to write every word written down on that piece of paper. It was even like God used that verse to talk to me directly. He talked to me and through me. From that moment on, I knew that this was the kind

26

of music I should be doing. It wasn't meaningless entertainment. It had a God-given purpose.

Before I knew it, my call to ministry took on a life of its own. I quickly jumped into performing at events and hosting my own. The first event that I did was at the church I got saved at called "King's Temple." From there, God began to send people my way that wanted me to perform at their church youth events. At every event, I would meet someone new. The circle of people I knew in ministry began to grow, and my opportunities soon increased. I had just gotten started and the next thing I knew, I was being asked to go into schools, alternative schools, detention centers, and the list goes on. While going into these places, I began to see the needs of our youth and still being young myself, I wanted to do all the things that I didn't see anyone else doing for them. My first official effort was to begin putting events together myself. This gave me the opportunity to get to know even more people that are advocates for Jesus, our youth, and our communities. In the process of all that, I can see now that God was grooming me to speak His Word. Over time I realized I wasn't only called to rap but also to speak God's Word and I saw that the Holy Spirit had anointed me in a way that I could connect with anyone on their level regardless of their age. The gifts God had given me to speak and to rap took me through doors I never thought I would be able to go through. These doors opening allowed me to share my gift in local neighborhoods, churches and even television.

It happened so fast, the only kind of training I got was on the job training. I had to learn as I went from place to place. I learned to rely on Christ's power, and I knew it was with me. He was showing Himself in and through me and developing me to be the "King" He had always intended me to be.

I have been set "on fire" by God for a great work and continue to burn with passion to minister to as many as God will put me in front of. Seeing how God touches people through me, drawing them to Himself, keeps me pressing towards the mark of the high calling in Christ Jesus. Many love my music because they can hear a little of their story in it. More importantly than that, they can hear God talking to them through my music. I've seen my music put tears on people faces. I've seen my music bring joy into people's lives and make them feel like they can conquer anything through Jesus Christ.

I have also learned that "ministry" isn't always pretty. Without questions, it has an ugly side. I've seen people using their God given gifts of authority and influence to exploit women. I have seen some operate with greed with a motive to get money for themselves. I've seen ministers and pastors focusing more on getting glory for themselves than focusing on ushering people in the presence of God.

I still struggle to understand why people that say they are of God and do those types of things but do my best not to condemn them because I recognize that at times I am even guilty. I keep pressing because I know it's not how you start your life or walk with Christ that matters the most, but it's how you finish. The Bible teaches that a righteous man can repeatedly fall but get back up again. I desire to become everything God wants me to be and am pressing to have a pure and blameless ministry to others. I am committed to the process of being transformed from glory to glory to become more like Jesus.

I hate the fact that I can look back over my life and my time in ministry and see the detrimental effects of my selfishness. I see that there were times that lives swayed because of my poor witness, and I could have done so much better to lead them in the right way. There were even times that I justified my behavior because of what I saw others doing but now I recognize that sin is sin, and we are to look to Christ as our measuring stick, not others. With all that said, it's just another reminder that It is God and God alone who deserves the glory for being who He is and doing what He does for even who the world would consider the worst of the worst.

In all I have been through, I have learned that God can take anybody and make them into a somebody through His power if they put their trust in Him. I have also learned that life in general and a person's walk with Christ is going to have ups and downs and it's an ongoing process of renewing your mind and allowing Christ to regenerate your spirit. I have made up in my mind that I am going to keep moving forward on this journey no matter bumpy the road gets, and I am going to keep giving God the glory when life seems to be its best.

For years, I lived in a world of mediocrity, doing things that were contrary to God's ways, but God in His mercy led me into victory. I thank Him today that He called my name "Antonio Leon French" all those years ago, so the world would know Him through who they know now as "King Antonio." A work in progress, yet already a display of God's power to save, heal, deliver and empower and I can't pay Him back but I can continue to pay it forward by sharing my life, my ministry and my message to as many as I can before I meet him face to face.

Billy Mason

*Trust in the Lord with all your heart and lean not on your own
understanding; in all your ways submit to him, and he will make
your paths straight. Proverbs 3:5-6*

My name is Billy Mason. I was born in Cleveland, Ohio.
At the age of five my parents and I moved to southern California.
My father, Bill Sr., was a big band jazz drummer and
photographer. He wanted to move to California to pursue his
dream. He was a press photographer for the local newspaper
during the day and played six nights a week at a local lounge. He
bought me my first drum kit when I was twelve. If it wasn't for
my dad and watching him play I wouldn't be here today. He even
took me to see Buddy Rich play at Disney Land. I had a picture
made of Buddy with me sitting on his drum set, which was
unheard of. I would go with him on most assignments and gigs.
My father also took me to a lot of nightclubs in California and I
sat in and played with a lot of big name players who played for
the Lawrence Welk Band and at the Disney Land theme park. I

was scheduled to appear on the Merv Griffith Show to play drums, but the show was cancelled due to Merv's illness. Who knows what direction my life could have gone? One of my fondest memories is when he was doing a story on the Osmonds and he took me with him to the California Angels baseball stadium where they were performing. I was able to meet and get a picture with Donny and Jay Osmond; I became a fan of theirs. Then twenty years later our paths crossed again at one of my concerts while playing drums for Tim McGraw.

My parents decided to move back to Fairborn, Ohio which was where my mom's family was living when I was sixteen.

Let me share with you some near death experiences so far at this point of my life. Once when I was five years old, I got pushed into a plate glass window with my right arm going through it. I was rushed to the hospital, nearly bled to death; if it would have taken five minutes longer to get there I would have died. Second time, I was fifteen at a party with some friends, and someone put some pills in my drink and I overdosed on the front lawn. I was rushed to the hospital again where they pumped my stomach and asked me "why was I trying to kill myself?" I said "I wasn't, I didn't take any drugs". They proceeded to say they found levels of eight reds (downer pills) when they pumped my stomach. I found out later my friends thought it would be funny to see me messed up because I didn't do drugs, but little did they know they almost killed me. My doctor told me if they wouldn't have pumped my stomach I would have died. Third, I was eighteen in high school, playing in a rock band called Jamaica Plains. We were getting ready to open up for Barbie Benton, she was a Playboy Bunny and singer, and we were scheduled to leave the following weekend. My girlfriend at the time, who later became my wife, was tired of me being gone every weekend playing music. We got in a fight and she said if I left that weekend she was breaking up with me. So I told the band I couldn't go. A drummer friend of mine, Vic Nan, filled in for me that weekend. Coming home, he and the leader got killed when a semi truck ran a red light, running over their MGM sports car. The leader and I always rode together with the rest of the band riding in the equipment truck.

In 1977 I graduated from Fairborn High School and was married shortly afterwards at the age of eighteen. I joined the Army, but was sent home early because my dad was hospitalized due to a heart attack that thankfully, he survived. I played in a disco band six nights a week, drove a school bus for Dayton city schools, painted houses during the day, and also during this time I played with members of the Ohio Players funk band. Then one night we saw the Imperials perform a concert and met Russ Taff. He convinced me to pray about moving to Nashville to pursue Christian music. We had $300 and an old yellow phone company van, but we loaded up the kids and moved to Nashville in 1980. I auditioned for several Christian bands and the doors just didn't open. I finally got a call to play for beach music artist Clifford Curry/Billy Scott who sang "You've Got to Treat Her Like a Lady". After that I played for blues artist Clarence "Gatemouth" Brown. By this point the country music gigs started happening. I played for Jo-el Sonnier, cajun artist, Billy Anderson, Grand Ole Opry performer, and Paulette Carlson, formerly with Highway 101.

In 1994 I got my big break being asked to play with Tim McGraw and the Dancehall Doctors right as his first hit "Indian Outlaw" was coming out. We traveled the world flying in Leer jets and tour buses. We played in every football stadium and arena you could think of, and we were the first country act ever to sell out Madison Square Gardens, where Tony Bennett got up and sang with us. As the band's drummer, the guys and I recorded his last seven albums including the biggest album of his career, which won a Grammy, "Live Like You're Dying". We played on multiple television shows such as Jay Leno, David Letterman, Ellen DeGeneres, Rosie O'Donnell, Jimmy Fallon, Good Morning America, the Jerry Lewis Telethon, and every award show including the Grammys. We even played with Elton John on the ACM awards.

This is a good time to tell you about another near death experience and a close call. On our winter break in 2000 I got a call to fill in for a friend on the Regal Cruise Ship. He had to have surgery and needed my help. It was supposed to be for two weeks and I ended up playing for forty days. While on the ship we got to do some fun activities like white water rafting in Costa Rica. It had just rained two weeks straight and their rain forest rapids were at level five and two people went missing the week before, they hadn't found them yet at the time; we didn't know all this until after the trip. The rapids were very treacherous. Half way down the rapids I was thrown from the raft. I was under water, got caught in the current and it was pushing me down and spinning me all around; I didn't know which way was up or down. I couldn't hold my breath anymore, my mouth opened and I started screaming, drowning, when all of a sudden something pushed me into a rock which threw me up to the top of the water. Talk about scary. Another close call was when Tim and the band were scheduled to play on The View a day after 9/11 in one of the twin towers in New York City.

After the Nashville flood in 2010, Tim and the band hosted a benefit called Nashville Rising where we backed up seventeen artists including Carrie Underwood, Amy Grant, Michael W. Smith, Taylor Swift, Miley and Billy Ray Cyrus, Luke Bryan, Blake Shelton, Lynyrd Skynyrd, Montgomery Gentry, Martina McBride, Miranda Lambert, LeAnn Rimes, Toby Keith just to name a few. It was such a great experience to play drums for all those acts. To this day the most memorable artist I've played with would be Kenny Rogers in Atlanta and Tony Bennett in Madison Square Gardens.

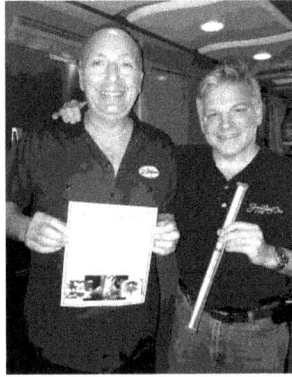

Billy featured with Astronaut Col. Greg Johnson.
My drumstick traveled to space.

Looking back on my career I always tried to be a light and example for the Lord. I never thought of myself as a world famous drummer because the Lord gave me the gift and I was doing what I was born to do. I always tried to touch lives at every concert by picking out someone in the crowd that looked like they were hurting. I would walk down to the front of the stage and give them my Pro Mark signature drumsticks; I even gave a guy one of my Zildjian crash cymbals. The Lord led me to buy a handicapped kid named David Boone a set of DW drums like the ones I played on stage. I've even signed my Remo drumheads and given them away on stage after the show. I've always tried to be a man of God and having a giving and compassionate heart towards others. Let me tell you about another way God has used me. I was on Facebook and a guy named Irving Scrible was online. He saw my personal phone number I gave out for a job contact. He called my cell and it came up as a LA number. I went to answer it and he hung up. So I was trying to decide to call it back or not. I wasn't going to call it back thinking it was a telemarketer, but I did and it was Irving. He said he hung up because he was going to take his life. He was an Ewok in two of the Star Wars movies and now he was out of work. He was unable to find a job and was calling me looking for advice. He said the posts I shared on Facebook really inspired him because I was always giving God the glory for everything I do. So I praise God for using me again to help someone because God gets the glory for it, not me.

Things were going great, I had just bought my new dream home, and in 2010 we were starting our Emotional Traffic Tour in January. All of a sudden my mother was diagnosed with cancer and was only given a few months to live. I felt like I needed to be with my mom, but didn't want to let Tim and the tour down. I stayed on the tour and saw my mom every chance I could. My mom passed away that February. Although the tour was a huge success it was very difficult for me.

Shortly after we got home, Tim had called each band member to meet with him separately and we assumed we were getting a raise or bonus, but instead Tim let us go saying he wasn't happy and needed to make a change, a new look, a new sound, etc. I had just lost my job, just bought a new home, my mother had passed away, and my marriage was falling apart all the while, I was asking God what to do.

A year later I had lost the house. I was working new jobs such as the Nashville airport for American Airlines loading and unloading airplanes, trying to play music, and trying to get back with another artist, but the doors kept closing. I did appear on the ABC hit show "Nashville" as an extra in the band of a few episodes. I was also playing percussion/harp in Luke Wheeler's band. Things got worse around the time I moved back in my old rental house. My father was getting ready to move in with me when he was hit with an aneurysm and passed away with me by his side. I obtained jobs at Nissan and Arby's for a short time. I also played drums in downtown Nashville for tips in local clubs. This was the time I thought about checking out. I didn't think my heart could take anymore. Then my sister Laura called me from Ohio. She was living in a hotel, out of money, and was going to take her life. I convinced her to come live with me telling her that I would take care of her until she got back on her feet. I felt like the Lord was using me in my time of need to help my sister. During all these experiences and loses I began to write songs with songwriters from Nashville. Some of the titles include "Kiss'em

While You Can", for my mom and dad, "They All Come With Me", after my divorce, "Was I Born to Do This", after I lost my job, and "Something's Money Can't Buy". When you lose the ones who gave you life, there is a part of you that dies also. Only God's peace can fill that void. The scripture I learned to love is *Proverbs 3:5-6 Trust in the Lord with all your heart, and lean not in your own understanding; in all your ways acknowledge Him and He shall direct your paths.*

After three years of sorrow, I started getting calls. Pastor John Collins contacted me to be his executive director for his Love That Cross Ministry. Also I am playing drums for country star Aaron Tippin and just did the Inspirational Country Music Awards, hosted by Ray Stevens, as the house drummer and I presented an award. I just did the Kevin and Treva Show and a Christian movie, *The List*, where I played a surgeon, which stars Montel Jordan who is a minister now that sang the hit song, "This is How We Do It".

So you can see God is turning things around in my life. I have two beautiful kids, David and Shanna, and nine amazing grandkids. I stayed faithful to Him through these hard times, which wasn't easy, but I give Him the praise, glory, and honor for the good and the bad. I think one of the things that helped me get through all of this is staying in church where I sing and play drums on the worship team at Creekmont General Baptist Church. I pray this testimony will touch someone's life out there showing that you can be on the top and lose it all, but in both situations God will never leave us or forsake us. As you can see God is not through with my life.

God Bless to all.
Billy Mason

Contact: Billytmason@aol.com

Also check out another book I'm in called Sticks'N' Skins-Drum Photo Book.

Carl Gassoway

Trust in the LORD with all thine heart; and lean not unto thine own understanding. In all thy ways acknowledge him, and he shall direct thy paths. Proverbs 3:5-6

    I was born late Friday evening, August 20, 1976 in a small town called Leesville. My mother was only 14 when she gave birth to me, but she had all the support she needed from my aunts, uncles, and grandparents. I know my father loved me, but I just don't think he was ready for kids. Although we lived in the same town, I never saw much of him. I enjoyed hearing stories about my father and how much I look like him. As a child, I spent a lot of time with my grandmother. My grandmother was old school and she believed in hand me down clothes. I don't think I ever had a pair of new shoes, pants, or shirts. All my clothes came from cousins that could no longer wear them anymore. I remember getting a pair of penny loafers and wearing them until I could not squeeze my feet in them anymore. I was the shy kid, known for wearing high water pants, mismatched socks, and talking shoes at times. We were not poor, but we were not middle class. I was constantly bullied and picked on as a child. Being skinny with big teeth and my wardrobe, it was not hard to figure out why I had low self-esteem. My cousins were my only friends at times and there are quite a few of us. My mother gave birth to my two younger brothers during the time I was living with my grandmother and she would pick me up to spend time with me. I lived with my grandmother on my father's side until I was in the 1st grade.

My mother got her first apartment and I was happy to be back with her and spend time with my siblings. I was the man of the house and I would watch over my brothers while my mother provided a living for us. She would work long hours to make sure we had what we needed. My mother had a party to celebrate one of my uncle's birthdays. Everyone was invited and you were welcome to bring a friend, as long as that person was not trouble. That party was the event that really changed things in our life. My mother met a gentleman, who was serving in the military at the time, which was invited by a mutual friend. He came around a lot after that party and I loved the way he treated my mother. We couldn't wait to see his car drive up because he would always keep us laughing and enjoying life. Exactly one year from the date of the party, he was proposing to my mother. Everything seemed to be falling in place for me. I was not wearing second hand clothes and my clothes fit properly. My mother married him and we moved into government quarters and a better school. I learned a lot from my stepfather. He taught me how to treat a woman and why it is important to work hard to take care of your family. Every weekend, my new father would allow as many cousins stay over as possible. We would sometimes make two trips to pick up my cousins and friends for a sleep over. My house had become the place to be for the weekends. There was not much to do in my old neighborhood, so getting away was a luxury.

By the time I was a freshman in high school, my new father had bought me a car. I was studying to get my driver's license so I could start driving to school instead of taking the bus. Everything in my life was great until Christmas Eve. My family had stopped at a red light, in my new car, and a vehicle struck us from behind. God saw it fit for me to see another day because the back seat had become the trunk. I walked away from that accident with some minor aches and bruises but my new father was not so lucky. The accident affected his back so much that he no longer could do his job in the military. I remember the family sitting at the table and my mother breaking down the news. My new father was medically retiring and the family was moving to his home town in Spartanburg, South Carolina. Everyone was excited to move to a new home and meet new people except me. Leesville was home for me and I was not ready to leave anytime soon. For days, my mother saw how displeased I was and she asked me what she could do to make me feel better. I immediately responded by asking to stay with my grandmother until I finish school. I was surprised she agreed to it. Although I got my way, I had mixed emotions about what was taking place. The day that my family dropped me off at my grandmother's house and drove away, I didn't know if I should chase the car or just sit there. It didn't help remembering the pain in my mother's eyes when she told me to take care of myself and continue to do well in school.

Because I missed my family, I immediately did things to occupy my mind. My new father got me used to wearing name brand clothing and shoes at this point. The thought of going back to anything less than that was driving me crazy. I hooked up with some childhood friends that were known for making money. These young brothers would drive by with their nice cars and always have the best looking females with them. For some reason, I wanted that lifestyle. As a matter of fact, I had to have that life style. Where I am from, it's not hard to pick up on a skill that can get you paid quickly. I hooked up with some people that taught me a trade that would later have me standing in front of a judge with my freedom on the line. I did things that I am not proud of to have things that I felt I deserved. As a result of my irresponsible behavior, I was at the mercy of a judge, facing some time that I was not sure that I was ready for. Thank God for my praying grandmother, because if it wasn't for her prayers, the judge known for giving young brothers 20 to life, would have never offered me a way out. I feared that I would spend the best parts of my life, caged like an animal, but the judge ordered me to find a recruiter and go to the military. I wish I could remember his name today because I would go back home and thank him.

The military was challenging, but it was what I needed. My first duty station was Fort Hood, Texas and I loved that place, simply because it was not that far from home. After being in the military for a short period of time, I did not have the desire to go back home, other than to visit my family. I looked at everyone and everything different now. I was growing up and growing out of my old ways. I got my first apartment and my first car that I could afford. It seemed that my troubled days were behind me. Every time that I received a paycheck, I made sure I sent money to my mother and grandmother. It's a blessing when God will put you in a position to take care of people that struggled to take care of you when you were not able. Because I am so grateful for what my family has done for me, I am constantly working hard to position myself, in case someone needs my help one day. After being promoted to sergeant, a few friends decided that we should go celebrate. I was having a wonderful time and I guess I had one too many Long Island iced teas. We danced and had a wonderful time together. I remember one of my coworkers asking me if I was okay to drive home. I felt fine and I did not think I needed an escort. Everyone parted ways and I headed home attempting to take the back road. About 10 minutes into my drive, I was blinded by red and blue lights. Apparently, I was driving recklessly and as a result, I was pulled over. The officer asked me to step out of my vehicle because he smelled alcohol. After stepping out of the vehicle, I was asked to perform a series of tests, which I failed. I was hauled off to jail and my car was towed. My blood alcohol level was twice the illegal amount. I never pictured my celebration ending like that. The next day, my supervisor picked me up from jail and it was a long ride back to my company. All I could think about is how I just got promoted and I threw it all away by not thinking smart. Over the course of time, there was talk about me getting demoted and I gave my life to God. I found a church home in Copperas Cove, Texas and it was almost like everything was supposed to happen to get me to that church. I stopped worrying about if I would keep my promotion or if I would get demoted and fully focused on building a relationship with God.

I remember throwing away all of my ungodly music and buying new music. I separated myself from people that were not moving in the same direction and speaking the same tongue as me. God revealed to me so many things that I was not aware of. People that did not like me would ask me to pray with them and share their personal problems with me. Because I decided to drive drunk, one night, my life had changed and God revealed to me my purpose. One morning, after almost completing a 24 hour shift, I watched the first plane crash into one of the Twin Towers. Moments later, the second plane had crashed into the Twin Towers. Our country was under an attack and it was mixture of fear, anger, and confusion. No one knew where the next plane would crash. My unit was notified that we were getting ready to deploy and because of such an event, me driving drunk was not so important. My supervisor came to me the day of the attack to let me know that I had orders to go to South Korea. I was given the option to get my orders deleted for South Korea or go on the deployment with my unit. I knew if I wouldn't have gone with my unit, it was a chance that I would get demoted for the driving while intoxicated incident. I chose to go to South Korea and keep my rank. As soon as I got my documents to clear my unit, I cleared in record breaking time. Not knowing what was in store for me on the other side of the world, I was happy to be leaving without losing my rank. God is so great, I got promoted and met the woman of my life.

I never would have imagined traveling to the other side of the world to meet my soulmate. I met a young lady that demanded respect and when she walked, she had my full attention. For the first time, I actually took my time to get to know her and learn about her likes and dislikes. This great woman of God had my full attention and I was willing to get down on a knee and tell the world. We became best friends and where you saw one, the other was somewhere near.

After building such an unbreakable bond, we decided that we should make it official and do things the right way once we got back to the United States. When my time was up in South Korea, I was leaving my love behind, heading back to the area where all my troubles started, Leesville. I got orders to go to Fort Polk where she would later follow. I found a place to stay and I was excited about the thought of starting a family. I had money to take care of the ones who take care of me and a beautiful woman to spend the rest of my life with. Shortly after she arrived in the United States, I suffered an injury that would cause me to be separated from the military. The one thing that saved my life was being stripped from me.

The military was all I knew and I gave it my all. I battled with this separation, but I tried my best not to show it. After all, God knows what's best and He always lead me in the right path. My new love wanted to go somewhere special to take my mind off of not having a job and to announce some good news. Anxious to hear what she had to say, I almost got a ticket trying to get to our favorite restaurant. We got to the restaurant and ordered what we always ordered. My love grabbed my hand and told me that I was going to be a father. That was one of the happiest days of my life. I was about to be the father that I always wanted in my life. This woman had given me more than she could ever imagine. We agreed on a wedding date and started telling her loved ones the great news. The pressure of being able to take care of my family was in the front of my mind. I had to find a good job that could support our lifestyle that I thought my family should have. I searched for jobs daily and I found something. It was not my idea job but it paid the bills. After a beautiful wedding, my son was born into this world. With more responsibilities came the need for more income. My new family and I were barely making ends meeting and I did not picture our new life being so stressful. A couple of years went by and we figured out how to get by with the income that we earned.

My wife received orders to go to Fort Campbell, Kentucky and I remember being so upset about it. Although I have never been to Kentucky, it just did not feel like it would be a place that my family would enjoy. On top of that news, my wife was pregnant again and I was stressing about having to look for another job. I went to my praying grandmother often when I had things on my mind. She would always be equipped with the right scripture when I needed it. My family prayed and we moved to Fort Campbell, Kentucky. My wife got promoted after being at her new duty station and I got a new job. I was excited to have a job and I could earn enough to take care of my family. So grateful about what God was doing in my life, I didn't realize that he was not done yet. I was so worried about a job and I didn't know that I would become a business owner. Through all I have been through, God never left me. He was there when I thought I didn't have anyone else. He has really taught me to trust him and lean not to my own understanding. My little family is blessed and we are now in a position to bless others.

Contact: Carl.gassoway@icloud.com

Christopher Kurtz

Blessed are those who hunger and thirst for righteousness, for they will be filled. Matthew 5:6

I was born on October 5, 1977 in Columbus Ohio. I am the oldest of three siblings. I have two younger sisters and a brother. The younger two are from my father's third marriage. At the age of six my parents got divorced. My father cheated on my mom. My mother finally separated from him when I turned five. My sister and I had to live with our father and step mother when I turned 6 because my mother had no job and no way of supporting us. There was just no way that I could understand why she made that decision. My father married the woman whom he cheated with. I did not like this new woman who was my "stepmother." I had no desire to even try to get to know her. I wanted no part of her, I wanted MY mother. I even prayed and asked God to change my mother's mind so that she would come back for my sister and I, however; that was not to be. I felt alone and abandoned. My sister felt the same way. It was us against the world.

Even though my mom believed she was making the best choice for us, after some time, my father realized he was not equipped to care for us either. He sent my sister and I to live with his sister for about a year. Her name is Sandra Kurtz. She was in an abusive relationship. She would sometimes vent on us, mostly Lynn. She was good to us most days though

At first things seemed like they would be okay with our Aunt. It did not take long to realize that she was in abusive relationship. Unfortunately for my sister, her way of venting from the pressure of her own abuse was to give my sister a hard time just as a way of entertainment. She would sarcastically say things to my little sister often. My sister could not understand that and took everything she said literally. When my sister would do something that would hurt her or make her sick (at my aunt's sarcastic command), my aunt would call up her children to laugh at her just to make the situation worse and make her feel bad. Although I was not really sure what prayer was or how it worked, I found myself a couple of times just saying, "Please, please, God. Just get my mother so she can come back and take us." This was not to be, however we were able to visit her some during the summer. Finally when I a bit older than seven, thanks to his experience in the Marines as a helicopter mechanic, my father got a job as a service consultant at Datsun (who was bought out by Nissan), bought a house and brought us home.

. But, while living with her we would visit our grandma Kurtz. Her name was Alvada "Kitty" Kurtz. To my sister and I, she was still just grandma. We enjoyed visiting with her. Grandma began taking us to the Methodist church. I started learning about prayer, the Bible and Jesus. I got to attend Bible studies and church events. My grandmother volunteered on a regular basis. She would stay and cook or work on fundraisers. I would get to go downstairs and play the piano they had in the basement. I did not really know how to play, but I would tinker with it. There is where my love for music really sprouted. I really enjoyed my time with my grandmother, unfortunately it could not last. She died of breast cancer Feb 9, 1995.

THINGS ONLY GET WORSE

We lived with our stepmother and father for four years. I had a bad feeling about my stepmother. I was torn however, because she was in nursing school. I thought that was really good. Her working to be a nurse lightened my view of her. I figured she could not be all bad if she wanted to do something that would help so many people. After some time in the home I realized I was wrong. She was quite racist and would say things in front of my sister that my sister would say at school. One day this black girl came up and almost kicked me in my genitals. She missed by just a bit. It was still in a pretty sensitive area though so I hit the ground. I laid there in pain not understanding why or how she could be so mad at me. I had done nothing. It was not until a few days later that I realized my sister had called her the "N" word. We had many more issues like this during school. My sister was just not handling the instability of our lives well at all. She was acting out in school and getting into all kinds of trouble. At the time I was a bit more easy-going and could cope better than she could, however I had not dodged a bullet, my internal struggle was just around the corner. We soon found out that racism was not the only issue my stepmother had. She abused both my sister and me sexually and mentally. There was also some physical abuse, but it was mostly sexual and mental. She manipulated my father in extremely subtle ways. She got him into such a rage at one point that he pinned my sister against the wall by her throat. We were finally able to move in with my mother in Indianapolis.

My sister begrudgingly moved forward with school work and just in general getting on with life. In that respect, she was much stronger than I. I had thrown in my towel. The abuse from my step mother was kind of a final straw for me. Then once we got into this neighborhood in Indianapolis, I discovered that it was predominately black, filled with gangs and just a generally negative environment. I got jumped going to the candy store at one point. I was the constant victim of bullying. I had not bothered anyone. I was not doing anything wrong. I was consistently messed with because I was the "white boy" in a black neighborhood. I became really hardened personally. I did not care about anything. I certainly did not care about school. I failed the sixth grade. I went and stayed a year with my dad, passed the sixth grade, but failed the seventh grade. I went back to Indianapolis and passed the seventh grade. In eighth grade, I decided that I was ready to get myself together and do better. I really was quite smart. I was not challenged at all. I would sleep during class. I had a neighbor tell me I needed to pay attention. I asked why, because everything she is saying is in the book and I can just read the book. When test grades came back I had a 100% and she had like an 88% she was quite impressed.

MOVING ON

Despite being smart, the school environment was just not my thing. When I was younger, I wanted to join the Air Force to become a fighter pilot, all until I heard of the height restrictions. Then I knew this wasn't going to happen; at "6'2," I was too tall. I dropped out of school later on when I was just 16, and moved away from Indianapolis so that I could remove myself from the gang life and that mentality. I ended up taking odd jobs. I started out in fast food restaurants and then I began working for an Ice Cream Company. I was pretty much the Freezer Supervisor. I did not have that official title, but I was usually the only one there working in the freezer. When the big deliveries came, I would get help. I worked there for three years at which point I transferred into roofing. I roofed for about six months. I then worked for Uhaul for about two and half years and then went back to roofing for three years. After that I became a bouncer at a gentleman's club. It was here that I realized that I had to get my stuff together and that I needed an education. This was just not my scene. I didn't like being there. Friends got me the job, so I took it, but I knew that I did not intend to make my living as a strip club manager. Don't get me wrong, they made good money, but morally it was just wrong. Everything about it was wrong. Music had been a great outlet for me. It got me through some of the hardest parts of my life.

I sang in choir in 4th grade, had a few vocal lessons and a general love for music. My friend suggested that we start a band. I was hesitant to the idea for many reasons. I could barely read sheet music. He listed off other artists that could not read sheet music either or at least did not know much about music. I sang for him and he said I sounded like a choir boy and he couldn't use that, so I needed to play an instrument. I started learning to play the bass. We were by no means a Christian band. We actually had a song called "Jesus Freak" that made fun of Bible thumpers. I played with these guys for 9 years; even though I had put a 5 year time limit on it. It was so much fun and I loved the music, but I realized that I was still going absolutely nowhere. I was in pretty much the same position that I started out in years before. It was officially time for a change.

A CHANGE IS GOING TO COME

I had a hard time getting decent work due to my lack of education. As a result I committed to earning my GED; which I obtained in 2001. It wasn't until 2008, while working at a gentleman's club; I became determined to join the Army. It just kind of happened. My girlfriend at the time was trying to figure out what she wanted to do in life, so she was checking out the Army. When she went to the recruiter's office, I went with her. She, unfortunately, did not see herself fitting into that role, but I did. It was the one thing I had always wanted to do. I was also 31 years old, and not getting younger. So they recruited me instead. I chose the MOS 19D Cavalry Scout. The jack of all trades they said; perfectly describing my life. I had done roofing, been to school for automotive tech, been a plumber's helper, small voltage wiring, etc., I fit right in. I signed and shipped in February, 2009. I started my training in an OSUT unit. That's

One Stop Unit Training. Combat MOSs train that way so they don't have two different places to go. In 17 ½ weeks, I finished my training and was awarded my MOS. I was then assigned to A Troop 1-75 Cavalry Regiment 2nd BCT, 101st ABN.

THE DAY IT ALL CHANGED

The moment that truly changed my life came about six months into my deployment. I woke up with déjà vu. It was not the, "oh this is the same routine" style déjà vu. I felt as if I had already lived that day. I felt like I was doing the exact same thing the exact same way I had already done it. In that moment, I realized that, "today was my day." I did not believe that I was going to die. I knew that I was going to be hurt. I did not know how, but I knew this was happening today. I had told friends back home that I believed something was going to happen to me. They just told me to shake it off, it was jitters about going. I was not nervous about going. I just had a feeling. Going back to the day, we were checking each other and making sure we had everything we needed: extra ammunition, water, spare batteries, etc. By this time I had become a Saw Gunner. I had begged for the opportunity. The other guys were not taking care of it the way it needed to be taken care of. I knew that I could do it. When I was given the opportunity even my team leader was impressed with how well I took care of it.

As we prepared to go my squad leader Staff Sergeant Simpson asked me was I ready. I said that I was and asked if he was. He gave me a strange look as if it was weird for me to even ask that question. Of course he was ready, he was born ready. We headed out on patrol. I was the last American in line. The Afghani soldiers were behind me. I followed protocol and walked in the footsteps ahead. I saw a spot that looked suspicious, but it had boot prints all over it, so I stepped there as well. The next thing I know, I was looking at the sky. My first thought was the sound. I was just thinking that someone must have gotten blown up. Then I realized that I was the one looking at the sky. I had been blown up. I had stepped on an IED. The next thing I saw was all this black smoke. I kept waiting on the pain, but the pain did not come. It was like my pain sensor had been shut off. When I hit the ground the first thing I thought about was my leg. With my right hand, I felt for my left leg, but all I felt was wetness. I could not feel skin, clothes, or anything. I just started yelling, "Bullshit! Bullshit! Bullshit!" I still had my wits about me so I reached over into my other pocket and pulled out my tourniquet. Before I could get to my leg I could hear someone telling me to be still because they got it. I argued and he insisted that I hold still. I found out later that I owe my life to Dr. Shius Hughes. Others came over as well. Saving me in that moment was truly a team effort. One leg was through me and the other was above me and my arm was damaged. They were trying to get me to the medivac chopper. I had lost a lot of blood. Once I was on the chopper, I died. I do not have a story of my life flashing before my eyes or anything of that nature. I just saw whiteness and then I felt a JOLT and was alive. The medic on the chopper was able to resuscitate me.

MINE EYES OF SEEN THE GLORY!

Once they got me to the hospital I died again. This time though it was completely different. I woke up in a field. I was looking down a path to a village. Out of nowhere there came a man that had to be at least seven feet tall. He wore shimmering armor, but I knew my focus did not need to be on him, but on the one he was protecting. There was a man behind him. I could not tell what race he was; I only knew that he had a beard. Once I looked into his eyes I knew that I was in the presence of Jesus! I fell to the ground in tears. I confessed my sins and begged forgiveness over and over again. I professed my love to Him. I told him that I had an unborn son that I did not want to make grow up without a father. He said to me, "By the POWER of MY FATHER you have more work to do!" I woke up on Christmas day 2010 from a drug induced coma in Landstuhl, Germany.

WHAT IT ALL MEANS

I have been through a lot in life. I could be angry and hold grudges. My family got together and had a discussion about things that had happened in our lives. At first I was angry with my dad. I did not want him to give excuses I just wanted him to own up to his part of what happened in our lives. The fact is, it was important for my own life to be able to forgive. I forgave him and moved forward. Understandably, every situation is different, but the one thing that should be common in everyone's life is the ability to forgive. ***If you don't forgive, you will have a black hole in your soul.*** You will have to continuously find something to fill it with and black holes, never fill up. Being able to forgive has allowed me to move on with my life. I married my beautiful wife Heather on March 24th, 2012. She has been my rock. I just pray that as you read my story, that you will realize that you need to seek Jesus and find out who He is on your own. Do not let things in life influence you and do not listen to others. Find the truth for yourself and pray on it.

Christopher L Kurtz / Sergeant U.S. Army Retired

Contact: chris.l.kurtz@aol.com

Luke 18:27 -Jesus replied, "What is impossible with man is possible with God.**"**

54

Calvin "Cylk" Cozart

"When you choose your friends, you choose your future. Because, It's okay to do what you want to do... until it's time to do what you were meant to do."
-unknown

"Be still, and know that I am God." Psalm 46:10

I was born on February 1st, outside of Knoxville, Tennessee. My family was relatively poor and I spent much of my young life going back and forth between the family of my teenaged Cherokee mother, and the family of my black father, who lived in a small hamlet outside of Knoxville, Tennessee. I chased farm animals and tended to crops on a daily basis. My name, Cylk; which is pronounced like "Elk" with the C before it; is a Cherokee nickname for "Running Water." I was honored to receive that name from the famous Chief Iron Eyes Cody, who was at that time close friends with Cherokee Chief Man Killer. He gave me that name from the lake that I was born beside. The hospital was racist and would not allow my Native American mother and black father in for my birth. My mother was in a coma for two days following my birth. Neither of us were expected to live. However we did. This was just the beginning of the racism I would face as a young child.

At the very young age of three, I was enrolled into an all-black school near Oak Ridge, Tennessee. Soon after that, National School Busing was enforced and after two short years at the small school; I was forced to attend Karns Elementary. It was an all-white school that was just a few miles way. I was younger than all my classmates, but no one seemed to notice. There was not a middle or junior high school so I went to high school two years early. At the age of twelve, I had my first encounter with the KKK. I danced with a young white girl at an elementary school dance. The locals were not pleased and they burned two crosses in my yard. In addition to burning the crosses in my yard, they killed my German shepherd, "King," and hung his body from a tree.

During high school, I really focused on my athletics. My ability to perform as an athlete in basketball and football was a way to mask most of the pain and prejudice I experienced weekly. My senior year, I helped our football team to a winning season. However, the issue of race played in there as well. I had to fight or get beaten up by people who were waiting for me after the games. Mostly from older boys or young men that lived in the community. I often had to sleep in the locker room on Friday nights after football games to avoid such issues. I would wait until the early hours of the morning to ease out of the nasty locker room. When it came to our basketball season, the coach called me in to tell me I could not play on the team my senior year.

I thought he was joking! This was very upsetting to me for several reasons; one being... It was my SENIOR year! And also, my teammates and I had basically grown up together, spent the night at each other's homes, played baseball and went fishing

56

together. We were all friends. The coach called me a "hotdog" because of my style of play. (no look passes etc...). I was just having fun playing the game the way I learned to play. Telling an athlete that he can't play his last year in high school, was like tearing my heart right out of my chest! The real issue however, was the fact that rumors swirled that I had been dating a white girl. I remember the look on the coach's face was like an evil monster as he spoke. I eventually was forced to move from Karns High School to Loudon High School in the middle of my senior year. I was only able to play in the last 14 basketball games of my senior year, because of the strict Tennessee rules. The impression I needed to make was still made. I received scholarship offers from more than 30 schools. I finally decided to first attend Montreal-Anderson Jr. College in North Carolina (close to home). I then transferred to King College (now King University) in Bristol, Tennessee. There, I studied child psychology.

It was in college that I truly learned to study. I had not realized how important studying was not only to school, but to my life. Studying made me a better athlete, professional, and even a better man. It really showed me where my strengths were.

There is a quote that says we learn more from our losses than our wins. When you are always winning, sometimes you don't work as hard after a few wins. You feel like you don't need to work on anything because you are the best. That is a hard place to come from. Being used to winning doesn't always mean you are going to win. When you lose, you go back to the drawing board and rethink things. In college I was shocked to find myself among people from all over the world. There were people who were better at things than me. You have to learn to surround yourself with those people. No one person can do everything perfectly. If I have ten ears of corn and you have 10 tomatoes; I'll give you 5 and you give me 5 and both of our families can eat a more balanced meal. That is the bartering system our country was created on. The same holds true for the advice you have to offer. You can learn from those that have gone before you and they can learn from you. I learned a lot from people older than me. I really didn't fit in with my black nor my white peers, so I often found myself with adults, or just alone. My mom taught me so much. I was able to watch her. We pretty much grew up at the same time because she was a teenager when she had me. My college basketball coach, Al Nida, (a GREAT man) taught me as much about life as he did about basketball. He taught me that celebrations were for the locker room. He taught me that when you jump around pumping your first in the air screaming about your victory (in front of the fans and the team you just beat), that sends a signal that you are not used to winning. Secondly, I would not appreciate someone jumping around in my face and after I lost a game.

I was able to translate that lesson to life. It really helped me learn how to deal with the media. I don't believe all of the press when they say I'm great at something and I don't take it personally when they write something not so favorable.

After college, I decided to prepare to fulfill my dream of playing in the National Basketball Association. I made the try out for the NBA's summer pro league and caught the eye of the then Denver Nugget Scout, (Ben Job). Mr. Job financed my entire summer while I played. I led my team in scoring and assists. Unfortunately in one of the final games of the season, I fractured my foot. That cut my dreams of playing in the NBA quite short.

I still had a plan; it just accelerated it a bit. My original plan had been to play about 10 years of pro ball after I finished college, then I was going to be a professional actor for several years and then once I felt it was time, I would end my career as a director. After my basketball injury, I changed my mindset and began focusing on acting and modeling (mostly acting). My first opportunity was with the Michele Pommier agency, when I moved to Miami, Florida. I was on the beach one day when a group of beautiful girls walked by and asked me to join the party. That party turned out to be an introduction to the modeling world.

I was quite fortunate later to be picked up by the famous Wilhelmina Modeling Agency out of New York. While living in

New York, I took advantage of opportunities to learn at some of the best theaters for the performing arts. I would find out where plays were and just show up! Sometimes, I would sleep inside the theater's back stage, just to wake up early for a chance to meet or see the actors, directors and producers coming to and fro. Soon, I tried out for the Actor's Studio and studied with the great teacher, Manu Tupo. At this time, I started to meet with agents and was fortunate enough to sign with Harry Abrams, of Abrams Artists. Next, I was off to the American Repertory Theater where I studied with Steven Strimpell. Soon I auditioned for the number one television show in the country, "The Cosby Show." It came down to two actors... myself and the actor who got the part.

I moved to California two days later. Upon moving into the Hollywood world, I learned directly from Robert Redford at his Sundance Institute (which was the genesis for the now successful SunDance Film Festival), that Mr. Redford created. I was able to be in two mainstream plays, "Diary of a Black Man," and "The Big Knife." I also learned during this time that no matter what your aspirations, it is good to start as a background person. When you are in the background or doing bit roles, you can do all the observing that you want to do. You can learn things like how to move around a set, what the "Best Boy" does, how to prepare for a role, watch and listen how the director sets up scenes, read good (and bad) scripts that reveal how the different writers write and observe closely how the major actors deliver their lines. Then when it is my time to perform in front of the camera, it is not so overwhelming and I would have an understanding about what I was getting into. I was able to do both theatre and film. I found one big difference is... theatre demands the importance of everyone's attention to detail as well as knowing each of the characters roles and lines. In theatre you have to do everything. Everyone is involved in cleaning up after rehearsals and shows. You may have to help prepare food for everyone. The person who cleans up is just as important as the person who pays for the theatre. In Hollywood, it's all about the star and everyone else kind of gets lost in the mix.

Even though I was unable to play in the NBA, I did not throw basketball out of my life. I was fortunate to be able to play in the NBA entertainment league. I was the back-to-back 3 point shooting champion, 3 years in a row. I was also team captain. Basketball gave me a jump into Hollywood. I was playing basketball with Denzel Washington one weekend, when he suggested that I play a role in his new film, "Ricochet." During that time the script for "White Men Can't Jump" was presented to Denzel. Because he was preparing to play Malcolm X, Denzel, turned it down but requested that the director meet with me. He was hesitant to meet with me because I was not a big name in Hollywood. He agreed because Denzel insisted. When I walked into the meeting, I met the GREAT Director Ron Shelton and we knew exactly who the other was. We had been playing basketball against each other in the YMCA league for two years. He knew immediately that I was the guy. Fox however was worried and unwilling to release a movie with a no big named actor attached to it. 20th Century Fox told Ron Shelton that if they were going to use me they needed to get a big name white guy. So the process began. One after another, I read with Tom Cruise, Keanu Reeves, and several others. But when Woody Harrelson and I performed in front of Mr. Shelton, we acted like best friends from the beginning. Fox had a production deal with Wesley Snipes so Ron was forced to rewrite the script, but he expanded another character and cast me as Robert (the Security Guard) who was in on the fix with Wesley's character to take "17... Hundred" from Woody.

My main focus now is being a really great film maker. I want to be a great director, period. I have learned from the best directors in film history. Ron Shelton, (Bull Durham, Blaze, Tin Cup) Richard "Dick" Donner, (Superman, Lethal Weapon, Conspiracy Theory, and 16 Blocks,) Currently, I have my own production company. I am directing and producing films, while bringing up young actors. I have learned how important it is to keep reinventing oneself. That's where a lot of actors fall short. They don't understand that they cannot have the same look and be the same character forever. I may take on a few roles here or there as things come up, but directing is my passion now.

I love acting, but I love even more what it has allowed me to do. I want to be remembered as the person who really cared about children and the planet. I'm in the process of a building an entertainment based school. We will be using a lot of acting techniques to teach the general education classes such as English, History, Math, etc. We will also have after school programs. I also have a 501c3 organization call Keeping Dreams Alive, known as KDA. KDA Foundation reaches out to communities that have a lower than 50% graduation rate. We focus on at risk teens, college-bound student athletes and low to moderate income students. The board members and staff are made up of ex-athletes, educators, community leaders and business consultants. I co-founded a program called Cure4Hunger. We have found a way to grow plants indoors, in cylinders, where light hits them a certain way, rotated hourly (so that the nutrients go all the way through the plant) and we use no pesticides. It grows three times the size without much water because it is condensation based.

I produced the "Wave to the World" All-Star Celebrity Recording and "Spirit of Life" video for the 2000 Paralympic Games in Sydney, Australia. "Spirit of Life" has earned, to date, the prestigious Videographer and Aurora Awards, the NY Film Festival Bronze Award, and the Telly Award. My friend Dolly Parton, put together an All Star cast of Super Stars in Nashville, including icons Charlie Daniels, for a "country version" titled "Wave to the World" that everyone loves.

Over the years, I have been the spokesperson and celebrity representative for The National Multiple Sclerosis Society, The National Make-A-Wish Foundation, The Boys & Girls Clubs of America, The Lupus Foundation of America, the National Tourette Syndrome Association and The National Indian Council, to name a few. I've also received the Golden Certificate of Appreciation from Los Angeles Mayor Richard Riordan.

I am blessed to have overcome the plethora of obstacles and the Byzantine machinations of Hollywood and am positioned to leave some deep footprints in the Hollywood landscape and hopefully throughout the world.

In 2015, a State Highway in Knoxville, Tennessee, will be named "Cylk CozArt Parkway" in my honor, and the date of May 6th is now the "CYLK COZART DAY" in Knoxville, Tennessee.

No matter how old you are, we all go through things. Find out what your passions are and really go for them. Never let anyone tell you that you can't do anything. Usually when someone says you can't do something, it means they think "they can't" do that. Everything we think about, we can do if we put it into motion. Always have empathy. If you are not empathetic, you will not go as far as you really can.

You have to be able to put yourself in someone else's shoes to experience the most of what God has given to you.

Contact: Calvincozart@gmail.com

Magnificent Man

Coach Sam Smith

The Lord is my shepherd, I lack nothing. He makes me lie down in green pastures, he leads me beside quiet waters, he refreshes my soul. He guides me along the right paths for his name's sake...
Psalms 23

Living Legend: 35 Years as Head Coach for the Continental T-Belles Girls Track Club

My name is Sam Smith, otherwise known as "Coach Sam Smith" and I'm a native of Canton, Mississippi, but I've have been a long time resident of Tennessee. I've spent my entire life dedicated to training young athletes and developing young people. I retired from the Metropolitan Nashville Public Schools system as the Head Girls Track Coach at Whites Creek High School. My service work has also included being the Assistant Women's Track Coach at Tennessee State University. I was named State of Tennessee Track Coach of the year, National Track Coach of the year Runner-up and McDonald's Coach of the year; and I'm a proud member of the Phi Beta Sigma Fraternity, Inc.

I have been a mentor and a coach for several well-known athletes such as Alexis Pekrosy--1987 Junior National Team, (USA Olympic Games) Yolanda Russell-Gurley—1991 Olympic Festival Team Gold Medalist, Kathy McMillian—Olympic Silver Medalist, Chandra Cheeseborough—Olympic Gold Medalist and numerous others who advanced beyond the Continental T-Belles Track Club to graduate from high school, college and post graduate school.

It's indeed a blessing to have many, versatile ties to the local and national athletic communities. Both my team and I utilize these relationships to provide educational opportunities to our athletes. This often consists of recommendations for academic scholarships at both high school and college levels. It's nothing to brag about, just a noted fact that 90 percent of the Continental T-Belles do prosper academically, spiritually and personally. Not always necessarily in a high financial sense, but as well rounded human beings, who infuse themselves into the community, give back and do well overall.

The "Continental T-Belles Track Club, Inc." is a non-profit Nashville, Tennessee track club for young girls' ages 8 to 18 years old. It's the brainchild and direct sweat equity of Coach Sam Smith, who tirelessly has developed this elite track program, further demonstrating that "even the sky is beyond the limit for the girls!"

The Continental T-Belles Track Club, Inc. traces its history to the "Tigerbelle Track Club Development Program", a summer track program started by the legendary Coach Edward S. Temple. The purpose of the original club was to provide track and field competition experience for young women, as sanctioned by the USA Track and Field Association

It is always my personal goal, led by the Lord to help our youth establish the disciple and self-motivation that is necessary not only for athletic competition, but also for life overall. My approach is said to be strict and the expectations are quite high. I promise you that they are always balanced with my heartfelt desire to see each athlete succeed within the framework of their own capabilities.

Any time which is not spent with the T-Belles is spent volunteering otherwise. My time and energy is always tied into helping young men and women develop their athletic careers. "Trust me that is minimal, because coaching and developing the T-Belles can be a full time, all-consuming but much appreciated job." Giving tirelessly and unselfishly is the core means to ensure the success of the Continental T-Belles Track Club, Inc. and the community at large.

This is a snapshot of my officiating record as it pertains to the awesome world of athletics.

A Snapshot of my athletic accomplishments over the years; Track and Field Officiating Record

1976 – 1979	Olympic Development Meets, Nashville, TN
1979-2004	High School Dual Meets, Nashville, TN
1980 – 1982	TSU Tigerbelle Relay, Nashville, TN
1980-1984	Director of All Comers Meet in Nashville, TN
1980 – 1989	Tennessee Amputee Track and Field, Nashville, TN
1980 – Until	District Regional Junior Olympics (various states)
1980 – Until	Tennessee Track and Field Association Championship (TN)
1981-1988	Tennessee Girls Regional State Championship (TN)
1981-1989	Optimist Track and Field Championship for Girls, Nashville, TN
1982 – 1994	Banner Relays Track and Field Championships for Girls, Nashville, TN
1983 – 1984	Atlanta Youth Games, Atlanta, GA
1985	Mason Dixon Games Championship, Louisville, KY
1985 – 1989	National Track and Field (various states)

1985 – 1996	Junior Olympics National Track and Field Championships (various states)
1987 – 1988	Tennessee Sportsfest Track and Field, Nashville, TN
1988	Para Olympics Track and Field, Seoul, Korea
1989	Volunteer State Track Meet, Knoxville, TN
1990 – 1993	Masters Track and Field Championship (TN)
1991	Director of South Regional Track and Field Championship, Nashville, TN
2000 – Until	Ed Temple Classic Track and Field, Nashville, TN
2002	South West Athletic Conference, Itta Bena, MS
2004	Olympic Trials, Sacramento, CA
2004 – Until	Morehouse Relays, Atlanta, GA
2005 – Until	SEC Championship Track and Field at Vanderbilt University, Nashville, TN
2006 & 2008	Youth Championships Track and Field (various states)
2008	SIAC Track and Field Championship at Morehouse College, Atlanta, GA
2009 – 2011	Tennessee State Track and Field Championship, Murfreesboro, TN

The aforementioned are basic statistics of my years of human interest efforts and input cannot be put on paper. I turned 72 this year and thankful for it. Every day that He wakes me up and allow me to rise and draw breath I do all possible to go above and beyond the call of duty. This is when it comes to pouring my all into the Girl's Track Team and in general; "I do not take this life on earth for granted at all." Making sure that every girl on our team receives the highest quality of training and is positioned for college and their lives afterwards. Rumor has it that I have been known to pound the pavement and keep a "hands on" relationship with my skeleton crew of parents and volunteers who help keep the Track Club running smoothly.

Many have gone on to become national champions, leaders of industry, commerce or to grow into the best woman and living proof that being a part of the T-Bells can offer. The

"Continental T-Bells Track Club" is clearly geared to providing every participant the best training, motivation and support possible to lay the groundwork for her to have overall productive life. Raising her confidence, helping her to push or exceed personal, societal expectations and dealing with life's realities as they arise.

After 35 years of service as the Head Coach for the Nashville, TN based Continental T-Belles Girls Track Club, Inc. I'm still known just as "Coach" to many. It's only the grace and mercy of God above that I am able to have this recognition. "He works through me and I know this all way too well."

My health scare of 2014 was a reminder at best. Thanks to Him and my instilled faith in God I am still going strong and can't say that I actually understand the meaning of the words "Quit or I can't." My team and I diligently teach the same principles to the numerous girls, ages 8 to 18, who we've been blessed to coach over the years; and still coach!

One of the platforms of the organization is that each girl who comes into the track club and stays in until she graduates high school has a 90 % chance of obtaining a college scholarship. The nonprofit 501(c)3 organization is highly dependent on donations and contributions to manage the program. Parent volunteers are encouraged and appreciated and over the numerous years, in wanting to see the girls succeed, I've dipped into my own pockets many times. "Anything (legal and moral) to ensure the program continues to exist and make sure any girl that joins the team can afford stay on the team. All in the sheer interest to help the program and some of the girls who join us, out."

Working with my team, we invite various speakers to provide workshops on character development and life skills every young athlete needs to be successful on and off the track. Topics include Teen pregnancy, smoking, violence, community service, etiquette or other things relevant to hindering their success may be an issue to shed light on.

Ongoing fundraisers are necessary to fuel the Continental T-Belles Girls Track Club, Inc. Funding is essential to ensure the program continues to provide the highest level of coaching, equipment, mentorship, and training facilities. Other major expenses include travel, lodging, meals, and training tools, the program running and advancing. Uniforms, hygiene items, track shows, travel and meal cost to attend track meets in other parts of the country, are just a few items relevant for the funding which is so badly needed.

My amazing T-Belles are trained to practice hard in preparation to compete and win, while keeping the "team spirit" flowing and practicing good sportsmanship habits and principles. At track meets generally they are decked out in red, monogramed "Continental T-Belles Girls Track Team, Inc." athletic suits. They show up ready and willing to work and know what to expect.

I am not known for being a soft touch, huggy feely type of coach. But my heart is always with the girls and their families. I am a fair man who remains dedicated to the cause, seeing the girls through to college and on to a productive life ahead. My proven track record of invariable results is what counts. For 35 years my tough love," straight up no chaser approach has cut the proverbial mustard and got the job done; and it still does.

They show up prepared and ready to rock and roll, some with their beautiful hair coifed and pinned out of the way for running to place and win. Each athlete is equipped with spiked track shoes; professional shoes or shoes with the detachable spikes added into the soles. Both types can adequately serve the same purpose, however, if the detachable spikes have to be added, that would no doubt stem from the lack of funding being in place for that athlete to purchase new all-inclusive track shoes.

This is just another key example why donations and fundraising is so necessary. It's all about "T-Belle Nation" dominance, but in a good sportsmanship way of course. After all, these noted girls are like any other 8 to 18 year old, with the same concerns. Making it through school and onto college successfully, combatting the buga-boos that can lurk patiently to grab our children away from His goodness and mercy. Teenage pregnancy, proper dieting information nutrition, dropping out of school, peer pressure and other factors are real, but they do not have to win over the good that we put forth.

Once again, "no one is paid staff, not even me." All service supporting the group is volunteer and the girls have been known to take up collections to help offset the Bus rental and meal costs. Parents. volunteers, and assistant coaches are sparse but well connected to the team and dedicated beyond measure. As Head Coach, I cannot stress it enough, "we have a high percentage of charted success with the girls. If they join the T-Belles at an early age and stay with the team throughout their school years, work hard and finish high school, chances are we can guarantee them a college scholarship."

The older girls are taught the ropes and how to pass the information and routines down to the younger girls. Every girl is treated with the same respect and are certainly expected to return that respect; work hard, be on time for practice and track meets, in or out of town and to keep their best foot forward at all times. It was heartwarming to hear and see the girls pray before practice, close out with prayer after practice and lock together to pray before big track meets.

The T-Belle Alumnus are very important to the program and organization, to say the least.

A Few Tribute Testimonials about Coach Sam Smith;

Anedra Henley-Logan

"A champion on and off the yrack" is one way that T-Belle Alumnus Anedra Henley–Logan describes Coach Sam Smith. Anedra is just one of many of his success stories and Alumni Club Members. She considers the 72 year old living legend to be a great maker of award winning athletes and a father figure in the interim. Coach Smith's drive, ongoing push, and heartfelt passion to see these girls succeed through the vehicle and discipline of sports is amazing! Especially for a man of his age who has overcome many obstacles in his lifetime. He could have relocated, traveled extensively (and still can) but yet he chooses to stay in Nashville and work with the parents, the girls and the community to help assure their journey in life. A man who doesn't hesitate to help anyone that he can and that puts new meaning to the words: "No child left behind!"

I love you Coach Smith and thank you for helping to make my life a success!

Anedra Henley-Logan

Catherine "Cathy" Bowers ~

I am not sure where I should begin because Coach Smith and I made state history years ago and it seem like we were a match made in heaven. I made history as being the first of his track and field accomplishments and was pivotal in the beginning of his coaching career. In 1978 Whites Creek Comprehensive HS had just opened and I had the opportunity to make history as a freshman achieving many accomplishments in the sport of T&F.
I lettered four years with Coach Smith and never knew I would be the first to catapult his coaching career for winning his first of many state championships. We both benefited greatly, I was his first state champion and All American as pentathlete and 100m hurdler in 1982. I am grateful to God to say I was his first All-American High School champion and his first USATF club athlete which was known as The Continental T-Belles. Coach Smith enabled us to excel through his guidance and strict discipline for the life of the sport. I am pleased to call Coach Smith my "coach for life". Not only does he guide young people in the sporting arena but also influences people in their everyday lives. It has been a blessing being mentored by him, and that has made me who I am today.

May God Bless and keep you always, Coach Smith.

Catherine "Cathy" Bowers

LaSonya McCutcheon ~

I was not a Tiger Bell but I did run track and cross country with Coach Smith while at Whites Creek High School. He was very tough and yelled a lot, but that was because of his tough love for us. As a result of this we became better women and State Champs. We were the team that every school wanted to be on. Coach Smith taught me that nothing comes easy, to be the best you have to work hard at it. He would always say "No Pain No Gain" and that is the way I approached life from all angles. I can truly say I am a go getter and hard working. I achieve everything that I put my mind to. I want to say **THANK YOU** for all the yelling, toughness, and for helping mold me into the woman which I am today.

Thanks, Coach Smith

LaSonya McCutcheon

When we asked "Coach Smith, why do you do this work Coach?"

It's been a blessing and a joy to pay it forward by tithing his time, experience and resources into these young lives. "Our greatest successes are young ladies who become self-reliant, disciplined, productive members of society.

Our greatest resource is the productive reinforcement of family, community and God."

~Coach Sam Smith ~

Contact: tbellestrackclub@yahoo.com
www.Facebook.com/pages/Continental-T-Belles-Track-Field-Club

Damon King

The Hardest Working Man in Gospel Radio
"Too blessed to be stressed by any negative test"

Introduction

My name is Damon King and I was born in Columbia, TN. My father was the pastor and bishop of the Church of God Sanctified. He served as a pastor for 50 plus years. My father was dependable and dedicated, and was the biggest mentor in my life. He taught me right and wrong. Although we didn't always do right, he raised us right. My father was big on treating others right. He taught us to put our trust in God. I have come to appreciate his guidance. It has helped guide me into the man that I am today.

My father taught me to love God, be a real man, and how to treat women. He taught me to focus on my relationship with

God and that other things and people won't matter, because if I love the Lord I don't have to worry about anything else because God is on my side. I was taught respect for my elders.

Today I enjoy what I do in life, because of my father. He taught me from an early age not to get hung up on being jealous of other people. Jealously is not of God. It can hinder you from what you are called to do for God's Kingdom. My mother also taught me to be gentle at heart and not be mean and hateful. Her words of wisdom allowed me to carry that into my adult life. My mother was a God fearing woman. She always taught me to love on people and treat them respectfully no matter how they treated me.

The bible says, ***Therefore all things whatsoever ye would that men should do to you, do ye even so to them.*** (KJV) Matt. 7:12 I believe this for my life. God has blessed me to build lasting relationships with people because I have strongly believed this verse. I am so grateful for the impact both of my parents had on my life and how much they invested in me. Both of my parents have passed on to Glory. I know that I will see them again.

When I first got into radio, I was playing R&B music over the air. I would often feel guilty about it. But my dad taught me that God can bless me to be where I am to do what I need to do. Because of his encouraging words, it changed my attitude and literally my life. I no longer felt guilty as a gospel announcer because I knew my heart was with God. It has brought me to the place where I am today.

Radio

I have very humble beginnings and I give all thanks and honor to God for making all things possible in my life. I am the Senior Account Executive, and Midday and Weekend Host of a Gospel Radio Show, Producer and Host of a new TV show, and successful concert promoter in my own right. I have promoted plays and concerts for many famous people throughout the years, from the Tyler Perry stage plays among others, to also include artists like Donald Lawrence, Shirley Caesar, Kirk Franklin, Vickie Winans and more. I have been known to sell out shows that I promote, as well as shows that I host. I am blessed that God made me to be a creative person and I like to surround myself with positive and creative people. I don't like sitting around doing nothing. I have to stay occupied. I don't think I would have earned the title *Hardest Working Man in Gospel Radio* if it had not been for a strong work ethic. This title was first given to me by Bishop Kenneth Dupree, Pastor of the Victory Church in Nashville, TN. I'll never forget it. All in all, I enjoy impacting people positively. Again this goes back to the teaching that I received from my youth.

Since my career first began in radio, I have been able to branch out into other things. I recently was hired a Morning Show Host, Producer, and Promoter for a local full time Gospel Station 760AM in Nashville. Here I will have the opportunity to connect with the community on a locally produced show and be more involved in my community. I also started an internet radio station at www.gmcawards.net with is carrying our music ministry nationwide. Before accepting my new position with 760AM, I was employed at the LIGHT Radio Station which is 102.1FM/101.9FM in Nashville andClarksville, TN. I served as Consultant Director for WPRT FM. My show aired on 101.9FM in Clarksville, TN and also 102.1FM in Nashville, Tennessee. I was with the LIGHT Radio Station for six years.
But before I tell you where I am today, I must first tell you of my humble beginnings. I would like to share with you about my career in radio before I even went to school for it.

We really had only one station in Columbia that played a range of music in 1976. WKRM radio played a mix of rock and roll, rhythm and blues, and country. I worked midnights there until I went off to school.

75

At Middle Tennessee State University, I was really able to advance my skills and learn more about the career I had already come to love. I learned about editing, voice overs and all aspects of radio. I had the opportunity to work at their college radio station from the beginning of my time there until I graduated.

Upon graduating from Middle Tennessee State University, I began working for WVOL. I started out on their night shift. I stayed there for a year before I was promoted to the afternoon drive. After WVOL I decided I wanted to go back to gospel. Dr. Morgan Babb gave me an opportunity at WMDB 880AM, also known as the Big Mouth. During my time at WMDB I was also able to venture into teaching at Fisk University. I was an independent broadcasting teacher. I also managed their station.
I worked for WFSK, at Fisk University where I was the gospel morning music host for 10 years. I was able to transform that station from a college radio show to a program that went out into the community and was very successful in the years to come. I was number one for many years and enjoyed my job and time there. I worked alongside Clarence Kilcrease and Sistah Willie Ruth Johnson before coming to 101.9FM. We were a great team until the management changed. Our popular morning show was called "Let's Talk" and in the afternoon we did fun creative programming for our listeners. My main job there was producing, promoting, and production sales.

New Places and Faces

In the early 2000s I had come to the city of Clarksville, TN to help build up accounts for my station and was on the air. The station was changing and I didn't want to do the job. This is what I called my wilderness experience. Every day I would drive 100 miles to and from Clarksville, TN. I began talking to God during that drive. God was talking and I was listening. This was a time in my life where God was making me. Being successful is all about Him and has nothing to do with you. Never underestimate what God will do in your life. I didn't understand how come everything around me at the time seemed like it wasn't in my favor or working for my good. But God opened a door for me to still be on the air. While our station was undergoing a transition, God was transitioning me for a new beginning. You have to trust the process and allow God to work in your life. I had to build a staff of people to help me. Soon I began making connections in the city. God would send people by the station to encourage me. All along He had a plan. The devil was mad and did not want me to be on the air, but God blessed me to run a successful morning show in spite of everything enemy attempted. He will send people to help you and He did. The station was still on the air in Nashville, but God was now using me in Clarksville. I am thankful to God for ordering my steps and placing the right key connections in my life; from pastors, to people in the print industry, to CEOs and Directors of various organizations. I was able to build upon many successful contacts in the area and eventually returned back to the city of Nashville at the same station. When I left Clarksville on orders from my job to go back to Nashville, many people from Clarksville were mad and thought I had left them. But I had nothing to do with the transition. Today God has reestablished those relationships. I have never left either city. My heart is to spread the Gospel to all people in all places.

FROM THEN TO NOW

Over the years I've become a better promoter and marketer. I've learned to market not only the station's name but my own. In my career I have learned that stations can go away. I see it happen quite often. They get bought and sold all the time, and so I learned that just as equally important for my listeners to learn the station's name, it was even more important that I began to build upon my name; the name that people tune in to early mornings or afternoons.

I began building my own brand; my name. In order to do that, I had to build a good reputation and a good name and do things in the right way. Connections are great to build upon. Always work at maintaining positive relationships.

A good name is rather to be chosen than great riches, and loving favour rather than silver and gold. KVJ Proverbs 22:1

Over the years I have been blessed to be the Founder of the Gospel Music City Awards Show (GMCA), and the owner of KIAD Productions. The GMCA is an annual event that celebrates artists and pastors in the community. This Nashville event has caught the attention of major gospel artist and promoters in cities near and far. This program brings out hundreds of people at a time in celebration of great gospel music. The people will vote online for their favorite artist or song, as well as pastors too. I believe we have great people who help add to the Kingdom. I am blessed to be able to provide a platform for artist and pastors as well as service to my community.

My ministry in radio has afforded me the opportunity to interview several mainstream artists throughout the years from Byron Cage, Shirley Caesar, Dr. Bobby Jones, Dr. Dorinda Clark Cole and more. I also work in my spare time as DJ to several events. I like old school music. If anyone knows me, they know I love old school music. That was great music back them. I think there ought to be a meaning in the song. Many people get caught up in the beat, but I think the words and the meaning have far greater significance. I get people who ask me all the time to play their music over the air. I cannot always do that. It is never personal, but songs have to be packaged and mastered professionally that are fit for airplay. I often try to educate artist who are looking to have their music played on mainstream radio. I know how to recognize a hit and I know what it will take to break it in to the music industry. The music business alone is a hard market to get into, but if you are blessed to make it in, consider that a great accomplishment. I will say to artists trying to make it into the industry, to not be discouraged. Also have other people to listen to your work other than your family; people who will be honest and tell you if your music is of quality.

In 2013, I married my wife Jewell Blackman. Our marriage works because we both have things that we deal with and go through, but we lean on each other, and trust in each other. It's more than just love, you have to have someone you can depend on and believe in who believes in you. I am thankful for my family and am blessed to have step children and now grandchildren. I see a lot of people who take their family for granted. If you have a spouse or children, love and cherish the time that God gives you with your family. A marriage works when love is involved.

Overall, I am a down to earth person. I love life. I love to laugh and have a great time. I am thankful for everyday that I awake out of bed. I am a Tennessee VOLS fan and enjoy outdoor sporting events and travel. I like meeting people and consider myself an outgoing person. Life is too short to spend it being unhappy. Find things that make you happy in life. A lot of people are single. When I was a single man, I kept busy with my job, church, and doing community events. Eventually God blessed me with a wife. Whether married or single, don't sit around feeling sorry for yourself, but find things to do. There are people around you who have it worse. Learn to count your blessings.

Learn to be happy at being you and don't sit around waiting for people to make you happy. Start first with yourself. Discover your passion and what it is that you would like to do with your life, and then pray about it. Remember to include God in all of your decisions.

Remember that you are too blessed to be stressed.

A passage of scripture that comes to mind is found in Proverbs 3:5,6.

[5] Trust in the Lord with all thine heart; and lean not unto thine own understanding.

[6] In all thy ways acknowledge him, and he shall direct thy paths.

As I close my chapter, I want to give God all the glory for my story. I would have never made it if it had not been for God.

Contact: gospelradio1021@gmail.com

Magnificent Man

Dr. Gregory M. Fryer, M.D.

Get Your God-Given Dream, Write It Down and Hold On To It

God is Faithful

Then the LORD answered me and said: "Write the vision and make it plain on tablets, that he may run who reads it. For the vision is yet for an appointed time; but at the end it will speak, and it will not lie. Though it tarries, wait for it; because it will surely come, it will not tarry.

Habakkuk 2:2-3 New King James Version (NKJV)

I entered the earth realm the last of four children to my mother and father in Greenville, SC, and my adventurous life began. My days were and continue to be filled with events that help fulfill my purpose. Each of us is uniquely created by God for a specific purpose. We are fearfully and wonderfully made and even before we were conceived in our mothers' wombs, God the Father knew us. Our God-given dreams and goals are for the fulfillment of our individual and collective purposes for which we were created. Our dreams and goals are orchestrated by God to bring about His majestic and symphonic will on earth.

The first step to discovering your dreams and goals is going to the source; going to the One who designed you. The Creator knows the reason why He created His creation. Today too many people do not believe in the biblical creation of the earth and the universe. Some scholars' state science as the reason for this false belief and that evolution is what brought everything which exists into being even though the scientific records do not support the theory of evolution. The evidence does support adaptation which still occurs, however evidence does not support one species evolving into another species. When people acknowledge that there is a Creator, God, then we have to acknowledge that we are here for a purpose and that we are accountable to God. When people do not believe in God, in essence they believe that mankind is not accountable for what we do in our lives. Those people who are violently against God and anything making reference to God want to cast off any and all moral restraint because they want to believe mankind decides what is basically right and wrong. Everything designed by an inventor and creator has a predetermined purpose. The Creator knows why He created you and acknowledging Him and earnestly seeking Him will help you discover your true dreams and goals, i.e. your purpose for being. You were created to impact this world for good because God is good.

I first recognized my God- given dream to become a physician at age eleven. Prior to that time I wanted to grow up to do various jobs but I had no idea or concern about purpose. However the road to the realization of my dream started well before then. A series of events in my life lead me to the altar of Jesus Christ to be reconciled with God, my Creator, and receive salvation.

The Right Path: The Start of the Journey

A journey of thousand miles starts with the first step. To go from where you are to a certain destination requires not only the first step, but also subsequent steps in the right direction. When I was seven years-old, my maternal grandfather, Marcellar Sheppard, died. "Poppa" which my siblings and I affectionately called him, was a spiritual pillar in my lineage. At the time, I did not grasp his impact in our family and on my life. Poppa was wise and a good provider. He loved to fish in his spare time. He was a deacon in our church who always had something good to say at the end of Sunday school. However, as a young boy eager to play, I lacked foresight to capture the priceless gems on paper. But unbeknown to me, God etched many of those truths upon my heart so that I reflect upon them often as an adult.

The next great impact on my life happened a few months later when my father was jailed and later sent to prison. My father was very smart, a hard worker and he was good at fixing and making things. He taught my brother and me how to fish and work hard. My father was a mechanic. After an injury, he started his own paint, body and fender business and built a garage in our backyard. I remember when he cut a car in half, removed the back seat section, reattached the ends and made it into a car-truck like those El Caminos in the 1970s. However, he abused alcohol and would often come home drunk. He had a violent temper and he would break furniture. I do not recall him ever physically abusing my mother or my siblings until one day in 1976. I do not know all the details. I was outside, my youngest sister was inside, my father came home, and I never saw him again outside of the penal system until after my high school graduation. After his trial my mother told me and my siblings that he would be in prison until I reached 18 years of age.

Without my two major, male, role models my world was rocked. Later that year, I received Jesus as my Lord and Savior and joined the Church. The redemptive power of Jesus Christ provides me a peaceful assurance which stabilized my spirit throughout the chaos and changes in life. I started on my right journey.

Statistics were against me being successful, but God had other plans. With my mother now a single-parent of four, our family was plunged further into poverty. Fatherlessness is the greatest cause of poverty and generational welfare enslavement. We were poor, but we did not have a poverty mentality. One of my fondest memories is when I got a job in high school and chose to get off the free-lunch program and pay for my own lunch.

My mother stressed to us to reach for the stars and she encouraged us to do and to be our best. She implemented daily reading of sections of the book of Proverbs for my brother and me. Even before our father was sent to prison, my mother ensured she took us to church and that we participated in church. Furthermore she insisted upon knowing our friends; if she did not approve of them she did not want us associating with them. God gave my mother great wisdom. Somewhere around my freshman year of high school, my mother and I watched a documentary of Dr. Benjamin Carson's journey to become the youngest chairman of John Hopkins' Neurosurgery Department and the first neurosurgeon to successfully separate twins conjoined at the head. Dr. Carson became an inspiration and mentor to me. I read Gifted Hands and I established and maintain a relationship with him by reading his other books.

Write Down the Vision

I wrote my goal to become a physician for the first time in the seventh grade as a journal entry assignment for my English class. I still have my seventh-grade journal. During my senior year of high school I made a banner, "Dr. G. M. Fryer, M.D." and I placed it over my bed and desk throughout college. I did not fully grasp the impact of this principle of writing down goals until I was in college and my professor of military sciences told me of the research study about the 3% high-achieving, ivy-league college graduates who wrote down their goals and over the next

50 years greatly surpassed and achieved their goals with higher success rates than the rest of their classmates who did not write down their goals. A few years later I got the revelation of Habakkuk 2: 2–3. Annually, I write down my goals and I review them frequently. I prayerfully consider them when I write them down and I keep them before me to keep me on track.

God Provides for the Dreams He Gives

Growing up, money was very tight. I had no idea how we were going to afford college and especially medical school. I was blessed to get a partial scholarship and a Pell Grant during the first year at the University of Georgia, however I took out a $2,000 student loan to make up the difference. The $2,000 student loan might as well have been $2 million. For the last three years of college I was blessed to receive a 3-year Reserve Officer Training Corps scholarship which covered all of my expenses and gave me $100 monthly stipend. During the summers I worked at a warehouse and at a trucking company. Over Christmas breaks I was able to work part-time at a department store as a stocker.

I learned about the Uniformed Services University of the Health Sciences, the military's medical school, from another ROTC student who was a year ahead of me. This information was definitely a God-send and a blessing when I was accepted into the school. Not only is this medical school free for everyone who attends but also all students receive full benefits and are paid as first level officers in his or her chosen service branch. For me it was a lieutenant in the Army. Praise God! I did not have to go into debt to go to medical school. Also I paid off the student loan from my undergraduate years during the first year of medical school.

Persevere

High school and college were relatively easy to me and I did well throughout those years, however during my first year of medical school I found myself really struggling in some of my basic science classes. Someone described medical school as "drinking water out of a fire-hose" but I soon realized that I was expected to learn and to know all of the information. What kept me hanging on through the first two years was my desire to become a physician and the fact that if I failed I did not know what I would do. Many of the professors offered tutoring sessions because the school was supportive and wanted you to succeed. The bright spots, which helped be maintain my eyes on the prize, throughout the first two years of medical school was my Clinical Concepts classes and when we were able to see and do physical exams on live patients. Although I was studying almost every waking-hour, I plugged into a local Christian church. My church small-group encouraged me to grow spiritually and deepened my relationship with Jesus. God sustained me and His Spirit guided me.

Forgive: Let Go of Bitterness

One of the greatest inhibitors of one to obtain his/her goals is holding on to past hurts or wrongs either real or perceived. I realized this when I was in my second year at the Uniformed Services University. My father's brother died and since I was close by Baltimore, MD where his family lived, I left class early to attend the family gathering after the funeral. My father and his two remaining siblings were there and I decided to go with them on a short trip up to Philadelphia to visit their father who was in the hospital. My uncle and aunt had received the forgiveness of Jesus Christ by this time and they had extended forgiveness to their father. When we entered into my grandfather's hospital room, the bitterness between my father and his father was so thick, one could cut it with a knife. The next day the Holy Spirit convicted me that I needed to forgive my father and ask for his forgiveness. I did so and experienced a greater freedom to be all that God had planned for me. I pray that my father comes to know Jesus as his Savior.

Trust God for Your Spouse

At the end of my junior year at the University of Georgia, I had the privilege to meet and befriend Erien Wynne, a beautiful young lady in my biochemistry class. I needed a date to the ROTC ball and she obliged to go with me. Erien was wonderful, smart and easy to talk to. She was in graduate school and moved to Augusta but we continued to stay in touch and she came back to UGA to attend my senior ROTC ball with me. In my third year of medical school, as our friendship grew, I prayed and asked God if Erien was the woman He had for me to marry. I needed God to answer me clearly like he answered Gideon in the book of Judges Chapter 6. God affirmed His answer clearly to me but when I broke the great news to Erien one afternoon over lunch, she did not seem so enthused. In fact her response made me question, "Did I really hear God say that she was to be my wife?" I continued to pursue my dreams, study hard throughout my clerkships, and trust God. Three years later during my internship when I asked Erien to marry me while sitting in a beach park in Honolulu, HI, Erien said, "Yes." Three months later, at the end of the internship, we were married. Our chemistry is perfect for each other and Erien is the perfect wife for me. It is important that you have a spouse who is equally yoked with you and who is an encourager of your goals and supports you, that you do the same for your spouse. The best way to find the right spouse is to seek God and have Him direct you to your spouse in His timing.

Continue to Grow and Dream

I graduated medical school on May 21, 1994 and finished my internship a year later. By August 1995 I had obtained my medical license but I had new dreams and goals already in the works. When I embarked on the journey to become a physician, I thought I wanted to become a cardiothoracic surgeon and then after I was 40-50 years-old I would change to family medicine. After the internship, doors for surgery residency did not open. Through prayers and evaluating pros and cons of surgery versus family medicine residency, I decided to pursue family medicine. Erien told me she had always saw me as a family medicine physician, and because of her spiritual maturity and grace she supported my pursuit of surgery and then rejoiced with me when I chose family medicine. Doors of opportunity immediately opened.

It seems like yesterday when I completed Family Medicine residency at Fort Benning, GA, moved to Clarksville, TN, and two years later Erien and I were blessed to have our son. Now I have been in the Army over 24 years, 18 of which as a physician, and recently retired. Opening an independent private practice, Medical Direct Care, eight months after my Army retirement was the birth of the dream conceived when I was eleven years-old.

God is good and He is faithful. Trust God. Commit your goals and dreams to paper. Put them in a place where you can see them regularly. Hold on to them. Press on toward them. They will come to past with God's help.

Contact: www.medicaldirectcare.com

Magnificent Man

Dr. William Luffman

**Senior Founding Pastor with Ginger Luffman of
Faith Outreach Church**

I have learned over the years that everyone has a story to tell. Each one is packed with highs and lows and is a gift from God. My story is one of these.

I am a native to Clarksville, Tennessee. My childhood family, and roots are in this city, which my love and dedication to my community. I have a passion for the military. Although I never joined the Armed Services, I have great compassion and a great deal of respect for all of our entire military.

I was the last of nine children born to my mother, Mildred Moore Perry. My mom was nearly 43 when she had me in 1958 and was a very poor, unwed mother. I was also a twin. They told my mom that my brother died after he was born. My mom never believed it. But in the 1950s, hospitals in middle Tennessee were notorious for taking babies from poor mothers and selling them on the black market. This was supposedly done because they felt the children would be much better off in a good home where they could be provided well for and they used this theory to substantiate these actions. It was mostly about power and money, maybe there is some truth to that theory.

My mom lacked an education and my dad was pretty much a non-factor, walking out on us on more than one occasion before leaving for good when I was 10. We struggled to survive and had it not been for governmental help, we wouldn't have made it. Looking back at these times I had a mother who was strong. She might have only weighed 95 pounds but was the strongest woman I have ever known in my life, until I met my wife. Mom went home to be with the Lord in 1993. I know that one day we will be re-united again.

I did not have a father in my life, so I understand what that is like for children growing up without a father. I know it first hand. I was blessed to have two men to be in my life who helped make a difference. I have to say I am thankful for these men who were like stepfathers to me. They have now passed away, but I would like to make mention of Steve Wolfe.

From a very early time in my life, I became a very avid reader. My mom, who despite her lack of education was also a very good reader. She read a lot to me and then had me read back to her describing what I read. It really accelerated me in just about every way.

Because I could read well and understood what I read, I was a very imaginative child. If I took an interest in something, I became consumed in it. I had a chemical laboratory in my bedroom when I was 12. I built a weather station in my backyard when I was 14. I had a "radio station" in my bedroom when I was 15. These passions still exist today in my life.

Despite being at the top of my class, I became disinterested in school in my sophomore year and dropped out. This immature decision was one of many more I would make in the next year. I got married that year (I was only 16!).

I didn't have many work options, so I did what most male high school dropouts do; I worked in food service (Dairy Queen) and construction (house painter). Needless to say, the next few years were a struggle in every imaginable way, except one; my stepfather, Steve, had been inviting me to his church for weeks. I never really seriously considered it until I had a dream one night. In the dream, I died and was slipping into a dark, dark abyss. I awakened and realized that if that dream had been real, I was lost. I went to church the following Sunday and became a born-gain Christian. In the next year, I heard and accepted the call to ministry.

Since that time, God has done tremendous things in my life. I am humbled when I think about how little I had to offer Him and how much He seems to be able to do with it!

Today, I pastor a church in Clarksville, TN called Faith Outreach Church. The church was established in August, 1989, and has an ever-growing membership of over 2,000 members.

At Faith Outreach Church, we strive to present the good news of Jesus Christ in an uncompromising, yet relative way through the consistent preaching of God's Word. The vision has always been to minister to people of all ethnic and social backgrounds, but especially to those who are hurting because of loss, divorce, or neglect. I believe God has a special plan for all of our lives and through the application of His Word we can have an abundant and fulfilling life here on earth. At Faith Outreach Church, we believe the following principles to be true. I daily live by the following:

Worshiping GOD as a Christian is not just about singing, fasting and praying. GOD is not interested in what you do as much as why you do it. HE does not honor hypocrisy - only a heart devoted to HIM. Worship is not something you just do on Sunday... it is a lifestyle. We are to love, trust, obey, praise, thank and live only for HIM every day. It is about surrender. It will cost you your self-centeredness. We are to worship in spirit and in truth. We were made specifically to bring GOD pleasure and glory.

Fellowship is all about living life together during the good and bad times. It is about being genuine, transparent and vulnerable in the things you share in confidence with others. It is about loving your neighbor as yourself. It is about encouraging others and sympathizing with their feelings. We are all part of God's family and He wants us to grow in our love for others. True love is about forgiveness and reconciliation.

Discipleship is about growing and maturing – it is the process of becoming like Jesus Christ. Growing is not easy – it takes work and commitment. It requires us to examine and change the way we think, feel and act. Thankfully HE also gives us HIS Spirit and HIS Word to transform us into the image of Christ. Additionally GOD uses other people and circumstances in our lives to help us grow through trials, temptations, and troubles. Through Jesus, we are more than conquerors! That means, no matter what is thrown our way, God will make us victorious!

Ministry is all about serving and giving. As Christians we are called to a ministry in the body of believers and a mission to the world. Each of us are shaped and gifted by GOD to fulfill our part in HIS great plan. Find the blessing of losing yourself in serving Jesus by serving others. Though we are saved only by HIS grace HE also calls us to good works – not to earn salvation but to encourage and equip the body of believers. Ministry is about serving an audience of ONE!

Evangelism is about sharing the love of Christ with everyone. We are all commanded to go and make disciples. This is our mission as Christians and it is not an option. In fact, it is a profound responsibility, the greatest privilege, and the most incredible honor in the entire world. This mission is the greatest thing you can do for another person, carries eternal significance, and is the true secret of being blessed!

I love our military community and families that we serve. A large segment of our congregation is active or retired from military service. We hold our relationship with our service men and women and their families very close to our hearts. We share their devotion to God and our great nation, and honor their patriotism and sacrifice.

I enjoy writing and have two books I have written. The first is called *Wake Up With The Word* and the second is *Turn In With The Word*, both books are devotionals and minister daily to the soul. I would like to think of it as food for the soul. I have also written three mini books entitled *Facebook, Who is This Man?,* and *Alcohol, Just One Drink*. These books are small enough to fit in your purse, and only takes a few minutes to read.

When writing these devotionals, I was inspired by the Holy Spirit to put them together. These devotionals were written to help people get their perspectives back and energize their faith at the end of the day. I pray that those who read my books will find them inspiring as they continue to grow in the hunger of Christ.

All in all, I have been in ministry for 38 years. I never imagined that my life would have turned out this way. God is always in control and has the master plan. Along the way I have had many people to speak into my life; powerful men and women of God from Kenneth Copeland, Dr. Hilton Sutton, Dr. Mark Barclay, Ed and Nancy Dufresne, Jim and Sylvia Miley, and many more. I have seen God move.

I would like to shine the light on my wife Ginger, who has stood beside me through thick and thin. We have been married for nearly 33 years. She is also a native of Clarksville, TN. Pastor Ginger spent many of her young years and a portion of her teenage years in Detroit, MI. She grew up in a church environment being in a singing group with two of her sisters. She felt the call of God on her life at the age of 15. She has obtained numerous certificates, recognitions, and accolades in the financial and administrative fields. Together, with my best friend and supportive wife, pastor Faith Outreach Church. She's walked by my side at some of the lowest moments of my life.

We have three adult children, several grandchildren and a great grand-son.

We also have one infant son who is now in Heaven. We love spending time with our family and especially our grandchildren. We treasure these moments.

In 2013, my wife and I introduced our plant church called Faith Outreach Community Church with Pastors David and Barbara Wesner. The church is our second campus and is growing.

If there is one verse that stands out to me the most, it is Mark 9:23: "With men, this impossible, but with God, all things are possible!"

God has truly been faithful to me over the years; He has provided everything I could have ever imagined my life to be and more.

I would like to encourage each heart today that is reading my chapter. I would like to share an excerpt from my book *Turn in with the Word*. This derives from page 235 and is *titled Born To Win* and was written on July 30th.

II Corinthians 2:14 – The Messiah, in Christ, God leads us from place to place in one perpetual victory parade. Through us, he brings knowledge of Christ, Everywhere we go, people breath in the exquisite fragrance." (MSG)

I heard a story about a little boy who stayed outside longer than usual. His mother came looking for him. She found him shooting basketball on the goal he had nailed on the big oak tree in the backyard. She asked him, "What are

you still doing out here playing? It's way past time for you to be inside." He replied, "I can't come in until I win." "Win against whom? She asked. "Against me!" he said. Later in life, this little boy becomes a professional basketball player!

People who have the drive to excel usually do. They are the first to rise and the last to go to bed. They are never satisfied with the mediocrity and set high standards for themselves. God wants us to become winners! He desires for us to live a life where we are constantly celebrating the victories He gives us. Those victories cost Him everything. He allowed His own Son to lose His life, so that we might gain the victory through Him.

If you know Him, do not ever buy into the notion that you are a loser. The high price has been paid and you are a winner in Him! You were born to win!

Meditation – "Lord, I will never again refer to my life as that of a loser. I realize you have created me to win in you, and I will! In Jesus' name, Amen!"

I believe my life is a reminder that no matter whom you are, where you were born and what you have done, there is always a way up and a way out!

Here are five meditations to leave you with. Say these on a daily basis or choose one each day to meditate upon.

#1 - Lord, remind me of the greatness of walking in faith. Remind me I do not need force to see victory, but continue in faith in what you have said about my life. Help me to walk in faith that shines so brightly others walk in the light of its path. In Jesus' name, Amen!

#2 - Lord, thank you for giving me the strength and the skill to earn what I need to bless your house and my family. I will fulfill my obligations. In Jesus' name, Amen!

#3 - Lord, forgive me for being lazy. I know you have great blessings for me when I work, and I will. In Jesus' name, Amen!

#4 - Lord, I will no longer wait for you to do something. I will do my part and take the actions I am supposed to take. I know when I do; you will help me to win. In Jesus' name, Amen!

#5 - Lord, I am so thankful that you have washed away the memory of my former life. I know I am new in you and no longer resemble the old person. I will never look that way again. In Jesus' name, Amen!"

God bless you for reading my chapter. I pray that you will be strengthened and encouraged in Jesus' name. I close with this; my life was nothing without Him and everything with Him. He is, of all men, most magnificent!

Contact: Outreachm@aol.com
www.outreachministriesinc.com

Dr. Albert "Al'Wayne" Miller

HEAVEN DRIVEN

I will bless the LORD at all times: his praise shall continually be in my mouth. Psalm 34:1

Growing up in LeFlore, Mississippi, parented by the late Carter and Ethel Miller, since age four I knew I wanted to sing but I didn't know that it would come at such a cost. Every day I would come from Headstart and put on our 45 Motown record by Stevie Wonder. The song was entitled, "Signed, Sealed, Delivered". I would use the coffee table as my make-shift piano. I would sing that song until I reached the 2nd grade. I came home one day from school and my record was broken in two pieces. My brother had stayed at home sick (yeah right!) and broke my record. I was terribly torn by this action and I needed vengeance. He was older and stronger than me so there was nothing I could do but cry. I never sang again when I was in elementary or middle school but I knew it was my destiny.

I began to dance and oh boy was I a good dancer. I would dance at all the home gatherings, Christmas, Easter, birthdays, reunions, etc. Michael Jackson was my favorite dancer. I later started doing my own dances. No one could beat me dancing.
In the fifth grade, I joined the band and played the saxophone. While in band, I began rapping to the white girls. They were fascinated at my skills. I was still entertaining. I entered high school at second chair over all the other upper classmen. I would never stopped practicing until I received a scholarship. Well, the college band I went to was nothing like my high school band. My high school band was ranked #1 in the state and #12 in the nation. The college band was like going back to the fifth grade. I quit playing the saxophone and joined the S.O.U.L. Club Gospel Choir (Society Of Universal Love) where I learned how to sing in harmony and break down the parts. I was so in love with this until later I started my own choir.

After receiving Christ and being filled with the Holy Ghost in 1992, I got married and moved to Clarksville, Tn. While married, already an ordained deacon, I received my calling to the ministry in 1994 and was ordained in 1996 after moving back to Mississippi. All I wanted to do was preach and sing. While in Clarksville, I started the Clarksville Multi-denominational Mass Choir. The choir was a group of singers that really couldn't sing and I did all I could do which wasn't a whole lot. Pastor Emmanuel Barnes began playing and helping teach the choir. Although we were great, we never made it to our first concert. I had to move back to Mississippi due to the illness of my mother-in-law.

In 1996, I began working at Mississippi Valley State University for the Department of Mass Communications. I met a group of singers who were highly anointed and super talented. They had already been singing and had a director. Their director needed a leader and chose me because I could get them in places they had never been. I have two siblings that are pastors who gladly welcomed us in their church during our only tour. The tour lasted for about a year.

I had already written over 70 songs. We later recorded our first studio recording and later did a live recording. We were also chosen to do a live recording, "Mississippi's Best Kept Secrets". I had already named them A Special Anointing.

The director was having salvation issues and later quit. I began directing and leading the choir. I was finally where I was called to be. The closer I got to God, the more trouble I encountered.

I had started my own church ministry in Greenwood and was appointed Bishop by other pastors in Greenwood, Mississippi. My wife grew weary of me traveling and doing revivals. She was a lead/background singer of A Special Anointing so we traveled together in that ministry. I also formed the Children of Life Community Mass Choir. It was a 150 voice group of disadvantaged and at risk youth. With two choirs, a church and an evangelism ministry, we grew apart because I was in such high demand. She could not go because of her job. I had resigned from my job to do full-time ministry at the age of 26. God was truly blessing me on the road but we paid the price at home. We closed the church in 1998, separated in 2000 and divorced in 2001. This is where the fun began.

I moved to Vidalia, Georgia with a ministry, a ministry like none I had encountered. It was a luxurious ministry but I wasn't preaching as much. We traveled by limo and tour bus and lived collectively in a 20 room mansion. I later realized that I had joined a cult.

Upon my departure from that ministry, I was called to a meeting where I was blamed for everything I had gone through. I left with nothing but a briefcase. My clothes, furniture and all memorabilia was left at that house. I left walking and a white couple picked me up and took me to their house and fed me. They paid for me a hotel room for a week. I had been blessed to buy a cell phone. One of the members of the church secretly called me and began to help me. She had a friend who took me in for about a month. I got a job and moved in my own apartment. I began going to church with a neighbor until I joined the First African Baptist church and was later appointed Associate Minister. I was still on my job to becoming a magnificent man.

After leaving Georgia, I moved back home for about a year and began preaching and singing everywhere. I sang at a festival in 2004, sponsored by Lee Williams and the Q Cs. It was an awesome experience that I would never forget. I was reassured that it was my calling.

During that event, I signed on a manager from St. Paul, Minn, I traveled to St. Paul a couple of times and later got a call from George Stewart, Founder of the Quartet Convention. He wanted to manage me. We never did connect and I moved to Albany, Georgia and continued preaching and singing until I met a bishop that needed a senior pastor at one of his churches in Smithville, Ga. I gladly accepted the position. I later determined that it wasn't where God wanted me. I moved to Americus, Georgia where I joined a praise team. I quickly shined and was obviously brighter than I should have been (in the eyes of the pastor). He was determined to do without me. He started turning my microphone down and turning his up while singing the same note as I. I left and continued working until I began to notice that my breathing wasn't just quite right. I began to walk shorter distances until I couldn't walk at all. I went from walking five miles from work to barely walking to the bathroom which was next door to my bedroom.

One night, I couldn't sleep for shortness of breath. No position was comfortable. I finally found a position, sitting up in a chair. I was awakened by the voice of God thirty minutes later. "Go to the hospital RIGHT NOW!" I went to the hospital and they took me to an emergency room immediately. I was alert but short of breath. I joked with the nurse and told her how beautiful she was. She left and I felt a feeling that I had never felt before. It was a roaring sound as if I was inside a large engine. It quickly turned to a sound as if it was winding down. All I can remember is slumping over toward the side of the bed. Before I landed, I was unconscious. I remember seeing a lot of doctors and nurses surrounding my bed and I was gone again. I finally awakened to see a nurse pushing the crash cart out of the room. I later found out from a friend who was rushing to be by my side that my heart had stopped and it took them forty minutes to revive me. For two months, I had a soreness in the center of my chest. It's been 8 years and it is still tender to touch. When the doctor was administering CPR on me, he broke my sternum. It is a common consequence of resuscitation.

I was diagnosed with recurring pulmonary embolisms (blood clots in the lungs). I have a protein c deficiency that causes the blood to be thick and consequently clot.

I was rendered disabled and received a check for six months until it was cut off. I had to go home to be by my mother's side when she got out of the hospital from having a mastectomy due to pre-cancerous cells. I stayed there for two weeks. When I got back, I had received a letter for a court date and had already missed it. It was now a warrant. A sheriff officer came to my house and arrested me but couldn't keep me due to my condition. I was placed in a Do Not Arrest file. I was placed on probation and wasn't getting enough money to live and pay the fine. As a result, the county contacted the Social Security Administration and had my check terminated stating that it would only help me to elude them. I struggled on with no income until I decided to move to Orangeburg, South Carolina. I was homeless, living in a hotel by the grace of God and the help of family and strangers. I stayed there for two weeks until a pastor took me to Columbia, South Carolina and paid for a hotel for two weeks. I knew no one and had no transportation. He also gave me $200 for food and beverages. I went grocery shopping and I had money left. After my time was up there, I had nowhere to go. I was extremely homeless, standing outside a grocery store. I did not feel defeated at all, in spite of everything that had already happened. My faith had grown and I knew that God would make a way for me. It had grown dark and I had nothing. Finally, I walked to the dollar store and met a young couple who took me to a hotel and paid for a week. Look at God! The next day, I went walking, yes walking. I was feeling great. I had a roof over my head and food. I walked to a church that was opened and I walked in. The bishop spoke to me to find out what was happening. I told him and he asked if I had any skills. I told him what I could do and also stated my title and gifts. He wanted to hear me sing. After hearing me sing and play, he took me to a better hotel and paid for two weeks. I was now his worship leader.

After the two weeks were over, he had secured an apartment for me, rent free. I stayed there for a couple of months and got sick again. The doctor recommended that she implant a filter to catch the clots before they reach my lungs. I agreed and it was implanted in my inferior vena cava, the main vein that carries blood to and from your head to your feet. I had to also take blood thinners to ensure that I didn't have another clot.

The bishop decided that he wanted to purchase a transient center and a church and allow me to manage and pastor. I was installed as the senior pastor of the church in Orangeburg. The center had to close and I was homeless again.

I found out that there was room in a shelter. I went and was processed in the same day. I stayed there for two months until the bishop in Smithville, Georgia wanted me to help him with a new show on the Word Network. I returned to help him. I was the worship leader, director and co-editor for the show for six months. It was an international show which got me lots of connections with the music industry.

After he cancelled the show, I began working as the general manager of his newly formed sandwich shop. The restaurant was in a small town with very little customers. I noticed that I was getting sick again. I was living in a small inadequate space.

During this period, two years ago, I had gotten a call from my sister telling me that my mother had passed. I went in a serious insane state for three days. I cried until I almost died. I didn't go to sleep for two days and when I did go to sleep, Death came in the form of my mother and was choking me with its forearm. God awakened me to go to the bathroom. The next night, God sent an angel in the form of my mother, telling me that she was alright and not to worry. She held me until I went to sleep and my mind was restored. The bishop only gave me $40 dollars to get home. I knew our relationship was OVER!

When I returned from the funeral, the lights were off in the restaurant and I had to move in the church for a couple of nights in Smithville. A pastor friend and her husband came and got me and I lived with them for two months. I began to play the keyboard and lead worship at her church. I had started making connections on Facebook like never before, using their computer at home.

I met a young lady who has a brother that used to sing with a famous gospel group. She said that they would produce me. I contacted them in Nashville and set up a meeting. I was quite ill when I left on the bus to Nashville. I made it to my meeting and the very next day, my heart stopped where I was staying. My friend came home to find me on the floor and he hit me in my chest and I awakened. He told me that I wasn't breathing and noticed that I had urinated on myself. I was rushed to the hospital by ambulance. I already had one filter implanted and I had to have another one implanted because the filter had tilted and a large life-threatening clot was hanging out of it. I knew that someone had to pay.

I moved with my sister, Pastor Dr. Jane W. Garland and in April, a lawsuit commercial came on tv and I called and am now awaiting a mega million dollar settlement.

I recently found out that I had been sought after by the Social Security Administration stating that they owe me back pay for seven years and that my check would resume.

I am now living in my own apartment fully furnished with my rent paid for a year. I have released my single, "Heaven Driven" and have almost completed my cd, **"#SOULREHAB"**. I have also celebrated 20 years in the ministry.

Out of all I've gone through, I still have joy. Victory is mine and I am on my way to being the man that God called me to be a Magnificent Man. This is my testimony for the last 41 years of my life. I am yet to be healed but I know God is a healer. I've been through the storm and rain but guess what, I MADE IT!

The lyrics to "Heaven Driven" are below.

HEAVEN DRIVEN
Accept my praise. Accept my worship. Lord I praise you every day.
For the ways you've made and your awesome power. I acknowledge you in all my ways.
I will serve you Lord with all of my might. Every battle I face I know you will fight.
I love you Lord with all of my heart. Nothing on this earth can keep us apart.
I'm totally Heaven driven. Heaven driven. Heaven driven. Heaven driven.
I'm totally Heaven driven. Heaven driven. Heaven driven. Heaven driven.
Good days are here. Better days are coming. I wanna be where you are in the end.
The Holy One. You are so righteous. You are my Comforter my Friend.
I will serve you Lord with all my might. Every battle I face I know you will fight.
I love you Lord with all of my heart. Nothing on this earth can keep us apart.
I'm totally Heaven driven. Heaven driven. Heaven driven. Heaven driven.

I'm totally Heaven driven. Heaven driven. Heaven driven. Heaven driven.

I'm HEAVEN DRIVEN!

No matter what I'm going through, I always find a reason to praise God.

Psalms 34:1 says, *"I will bless the Lord at ALL times and His praise shall continually be in my mouth."*

As you have walked on this journey with me, I pray that you have been encouraged by the outcome. I hope you've realized the awesome power that God has to turn your life around so that you will have a testimony that will lift you up and give God all the glory.

May God bless and keep you.

Contact: heavenzgiftnd21c@yahoo.com
Facebook.com/minalwaynemiller

Magnificent Man

Edward Eick

For he will command his angels concerning you to guard you in
all your ways. Psalm 91:11

I was born the seventh son of a family of eight boys to
very devoted Catholic parents and was named after my father. My
father studies theology and has always be a powerful figure in my
life. I have always had a sense that I was meant to be a positive
influence in people's lives. At two years of age, I died in my
mother's arms after a terrible cold and was revived by an
emergency tracheotomy. It started when our neighbor stressed to
my mother that I did not look good and that she should take me to
the hospital. She called an ambulance and they rushed me to the
hospital with an emergency tracheotomy, which saved my life.

I became very close to that neighbor throughout my life,
she always made a point to spoil me with extra Halloween candy,
the biggest Christmas gift, and always gave me that special smile
each and every time that I saw her. I was much too young to
remember my vision of God, but always felt that I was touched
by an angel or even possibly by the hand of God.

Due to the surgery it stunted the growth of my adam's apple causing it to become pointy. My voice box became disturbed resulting in a high pitched voice. The surgery left a medium sized scar on my neck. This made me feel like an outcast, so I became a quiet child and always stayed in the shadows. In my teenage years I discovered girls and drugs, which gave me a boost of confidence, but also made me violent. As I continued to hang with the wrong crowd, I eventually ran away from home.

I thought that I was not loved enough or even worthy of my parent's love. I felt like God over looked me as I saw my outgoing brothers excel in sports and love, while I did not. I ran away from home and was starting a life of shame, doing drugs, and giving into temptation with things I knew were wrong.

Deep down I knew that I did not belong and just could not figure out how to get out of the temptation of the Devil's grip and evil ways of the street. I can remember a day sitting away from the crowd that I was living with in a corner of the kitchen. I felt as if life had no purpose and just wanted to end it all, but was just not sure how to do it and why I felt like this. I was sinking into a deep depression and was becoming more isolated and just wanted to get drunk, high off marijuana, or whatever that I could get a hold of.

I never tried to contact my family. I had moved from Florida to Arizona and figured that happy part of my life was behind me. Just when I thought that my life was on the path of despair, one day out of nowhere, I received a call from my oldest brother's wife. I was not sure how she found me and never asked. Looking back I think it was the Lord because it was at time that I was feeling suicidal, alone, confused and scared. We talked and my parents sent me a plane ticket to come home, so with caution in my mind, I decided to go ahead and visit my family back in Florida. After the fear and confusion passed and their warm open arms embraced me, I realized that I was indeed loved and they did care for me – all of my seven brothers, my parents and my entire family.

It took my family finding me and showing me the love that I thought I had lost for me to gain clarity in life. My father enrolled me in art college, and I again started to attend Sunday mass and receive the sacrament of the Holy Spirit.

I graduated and was at my second job as an Art Director / Floor Manager one day when a young woman walked in and I greeted her. The woman stepped back and gave me such an odd look. As I gazed upon her, she proceeded to speak to me and asked me what had happened to me in the past? With much surprised I said "excuse me?" and she continued to tell me that she has never seen such a powerful angel above anyone (she compared him to the angel Michael) and that she was clairvoyant. In disbelief I asked her, "if that was true, why did he appear above me?" She look up with a tilted head, then looked back at me and told me that he would not tell her other than I was here for a higher purpose. When I asked what that purpose was, she again told me that he would not tell her. She also talked about some of the family angels around me (which I had always felt) and they were there to guide me into happiness and a calm.

Years earlier I had indeed felt my Grandmother, I smelled her and felt her presence as she lay on the floor with a broken hip at the exact time that it happened and then again with my Grandfather when he died (as I was shaving in the morning on a business trip in Europe). I realized after talking with the girl that was in my office, whom I never knew her name that I truly felt that I was blessed and I was here to spread happiness to all that I can help, but still did not know what that "higher purpose" was.

Growing up with a scar on my neck and my voice a bit higher, I always covered my neck and was reluctant to speak a lot. But after that experience of meeting the stranger that could look into my eyes and tell me so much about me my fear just seemed to go away and a calm came over my life. That was 20 years ago and I still have a strong faith. I believe that with faith and constant prayer your life can be what you make of it – full of smiles and full of love.

I have a habit of talking to my angel, the Virgin Mary and our Lord Jesus daily before I put my feet on the floor from bed as well as on my morning drive. It is good to give thanks and praise. So you see my life is not that magnificent, but I do try to make everyone I meet smile and feel special.

Psalm 91:11 – For he will command his angels concerning you to guard you in all your ways.

Contact: esquared@glasgow-ky.com

Magnificent Man

Gary E. Bender

Favorite Life Quotes

"Experience is the best teacher but some things are best not experienced."- Gary Bender

"Young men think old men are fools, but old men know young men to be so."-Truman Capote

Background

I discovered America in Nashville, Tennessee on January 25, 1954 in the historical Meharry Hospital. Meharry is located directly across from Fisk University. I was born to the Reverend Curtis E. Bender and the late Willa J. Bender. And as I recall, growing up in Nashville was quite an experience.

Precious Elementary Days

I began first grade at Glenn Elementary School, seven years after integration began in Nashville. As I reflect on those very tense and trying days, I realize those experiences helped make me who I am today. I can remember a multitude of events that would change my life forever.

The Brokenhearted Second Grader

In 1962, my second grade class collected money for a field trip that was called "Day Camp" at the YMCA located on Gallatin Road in Nashville. As the class waited on the bus to arrive, I was the only African American child out of 40 going on the trip. Witnessing this event, my mother Willa Bender stood by and patiently watched to make sure I was taken care of. .It seemed like hours before the buses would arrive, and when they did, oh, the shout for joy from a group of second graders! As we loaded the bus with great anticipation, the next event would change my life forever as it related to the color of my skin. As we loaded the bus and were seated, it still seemed as if it was taking forever just for the buses to start moving. As I looked out the window, I saw my second grade teacher, the principal of the school and the bus driver approaching the bus. They entered the bus and began to walk directly towards me. When they reached me, my heart became paralyzed and fear ran through me as my second grade teacher looked me in the eye and said, "Gary, you cannot ride this bus, nor can you go to the YMCA this time. She then stated, "President Kennedy is working on a plan to let all colors ride the buses and go to the YMCA, but as of right now, you are not allowed to go and you must exit the bus." Tears began to run down my cheeks, my voice was quivering and I could not wait to get off the bus and run into the safe haven of my tearful, precious mother's arms. The other children rode off in bliss as I looked at the bus rolling off. I quickly put my head in my mother's lap and began to weep.

Although this story saddened my heart, the joy of this story is that the end of this strict segregation would end before I entered Junior High in 1967, and integration would grow into full motion. And when I became of age, almost 14 years later, I would become a proud member of the YMCA that would celebrate membership by showing my membership card to the clerk at the front desk every time I walked in. I remember staying all day, taking my time in the swimming pool and taking a shower while smiling in victory. As the saying goes, "truly time does heal old wounds."

The Shock of a Nation

In 1963, I remember receiving the saddest news, as we were all called into the student auditorium on a cold Friday in the month of November. With teachers upset and crying in an atmosphere of insidious calm, the principal announced over the microphone that John F. Kennedy had been assassinated in Dallas, TX. Feeling the grief at such a young age, this second grader was forced to deal with real life issues and events that would change his life and alter history forever.

History in the Making

In 1967, the Black Panthers, who were headquartered in Chicago, started a student non-violent coordinating committee. During this time, the Black Panther leaders were H. Rap Brown and Stokely Carmichael. These leaders gave a speech at Vanderbilt University in Nashville, and after they had finished speaking, Nashville had one of its biggest race riots in its history. The rioters and looters ravaged, burned and pulled Caucasians out of their cars while severely beating them as they fell out. The rioters burned buildings from Fisk University all the way to the East Nashville bridge. Some of these historical buildings included the Ritz Movie Theater, which was the only African American owned theater in Nashville at that time, homes, restaurants and barbershops along with some of the main African American night clubs such as Club New Era and Goodjellys. The riots were so intense that I can recall memories of our parents staying up all night long armed with weapons for fear of break-ins and danger. After all of this, more events would happen that would also go down in the history books. As time passed, Martin Luther King, Jr. would be killed on April 4, 1968 in Memphis, TN and Robert Kennedy would be killed on June 6, 1968 in Los Angles, CA. Although the times were seemingly tumultuous, we overcame and kept pressing on. More history would be birthed through an active military draft, the Vietnam War and the first color broadcast of the Wizard of Oz that hit the television creating a new phenomena that would compel loyal church goers to stay home that Sunday to witness the event. Also around this time were rising artists and bands that would shape music in American history. Recording artists that were booming during this era, to name a few, were Aretha Franklin, Jackson Five, Temptations, Smokey Robinson, Miracles, the Beetles, and Elvis Presley. These artists and bands were truly taking America by storm.

Racism & Riots

As stressful and intense times continued to grow, racism proved itself to be in full bloom. I can remember my mother and I standing in line at the grocery store. As we waited in line behind a Caucasian woman, I watched the cashier place the woman's change directly in her hand. However, when my mother stepped to the counter and it was her time to receive her change, the cashier threw her change on the counter. While I became angry, I looked up and saw my mother smile politely and say, "Thank you." This said so much about the Christian woman she was and the life she lived before me as an example. I will always cherish her memory and I truly thank her for her witness and legacy that I was able to pass on to my own children.

Racism seemed to be extremely rampant during my childhood. I can recollect downtown lunch counters that African Americans were forbidden to eat at. I can even recall water fountains in the courthouse that had large signs labeled, "White

Only," "Colored Only." In addition, there were even certain parts of town that African Americans could not go into after dark. Although these strict limitations would create a rift between races, one of the most disturbing events occurred at a local swimming pool that was located inside Centennial Park, which was located across the street from Vanderbilt University. This particular swimming pool did not allow blacks to swim and the culminating event was a heated race riot that ultimately closed the pool in the late 60's or early 70's. Little did we know, the pool would be closed forever and filled in with dirt. A brick, red and white building, which housed the showers people took before entering the pool, now serves as a reminder of days past. Although this building was converted into some other use, I never wanted to enter that building again to go back and find out what they had remodeled it into due to the disturbing angst I experienced after the riot. After all that I have experienced, I can honestly say that I have dealt with my share of discrimination. In the workforce, I have been a part of the group "last hired," and I have also been a part of the group "first fired." I have even been betrayed by my own race, or "house boy" as they call them, just so that they could look good in the eyes of the boss. Although I experienced these hardships, these experiences made me who I am today. It is because of these experiences that I am not afraid of hard work or getting my hands dirty. These experiences humbled me and I don't regret my struggle, nor do I regret the era that I grew up in. As I write this, I'm reminded of Maya Angelou's book, "I Wouldn't Take Nothing for My Journey Now." And through all of this, at this junction of my life, I too can boldly exclaim, "I wouldn't take nothing for my journey now!"

Medicines & Cures

As a child growing up in this era, I remember many of the "ethno-medicines" that were used as remedies to cure certain or all diseases. There were the "asphiditiy bag" that hung around a person's neck to help prevent poliomyelitis. This bag was a compilation of herbs and pungent substances to ward off diseases. The truth is, as a boy, I did not realize it was for warding off disease. My deduction was that it was meant to ward boys away from girls because when I smelled it, it made me want to vomit.

Another medicine was "coal oil." Coal oil was given to me to help cure coughs, flu, cuts, abrasions and wounds. And if mama gave it to me by mouth, she would use sugar cubes and molasses honey to mask the taste. If I had a bad cold, I had to have "cow tip tea." The main ingredient in cow tip tea was dried cow manure. I also recall "Sassafras" tea. Sassafras tea was given to ward off evil spirits, treat toothaches and menstrual disorders. My grandmother used it for rheumatism, but she also said, WV-40 was good to spray on your back when you had back pain. As another remedy for back pain, I can remember her instructing us to get a small child who weighed about 20lbs or less to walk up and down your back. Eventually, this would end and cure your back pain. Needless to say, we found all of these "ethno-medicines" quite interesting.

Junior High, High School & College

In May of 1968, I was voted the first black president of the student body of Highland Heights Junior High School in East Nashville, TN. This would be the first of many leadership positions that I would have in my lifetime. In 1972, I graduated from high school at East Nashville High School. During my matriculation through high school, I served as a basketball manager for 3 years, I played the trumpet in the marching band and I was Co-Captain of the football team during my senior year. During my junior and senior year in high school, I worked as an Orderly at Miller's Clinic, which would eventually become a hospital. After graduating from high school, I was chosen to be an ambassador of the United States to travel throughout Europe and stay in youth hostels during the summer of my senior year. This travel tour would include France, England and Canterbury.

After completing this tour, I went to work at Peterbilt Truck Company in Madison, TN. After the summer of 1972, I entered Middle Tennessee State University (MTSU) and graduated with a double major in Criminal Justice Administration and Psychology. It was my personal aim to go fight in Vietnam War, but taking the guidance and counsel of my godmother would encourage me to stay home and enter in the MTSU Army ROTC program. And upon graduating from this program, I commissioned as an officer in the United States Army. I entered active duty as a Second Lieutenant and became an Infantry officer that would grow into a well-developed leader.

Family

On May 22, 1976, I married my high school sweetheart Linda Diane (Overton) Bender. As of this writing, Linda and I have been married for 39 years. To this union came three wonderful children and two granddaughters.

Look at God

With faith in God and trust in Jesus Christ, I was able to succeed in my calling and purpose in life. One of my favorite verses is Proverbs 3:5-6. These verses simply say to me, "Trust God in everything." Trusting in the Lord's guidance through His Word and trusting in the counsel and wisdom given to me by my elders aided me in many accomplishments while pursuing a higher education such as graduating from Southwestern Baptist Theological Seminary in Fort Worth, TX with a Masters of Religious Education and graduating from Trinity Theological Seminary in Newburg, IN where I earned a Masters of Divinity in Expository Preaching and Pulpit Communication.

Work Experience

The occupations that I have acquired in my lifetime have been sundry. These occupations include: MTSU Campus Police, United States Army commissioned Infantry officer, Frito Lay Manager in Louisville, KY, Kaiser Aluminum Chemical Company Production Foreman in Ravenswood, WV (this position consisted of casting aluminum ingots from South Africa), Wage

Grade Supervisor for El Reno Federal Prison in Oklahoma, Parole Officer for the State of Tennessee and a certified Chaplain for Caris Healthcare in Chattanooga, TN. Currently, I serve as the Chief Bailiff for the 3rd Division Criminal Court of the 11th Judicial District of the State of Tennessee.

Pastoral Experience

I served as the full time Assistant to the Pastor at the Faith Memorial Baptist Church under the leadership of the Senior Pastor, Morris A. Curry, Sr. in Oklahoma, City. In 1989, I became the Senior Pastor of the Holiday Hills Baptist Church in Abilene, TX. And from 1995 to 2008, I would serve as the Senior Pastor of the Bethlehem Baptist Church in Lawton, Oklahoma.

Civic Organizations & Christian Leadership

I have been a lifetime member of the Omega Psi Phi Fraternity, Incorporated Mu Zeta Chapter since 1973. My Christian leadership positions consist of: Former President of the Lawton, Oklahoma NAACP Chapter, Former Dean of Congress of Christian Education for the Western District of Oklahoma, Former 2nd Vice President of the Oklahoma Baptist Missionary Convention, Former New Testament Instructor for the Congress of Christian Education for the National Baptist Convention, U.S.A. Incorporated, Former Treasurer of the Concerned Clergy for Spiritual Renewal (CCSR) in Oklahoma City, OK, and the Former Adjunct Professor at Oklahoma Baptist University in Shawnee, OK.

Words of Wisdom

If I had to leave you with words of wisdom, I would leave you with this. There is so much wisdom resting in retirement homes, senior citizen homes and Foreign Legion Veteran organizations. I believe that this wealth of wisdom needs to be tapped into by America's young people. A lot of the travesty, torment and tragedies that our young people are experiencing could be avoided if they would only listen to the tried wisdom of the elders who care for their well-being rather than pioneering life's landscape by themselves without consulting other people who have ploughed through the same territory years ago. When our young people run into massive complications after following their own ways, they really find out that "Experience is the best teacher, but some things are best not experienced." It is my earnest prayer that my chapter will help someone realize the potential and valuable resources that they have at their disposal in the personality of the senior citizen. And if by chance these people have moved on to a better life, befriend one that is living in a senior citizen home or a retirement village and let their drops of wisdom fall on the dryness of your soul as the rain falls on parched land. Who knows, the light of your creativity may be lying dormant, just awaiting someone to awaken it and turn it on.

The Third Eye

Having experienced all that went on during my growing up in the 60's gave me a tremendous "third eye." What's a "third eye" you ask? Well, I'm glad you asked. When the notable comedian Steve Harvey was asked what made a good stand-up comic, he replied, "Comics have to have a third eye." When he stated this, he meant that good comics could transcend the obvious that would make people laugh hilariously. There is no doubt that my era has done the same for me by teaching me life lessons that I may have never learned had I not grown up during that time. In particular, some life lessons that the old folk taught me was how to save my money, how to give my entire paycheck to my wife and family and how to send my mother "a piece of money" in every pay period. Little did I know, these would be lessons that that would stick with me for the rest of my life.

Conclusion of the Matter

I heard the late great Pastor, Dr. E.V. Hill, Pastor of Mount Zion Missionary Baptist Church say at a conference, "About the time you learn the most of life, most of life is gone."

Over the years in my life, I have not always made the right decisions as it relates to always taking the right path. In retrospect, having thought about all the elders that were trying to teach me to avoid the path that I took, I may have been able to avoid the school of hard knocks. However, it is at the school of hard knocks that my personal quote, "Experience is the best teacher, but some things are best not experienced," was birthed and would later become the fundamental life lesson that I would never forget. Realizing that I am not perfect, while also realizing that on this side of Heaven I will never reach perfection, it is my resolve to keep pressing on and encourage others just as others have encouraged me.

There have been many leaders and philosophers who have lived and died that have left an impact on my life, but one in particular stands out in the great legacy and legend of Nelson Mandela. Near the end of his life, reporters were asking Nelson Mandela how he would like to be remembered. They asked him, "Would it be your Nobel Peace Prize or maybe your many accolades people gave you?" Nelson Mandela stated very calmly and with great resolve, "I want to be remembered for how many times that I got knocked down and got back up!" I shall never forget these words. Well, it is not my intention to match Nelson Mandela or be one of the great philosophers of life, however, I would like the summation of my life inscribed in two words on my epitaph, "I tried."

Contact: benderministries@gmail.com

Magnificent Man

Jerry Silvers

I can do all things through Christ which strengtheneth me.
Philippians 4:13 KJV

Music has been a part of my life since listening to Disney records as a child in the 60s. My old portable record player was the window to a world of sounds. My mother noticed my gift of music and she quickly placed me in piano lessons at the tender age of four. My exploration of music in those days took me through Blues, R&B, Rock, Pop, Gospel and Classical music. Because my parents were in the military and stationed in remote places in Upstate New York, Alaska, North Dakota, California, and Ohio, by the time my father retired to Clarksville, Tennessee I was well-versed in all genres of music.

By the early 70s I was exposed to The Beatles, Mississippi Mass Choir, Parliament/Funkadelic, Denise Williams, Earth Wind and Fire, The Eagles, Shirley Caesar, and George Benson; just to name a few. I did not see color nor did I see a dividing line between genres of music. I was just as happy singing Muskrat Love as I was uttering the lyrics to Amazing Grace.

When my parents moved to Clarksville in 1972 and bought a house in North Clarksville I attended a local elementary school. It was my first dose of being immersed in the so-called integration that was going on in the south. I had grown up on Air Force Bases around people of German, Irish, Asian, Latino, and African descent. It was a rude awakening for me to attend school in Clarksville, go to recess, and was encouraged not to play with the white kids. I was also paddled severely by the gym teacher who called me the "n" word because I was a chubby kid who could not climb the rope to the ceiling in gym class.

In 1974, my dad returned from Vietnam and our family moved to North Dakota. I loved the flat prairie and adored the fishing experience. As I progressed through my teens I experienced many forms of music and as the flower power era gave way to disco I was delighted to listen to KCJB Radio Station in Minot, North Dakota. On the weekend there was a DJ named The Baby Rabbit whose broadcast tickled the ears of the soldiers and their families, at Minot Air Force Base, with a variety of music and information. Coming home from a fishing trip my dad said he'd like me to pursue radio one day. Little did he know I was way ahead of him. I knew becoming a DJ would be my destiny.

While deployed to Vietnam my dad purchased, and sent home, a reel-to-reel recorder and I spent many hours recording The Baby Rabbit Show. I mimicked the way the DJ spoke and practiced introducing records at home.

In high school I gravitated to the kids who were into music. Although I never took chorus or band, I hung out in the music classrooms before and after school. It was there I experienced groups like: Air Supply, The BarKays, Pink Floyd, The Brothers Johnson, and The Commodores.

During the 12th grade at Northwest High School in Clarksville, Tennessee I was delighted to know there was a mock radio station that broadcast through the intercom before classes each morning. There I found many friends from my neighborhood who were in a class that created that station.

One day the class gave a report about school activities at our high school and we were invited by the weekend DJ, at Clarksville's new urban formatted AM station, to participate. I went to the station and met Lee Erwin, one of Clarksville's legendary broadcasters. After nervously doing my part for my class, I spoke to Mr. Erwin about radio and he suggested after graduation I should apply to work there. From the Fall of 1979 until 1982 I found every excuse to visit the station and acquaint myself, even if I had to walk.

I applied for a part-time announcer position at WABD 1370 AM, Fort Campbell, Kentucky in the fall of 1982 and was immediately hired. I will never forget choosing a radio name within 30 minutes of my first air shift. As the seconds ticked away to announcing my first song a radio stage name popped into my head. I opened the microphone and announced my first record saying, "Hello everyone I'm Jerry Silvers and I am very happy to be here today. Here's George Clinton with the Atomic Dog." The name stuck and some 30 years later I have answered to both my real name and my stage name no matter where in the United States I am.

The company I worked for had owned other stations in the same building; but I programmed the AM station and adored commercial production and sales. I also assumed the name of Terry Donovan of WCVQ, Q108 FM for many years where I was the evening DJ on that station too.

Since 1979 I had been a member of a traveling DJ service called the Funkerteers. As the years passed I became a club DJ on Fort Campbell and off post too. Years of experience through the 80s and 90s taught me to do high school dances, provide music for skating rinks, wedding receptions, family reunions and run sound for many events on and off post. My most memorable event was DJing at Northwest High School, Northeast High

School, Clarksville High School, and Montgomery Central High School all in one night. Of course I had the help of the Funkerteers; but the experience groomed me to manage large groups of people.

My most memorable experience of DJing in the community was performing a program called Taking It to the Hood in Middle Tennessee and Western Kentucky. I was honored to work with some of the area's most-talented artists. Most noted are: New Beginning of Chattanooga whose lead singer was Usher Raymond, Tina Brown, and Budda Fly who went on to perform an on air shift stint on 101.1 The Beat in Nashville. There were many others and many of them I am still in touch with today.

By the late 90s the landscape of music was changing. Rap music went from Grandmaster Flash to the Wu Tang Clan and gospel music changed from The Clark Sisters to Trinitee 5:7. When I started in radio there were turntables, then CDs, then computers.

In 1997, I finally decided I'd had enough of radio because there was nothing to do but hit the space bar on the keyboard to stop and start songs and answer the request line. I left WABD, my home for 16 years and went to WHVO, 1480 AM in Hopkinsville, Kentucky where I co-anchored a morning show, was news director, and Sunday morning DJ. The experience of gathering and writing a news cast has never left me. The memory of how friendly the people of Hopkinsville were also sticks with me to this day.

It was the dawn of a new millennia and I wanted to do something different. I recently was divorced and lost my mother to cancer in 2002. I decided I'd try to work a manual labor job or two so I went to work at Cumberland City at the steam plant. I also worked at Stone Plastics in Cadiz, Kentucky and Frigidaire in Springfield, Tennessee, I liked the jobs and loved the people until I had a stroke.

Years of sitting in the control room at the radio station puffing cigarettes, and eating free pizza and burgers took their toll on my body. I was admitted to the hospital in 2006 for stent surgery. The doctor told me that I was two weeks from a massive heart attack. Years of lifting heavy speakers took a toll on my back as well.

I took a hiatus and physically my body was mending; but, mentally my mind was a sponge and I could not wait to get back to work. I started studies at the Tennessee Technology Center in Clarksville and graduated in 2008.

While attending classes I was wondering why some students were wearing headphones and bopping their head to the music they were listening to. After asking, a classmate responded, "That is internet radio." I put the headphones on and was blown away by the clarity of the sound coming from the computer. I found out it was not just clear; but, better than CD quality. Well! I went home and studied everything the internet had to offer about internet radio.

In October 2008, I launched New Praise Radio, a full service 24 hour a day internet radio station. The mission was to restore local communication between small business owners, non-profit organizations, churches, and the community because the local stations were sold to corporate companies who raised the rates and made it difficult for those aforementioned entities to survive and prosper. I soon found out that this was happening nation-wide.

After launching the station I met Jodi Serino, a Chicago native, who was in Clarksville assisting her daughter who was not only in the Army, but just had given birth to Jodi's grand-daughter. Jodi was working for Convenient Shopper Magazine and attending Ministerial Training School at West Gate Christian Center in Clarksville, Tennessee. We spent many hours working together on media, and promotions, then were married in 2011.

Today Pastor Jodi Serino-Barbour and I live in Harrisonburg, Virginia with two of our 7 children. New Praise Radio has opened a branch location of our station here and serves the East coast. The station now has offices in Clarksville, Tennessee, Tallahassee, Florida, Dayton, Ohio, St, Louis, Missouri, and Baltimore, Maryland. Pastor Jodi and I are ordained through West Gate Christian Center and I, with roots in the AME Church, am Minister of Music at Bethel AME Church in Harrisonburg, Virginia.

I currently host The Jerry Silvers Morning Show, a daily show that airs Monday through Friday at 6 a.m. Eastern on the New Praise Radio with my co-host Minister Anna Godfrey. The station, which has run for nomination for a Stellar Award for three consecutive years, continues to serve the United States and nations abroad as each community's hometown radio station.

Over the years my community has molded me into the person I am today and I am grateful to the elders of the Middle Tennessee and Western Kentucky region who took the time to mentor me about God, community, and music. I am grateful to God for taking everything I was exposed to and using it to lift Him up. To God be the glory.

Contact: praiseradio@live.com
http://praiseradio1.webs.com
Twitter: @jerrysilvers

Magnificent Man

John "John Keith" Montoya

"And when you stand praying, if you hold anything against anyone, forgive him, so that your Father in heaven may forgive your sins." Mark 11:25

Introduction:

Hello my name is John Montoya. Thank you for taking the time to stop by my chapter. I am grateful that God has given me an avenue to express my life and thoughts. My prayer is that what you find in these words will inspire, encourage and entertain. It is fairly unknown that I have a great love for poetry. The story I wish to share will introduce this part of me to others. I am ecstatic to be both a vessel and reference as proof of what God can do.

This life of mine

The summary of my life is Lord, Love and Maturing. I hope others find inspiration as they read though my story. I started the same as many kids with a dream. I dreamed of being a big star and it didn't hurt that I could sing! Born in Hollywood, I was designed to be a star. I was mesmerized by the glamour, fashion, and the cars. There was something inside me that wanted more than the fame. I wanted to give a voice to those with no name. I wrote songs in my youth about God's judgment day. I didn't really understand what it meant, but momma raised me that way! Evangelist Eva since before I learned how to speak. Evangelist Eva, now that I have a son to teach! But I'm getting off course, let me get back to the meat. Welcome to this life of mine.

Sins of the father:

My family was burdened with a low income and broken home. My biological father left me, my mother and older brother alone. He didn't see value in marriage or family, so he didn't feel obligated physically or financially. It hurts as I write this and it's sad to say lots of women have to raise their children this way. Was my father a bad guy? No, not really! We just lost the battle between fatherhood and public imagery. Why be tied down to just one lady? When you can have many and she raises the baby....huh! This is the lie some men tell themselves. Hoping the decision doesn't hinder their wealth. Hoping that years later missed birthdays and holidays of the past, all is forgiven and you get a pass. See I do forgive my father, because God is my source, but the scar is still there from when he took mom to court. All because he wanted to prove she was wrong to her face. He would say "you're a woman of God but you made this mistake!?" He was very convincing, yeah his game was good. I don't blame him fully my mom understood. Consenting adults both sharing a moment, the difference, when responsibility came Mom stood up to own it! Its fine, the relationship between my father and mother ended, but why deny a seed when the fruit is a spitting image.

Some days I would wonder why my father didn't want me. When I would lay down to dream, it wasn't the monsters that would haunt me. It was nightmares of not being good enough and not being accepted. Is it wrong to want your father's love when you weren't what he expected….and the feeling is progressive? It felt like chasing a mirage, you know you never will possess it. Sometimes I would call just to see if I would hear his voice. I would get on a plane and fly there instead if I had a choice. Over the years I thought about my older sister that I barely even knew.

After a call one day, I heard her voice on my father's answering machine; the curiosity inside grew. I left a message and to my surprise my sister called me back. We talked about what life could have been if my father was on track. We laughed, joked and told stories as if we knew each other for years. The feeling was exhilarating and eased all of my fears. I thought for sure when this moment came, that I wouldn't be considered family. I was grateful to God every time we talked and for this new relationship he had granted me. Through our talks I soon discovered more siblings were to claim, 2 older brothers, 2 older sisters; now we're like links that form a chain. We have become unbreakable no matter how distant we may be. This is a testament that God can fix the broken and wash away any stains. With my family getting closer, my father decided to join in. When we talked I asked him, "Why?" He asked forgiveness for his sins.

The Valiant Knight:

As a single woman with two kids, my mother continued to raise us the best that she could. One day she thought she found someone willing to stand up for good. He was her knight in shining armor here to rescue her heart and her mind. It all became different when marriage papers were signed. I often daydreamed of being on stages, movies and music videos as I washed the dishes. One day they were interrupted by a smack to the back of my neck with a vengeance. "What's taking so long," my mom's so called knight would shout, as curse word after curse word spewed right out his mouth. Like all siblings, my brother and I fought and threw words in the air. It came to a stop when my brother was pulled by his hair. My mom's new "knight" had taken a hold; determined to prove he was king of this throne. I remember staying late over at my friend's house on school nights wishing that I could stay. I knew that I would be in trouble, but I just had to get away. There were many other times that we felt the knight's wrath. I won't dwell too long because that was the past.

At the age of 15 I decided enough was enough. It was time to escape so I gathered my stuff. My plan was to clean up the house and then I would leave. My mom's "knight" was no dummy, he knew something was up my sleeve. I tried to walk past him as I made my way out the kitchen. Suddenly his hand rose up and extended. He started to choke me but he caught hold of himself. I affirmed my manhood by re-positioning myself. With an elevated chest, I stepped back and said "Hey man" as I pushed his hand and raised my fist. He could tell something had shifted inside of my wits. In my mind I thought for sure this is it. I am about to experience his anger to the full extent. What I saw instead was his eyes repent. His mouth showed anger for the retaliation. His heart showed remorse for his violent illustration. I was shocked when his only remark was "go to your room!" I could tell that God protected me that afternoon!

Soon after that I could see a change in his ways. I'm not saying things were perfect, but was Rome built in a day!? Through prayer and forgiveness my mom's knight has changed a lot. I am now proud to call him "POP!" I know it seems stupid and crazy of me. If God forgives, then so shouldn't we? Over the years our family continued to grow. I was far from the youngest with 3 more children for my mother to tow. Things were going good, "Pop" was trying to change. Some things in this life are harder to rearrange. Though we stayed a close family with these new additions, after 25 years my parents' marriage ended by another woman's admission. It was sad to see something that had been so hard to build, crumble. The act of my mother was to always stay humble. She never once boasted about the faithfulness to her knight. She knew God would take care of her as the valiant knight walked out her life.

Mistakes and Forgiveness:

What happens when you try to do right? At age 19 I decided to make a change in my life. I started trusting God more and he rewarded me with blessings. Like with most change there was a time I was tested. See I promised God and myself to remain abstinent and stick to my word. Then along comes temptation that caused my vision to blur. My intentions were loyal, I stood strong for 2 years. Well, I thought I was strong until she whispered in my ear. My ex-girlfriend was in town for a visit. She was a familiar face, an old flame that I couldn't extinguish.

We talked about life for hours to one another. Next thing I knew, we were under the covers. I woke up the next morning with remorse of great measure. I had traded my vow for a moment of pleasure. God did forgive me and accepted me as his son. But he didn't exempt me from the wrong I had done. New Year's Eve, while spending time with my now wife, I received a call from my ex-girlfriend with a plight. She explained she was with child and was sure it is mine. God had given me consequence for committing my crime. She promised no matter what our friendship would remain the same. I told her I would be there for her since I too was to blame. Weeks went by, things seem to be going well. It was about 6 months later things went all to hell. I started to get pressurized calls from her and her mom. Though I extracted my time and heart, it was my bank account they wanted withdrawn. My reply was "of course I don't mind providing what I owe. I just don't want to do that till the true father is known." She became outraged. Then her mother chimed in. "You can tell him we don't need his help, we can do badly all by ourselves! He is just like other men!" Then the call came to an end.

When the baby was born I made a 6 hour trip to view the child. I arrived to see her family gathered around. Lectures were presented of my new responsibility as a father. A woman in her family spoke down at me. Why didn't she stop her! Wasn't I

131

there? Wasn't I present? Why crucify the one that's trying to be a blessing? She declined and made excuses when I asked for a paternity test. One day she finally agreed to do what she knew was best. This entire lesson in my life lasted a year. Now hold on to your seats for what you're about to hear! The test results were in and I couldn't believe the answer. A voice mail left on my phone cried out, "I'll pay you back for every Pamper! I am so sorry for what I did to you." I guess she wanted the baby to belong to a friend who had proven to be true. I told her not to worry for I knew what God was doing. He was teaching me how forgive so that he could give forgiveness to me.

The Departure

They say God never puts more on than you can bear, but for my younger brother Aaron's death I just wasn't prepared. Only 19, there his body laid in front of me, no trumpet sounds, no rapture. A gun he had placed in his grips silenced out his laughter. Tears started to fall as I pounded my chest, but I had to understand this was a kingdom request. See my brother had struggled for about a year with depression. Caused by medication that was supposed to give him perspective. A troubled teen is what the state of Kentucky would say, about a kid who just wanted to smoke weed all day. No violence no crime that required a bounty, with just assumptions of what could be, they sent him to McCracken County! A place where young teens were supposed to learn how to maintain, funny, the majority of them went insane. Tell me again why he needed a pill to make him chill? The side effect of weed has the same appeal! Oh, I get it that substance is illegal, but the medication that causes thoughts of suicide is for the good of the people!? I digress. Let me stop making this boring. I had to vent for the people who share the same story. My brother lives on through a song that I wrote for my youngest brother Joel's album. The song is called Altar. Arron may have left this earth but in my heart there will never be a departure.

132

Conclusion:

I am happy about the next chapter in my life; God has now blessed me with a beautiful son and a wife. I have traveled to many places and accomplished many of my dreams. More doors continue to open, God is not finished with me yet so it seems. The broken bond with my biological family has been mended. The reign of confusion in my mother's life has now ended. God is working with my "POP" and making him better. Though he may not be perfect I feel a change in the weather. The message I wish to send is don't give up on yourself, others or God. The outcome you will see is more than a facade. I know there is more out there who have endured more than I have. This is meant to inspire those with a similar path. I ask that what you take from this is a way to forgive. Let God handle what you can't; find a new way to live. Don't be a prisoner to your grudges; in time you may find, the one you held dislike for will change in due time. So I hope this reaches you well. Remember this as I close. No matter your struggle God sees and he knows.

Contact: johnk.montoya@gmail.com
Twitter: @johnkeithman
Vine: johnkeithman
Facebook: johnkeith.9022

Magnificent Man

Joshua Rogers

But seek first His kingdom and His righteousness, and all these things will be added to you. Matthew 6:33

The Beginning

      I was born on March 22, 1994, and raised by my mother in Greeleyville, South Carolina. I grew up singing and playing the drums in an apostolic church pastored by my maternal grandmother. I have always had a love for music, and although I was not in the "in-crowd," music is what my peers knew me for. At the age of 17, I competed in a local talent show and won the grand prize. After winning the competition, I was encouraged by my friends and family to audition for Sunday Best, and I did just that. My family and I drove to Atlanta to audition for a slot on the show along with 10,000 other competitors. At the age of 18, I graduated from C.E. Murray High School, and days later I received news that I was selected to become a contestant on BET's Sunday Best. My love for and commitment to music is what landed me such an amazing opportunity. God was up to something big. This was just the beginning.

There are no words to describe the experience of being on the Sunday Best stage. I auditioned for the fifth season in Atlanta, and it was just mesmerizing and unforgettable. It was an honor to be evaluated and mentored by gospel greats such as Yolanda Adams, Donnie McClurkin, CeCe Winans, and Kirk Franklin. It was Kirk Franklin that gave me the nickname "Young Buck." For several grueling weeks, I performed songs such as "Peace Be Still" by Vanessa Bell Armstrong, "Well Done" by Deitrick Haddon, and "We Expect You" by the late Andrae Crouch.

I landed in the finals of Sunday Best alongside Alexis Spight, another teen contestant. I became the season's winner and made history by becoming the show's first male and youngest champion of BET's highly successful reality singing competition. This South Carolina native of a small town called Greeleyville, was placed on the map for all the world to see. I was also blessed to win a 2013 Ford Escape, and a recording contract with Music World Entertainment.

Sunday's Best Lessons Learned

My experience with BET's Sunday Best has a lot to do with who I am today as a person and as an artist. All of the rigorous training that I received as a contestant on the show has prepared me for my journey. I embraced it.

Before Sunday Best, I rarely paid close attention to the way I connected with audiences when I sang. Since the show, I've become more in tune with how I convey the message I am singing about. My vocal quality has also improved because of the conventional training I received while on the show. I am thankful and remember all of the positive feedback and constructive criticism I received. What I would say to myself was this:

"When you really want something, you take all the criticism that comes your way. You want what you want and you do what you must to reach that goal." Through the determination, dedication, and drive to stay, it all paid off by not only winning the show, but also in building the necessary groundwork for a firm foundation in the gospel music industry.

Now in the gospel industry, I am fully embraced by the industry's gatekeepers after my win and have continued those relationships. In my own words:

"It's such a great and inexplicable feeling to be able to work with artists who have been in the industry for years; it's mind blowing to know that they respect me."

I keep counting my blessings. I have made my national appearance on TBN, performed on BET's Celebration of Gospel, Nominated for a Stellar Award and more. I have many ventures in the works including the launch of my own radio station on UGospel, in addition to getting more work done in the studio.

I am doing what I love to do. I don't consider it work; it is my ministry. This is where I want to be. I am happy and will continue traveling weekly across the nation ministering to audiences through song.

Concern for Today's Christian

I feel like we are under attack. Recently, they have removed Bibles from naval bases. The devil is getting stronger and stronger, and the Church is becoming weaker and weaker. We worry about things that should not even be on our minds. Instead of standing up for what we know to be right, we are more concerned about public opinion. We are not praying as we should be for our nation, its laws and its law makers. We need to be praying for this generation to seek God first. Our youth are coming up ignorant of who God is and who they are in Him. We have got to get them to understand that they are vital to what is coming.

Life did not slow down; it only sped up for me. After Sunday Best, I was busy hitting the recording studio and touring across the states, and quickly became a household name to gospel music lovers across the nation. Today, I would describe myself as a traditional/contemporary gospel artist with a touch of soul, who has been intentionally diligent about taking my time with my music; I am particular. "My music is more than just a groove or something that is appeasing to the ear. I want to take people back, usher them into worship, and connect to the core of who they are."

I released my first album, Well Done, on December 4, 2012. The album debuted at #1 on the Billboard Gospel Album Charts with 5,917 sales in its first week. I am most thankful to God for being faithful, and I know that it is truly by His grace that he allows me to be who I am in Him. I am confident in Him because He loves me. I am grateful for the support from loved ones and fans that I have received from everywhere. God is good. I am standing on His promises because He has been so good to me, time and time again.

Encouragement

The people who encouraged me the most to sing was my family. They didn't sugarcoat things either. My mother would encourage me and tell me straight like it is. This allowed me to work harder and I will always love her for that. Some people will get mad and quit when they don't hear what they want to hear, but I know that the people whom God has placed in my life, genuinely care for me and will keep it real with me. All in all, I stuck it out and didn't quit; I had to keep going. Not to say that things were always easy, but somehow God always worked it out. I continued working diligently on my craft.

Ministry

I am young, but God is calling me to be a bolder, stronger and more courageous witness for Him. Naturally, I am quite shy and He is pushing me out of that comfort zone. It is on my heart to reach out to other young artists like myself. I believe that God is using me for my generation. I have begun a monthly conference call entitled, "Teachable Moments with Joshua Rogers." I just want to be able to mentor other artists and bring in other seasoned veterans of this industry for them to hear as well.

My passion is our youth and reaching our younger generation. I feel that we have to bring about change. It's time to involve our youth in all that we do, and if we don't, we will lose them. I desire to help, mentor, and support our youth who are working to bring about difference. As an artist, I did not have anyone to mentor me in my earlier years, to show me the ropes. That is why I founded Teachable Moments. Ever since I was declared the winner of BET Sunday Best Season five, many questions poured in from other artists, near and far, about how to become successful in the music industry. So I started Teachable Moments, which is a free series of teleconferences to answer questions about the industry, how to break in, and to personally share from my own experiences. Many celebrities who have given their support to offer advice on the line thus far include Dr. Dorinda Clark-Cole, Vanessa Bell Armstrong and more.

My Vision

Everyone has a purpose in life. We have all been divinely created to fulfill a significant task while we make our days through this journey called life. For me, for as long as I can remember, I have loved to sing! Singing has been my way of expressing my gratefulness for all that God has done and continues to do in my life!!

To that end, I truly believe that "The Vision" God has given me, is to spread the good news of how awesome He is through songs. By sharing my testimony of His greatness as He manifests in my life, I am living on purpose. The purpose of reminding older generations of God's grace and mercy, and letting the younger generation know that they can accomplish anything if they trust and believe in God! "The Vision" for my life: To live on purpose for God and to do His will!"

I am looking to enlarging my steps more and more; from changing my record label, to reaching out more than ever to my peers. I desire to be financially well off by the age of 40. So therefore, if I decide to retire, I can. I want to do things God's way and not waste years and time.

I am just a young man that loves God and love being used by God. I'm consistently learning and willing to learn more each day. I'm not prideful or arrogant. I've made mistakes and am not afraid to admit that I'm thankful for trials and tests. I am thankful to everyone who has loved me.

Through it all, I will remain humble, counting my blessings, and will be committed to all that God has in store for me. Even in my travels, I still make it a point to be home every Wednesday to attend my church's weekly bible study, and while on the road, I create time for spiritual rhythms such as praying and fasting. I plan to pursue college in the near future, likely majoring in musical performance. In my hometown, my city celebrates me with a day on September 13th. It has been deemed Joshua Rogers Day in Manning, South Carolina.

If anyone reading my chapter doubts God right now, you should look at what He has done for me. If He can do it for me, then He can do it for anyone. I am just a living example.

I started out my chapter with the scripture of Mathew 6:33, and in closing, I urge you to read the entire chapter to encourage your faith and walk in Christ.

Contact: Booking@thejoshuarogers.us
Follow me: @thejoshuarogers
www.thejoshuarogers.us

Magnificent Man

Kelvin Braxton

Blessed are the pure in heart: for they shall see God.
Matthew 5:8 (KJV)

Photographing from the Clubhouse to residents of the White House

Reflecting on the places I have been and the people God has brought me in contact with, growing up, one would have never imagined all of this. I am the proud owner of Braxton Photography, LLC in Clarksville, TN. In my chapter, among other things, you will not only discover my love and passion for photography, but also how I got my start and more. But most importantly, I would be remiss if I did not mention my beautiful wife Adrianne, of 32 years. God has blessed us to stay together all of these years. I am thankful for our relationship. Marriage is a gift from God. With so many marriages ending in divorce, I am very proud of the work and commitment that it has taken us and we still enjoy our time together. We have two sons who are now grown. Growing up we had lots of good times in our home as a family. God is good.

My story begins in a Virginia county called King and
Queen. I was raised by my mother, brothers and grandfather. I
am the youngest of 5 boys. Our family is very close. We love
each other. My father was not in the home, so as boys, we
learned to be men from the upbringing of my grandfather. My
grandfather was a wise man and full of wisdom. He would say
things like, *"Whenever you pray, pray sincerely for wisdom and
understanding."* I know this works. I know in my lifetime, God
has blessed me in so many ways and so I am only giving the glory
back to Him for the times He has pulled me through.

Growing up in King and Queen County, Virginia, I
graduated from Central High School in 1978. After graduation, I
left home and joined the military where it brought me to Ft.
Campbell, KY. My decision would eventually lead to a
commitment of 25 years of military and civilian service; I am
proud to have served. I do believe God directs our paths, and this
is where it has led me. In the military I was trained as an Ear,
Nose, and Throat Medical Health Technician. Back then, in
1980, going into the medical field was a safe bet because it was
almost guaranteed you would find a job. I thoroughly enjoyed my
job and especially liked working with my patients.

In 1992, I left active duty military, joined the National
Guard and continued working in the same military hospital as a
civil service employee. It was during this time that I became more
involved in professional photography. This would be only the
beginning of many rewarding years to come.

The Journey

My story about photography begins with a single camera.
My journey started by taking a Polaroid camera to the clubhouse
and from there going all the way to photographing residents of
the White House. I first began photographing couples in
nightclubs. People would get all dressed up and I would take their
picture with my Polaroid camera for $5. From there, I was
invited to take pictures of birthday parties and get-togethers, as

well as other nightclub gigs.

When Polaroid cameras started losing popularity, I switched to a 35mm, which meant I had to adjust my business model to have photos professionally processed and then I delivered them to customers.

At this time, I had no idea of how far this would go. As my business grew, so did my clientele. I was asked to cover family reunions, weddings, and military functions and other events for all occasions.

In the early 2000s, I started networking and met fellow professional African-American photographers while photographing an episode of the Tom Joyner Morning Show. These photographers were from Washington DC and worked on the national level. They told me to meet them in a month and be prepared to work. The rest is history. I have been with these professionals ever since, and we have covered award shows, national conventions, and more. I would like to give a special thanks to Paul Thompson, owner of Photographic Services and Cornel Taylor, owner of C It Visual. These two have played a great role in my career and who I am today. They are my best friends. I am grateful for their presence.

Recently, my local hometown newspaper, The *Tidewater Review*, put together a great article that captured my years in photography. The people back home from my community were very proud. In the media we see lots of stories about the bad things happening all around the world, so it was great for my hometown to have the chance to read about one of their own doing great and positive things around the country in the field of photography.

The Tidewater Review wrote, *"Braxton's subjects include some of the most influential people in the world. He has photographed former presidents George W. Bush and Bill Clinton, current President Barack Obama and Vice President Joe*

Biden, as well as the late Maya Angelou, the late Johnnie Cochran, Rev. Jesse Jackson, and Magic Johnson." Every two years I travel home to photograph and attend my high school reunion and everyone is happy for me and proud of my success.

Throughout my years, I have photographed many influential people and some of the world's largest conventions and gatherings to date, such as The National Urban League, The National Conventions of The NAACP, The National Minority Supplier Development Council Inc., The National Rural Electric Corporation of America and others. There was a gentleman whom I met while photographing from the podium who said to me, *"There are many people who do what they do, but you are not just here doing it, you were chosen."* I believed this to be true, and I am humbly thankful to still be doing what I love to do.

"When you have the opportunity to ride in motorcades with national presidents of key organizations, it gives you a sense of accomplishment. It has taken me to another level in my career." – Kelvin Braxton

President Barack Obama

One of my favorite photos is that of President Barack Obama, and Vice President Joe Biden and soldiers from Fort Campbell, KY, in May 2011. That photo was taken four days after the president announced to the world in reference to the raid on the Osama Bin Laden compound. President Obama thanked the 101st Airborne Division and Seal Team 6, who captured Osama Bin Laden.

I knew I would photograph the President again, so I enlarged the print and placed it on a 20x30 canvas. When I went to photograph the President a few years later in Nashville, I was hopeful that the President would sign the photo even though I was told it wouldn't be possible. According to one of the White House staffers, the President agreed to sign it after seeing the picture, which he did following that event.

144

I was able to get Vice President Biden to sign an additional 20x30 canvas of the same image at the 2014 NAACP convention in Las Vegas. Before the event, I was told to have the picture on hand if I wanted it signed, but then I was later told he wouldn't be able to sign it because he was running late. As Vice President Biden was leaving, a member of the NAACP leadership mentioned to him that I had a portrait that he may want to see. After seeing the print, Vice President Biden turned around and yelled to his entire staff to "hold up." I was then afforded the opportunity to sit with the Vice President to explain my photo as he signed and dated the 20x30 print that I had enlarged, even after being told by a staff member that was not going to happen. But it did.

Mr. Braxton sat down with U.S. Vice President Joe Biden to autograph portrait.

I will tell anyone, *"Do something you like to do."* How could one go from photographing in the clubhouse all the way to photographing occupants of the White House? All in all, it's all God, but not everything was always easy. When I first started out I had very little support or help. I was thought of as the underdog. There were people who actively worked against me but nevertheless, I kept being persistent. Over time what I found is that the very same people, who were against me at some point, actually needed my help and support as I advanced in my career.

Blessings & Thanks

I reflect upon the memories of the late Dr. Maya Angelou and former Washington DC Mayor Marion Barry. I had photographed them both at the Essence Musical Festival in 1998. I had taken a picture of Dr. Angelou and Mr. Barry at that event, I had it enlarged to a 20x30 canvas and Dr. Angelou had signed it. She commented about those in the picture saying, *"Those are my closest friends,"* she also said to me, *"Hold on to this picture and it will mean something someday."* I still have it until this day. She also dated it. I will never forget this moment for as long as I live.

Mr. Braxton poses with autographed Image of Maya Angelou, Jesse Jackson, Marion Barry, Susan Taylor, and others.

As I look back on photographing previous national events, to include photographs that captured the last three Presidents, Vice Presidents and First Ladies, I have a lot of memories from over the years and images of different leaders as they were going through their key moments in history. These images are important to me and allowed me to capture them at their peak.

It is always great to network with other photographers, business and church leaders, organizations, politicians and more. You never can tell when you will be in their city. I have been blessed to travel all over the country providing my services. I have friends in Tennessee and throughout my local community who support me such as The Tennessee Tribune, in which I have been blessed for many years working with the Editor in Chief, Rosetta Perry. Also, I've been fortunate to work with the Boyd Publishing Company, Dr. Bobby Jones, the Churchwells, Connie and Rhea Kinnard, and Treva Gordon with Convenient Shopper Magazine. These are some of my greatest friends.

Of all of the photographs, the one that is the most valuable and important to me is the last photograph of my mother that was taken right before she passed. She said, *"Boy don't take that picture of me."* At the same time, she was posing, smiling, and knowing I was going to take the picture anyway. I am so glad I did. I was fortunate to take that picture and still have it to this day. It is the most precious of all my photos.

As you take time out to count your blessings, be sure to enjoy life and take the time to love others. In my pastime, I enjoy fishing. Even when my boys were young, I would carry them out to the lake for some great times. I call the lake my get away spot. Whenever I can take the time to get away, especially spring time, I go to a little place that is calm and serene. Every person should have a private quiet place. I am not trying to tell everybody mine because it is a place in this world that God gave little ol' me.

God

God is the Creator of the heavens and the earth. It all belongs to Him. He is the most important in our lives. We were all pre-destined by God to be here. Our parents are the vessels that got us here. Even though we are here in the flesh, we have to die in the flesh to live in the spirit. In these human bodies, we are only familiar with our six senses. But there is more. It is The Spirit of Holiness. It is important to understand that the God who created us is also the architect of the entire universe. He has a perfect plan and God's perfect plan works.

It is important to know that God gives us a free will. If you have the faith and believe, God's love is limitless. So don't doubt the power, embrace it. If it's one thing I know, God is the maker, the shaker, breaker and taker of life.

I pray that everyone will grow stronger in the faith and in God. One day we shall all behold Him. We are all going to leave here and will die. If you think about it, our spiritual being has to go somewhere. It is important for us to know that the Spirit of the Lord cannot dwell in any unclean temple. Once it's clean, we can allow God to come in, and He will give us a sense of direction through the anointing of the Holy Spirit.

Reflection

As I look back on growing up in Virginia, I never thought about pursuing a career in photography. God had a plan. From being raised in a loving home by my family, God was setting the course for my life. From my military career working as a medical technician tasked to take pre-op and post-op photos and working with patients undergoing cosmetic procedures, I never knew that even taking those photos then, would lead me to where I am today.

Because of that job, I had to know my cameras; especially how it should be set in various setting positions. God always has a plan, even during the times when I was trying to figure it out. From photographing from the clubhouse to the White House I cannot take any credit because it was God who gave me the strength, availability, skill and knowledge to travel, and meet the most influential people in this world.

I pray that my chapter will bless people just as my images have blessed others throughout the years. Know that in God all things are possible. Phil 4:13. Whatever you desire to do with your life, allow God to lead and guide you. I am thankful to be among other Magnificent Men inside this book. Again, I give all glory to God.

"I really love what I do and plan on doing this for a long time. There is something about capturing a really awesome image." I will continue photographing until God assures me another gift to pursue for the choosing of His kingdom.

Contact: braxtonkel@aol.com
Owner of Braxton Photography LLC

Magnificent Man

Kevin C. Kennedy

So shalt thou find favor and good understanding in the sight of God and man? Trust in the Lord with all thine heart; and lean not unto own understanding. Proverbs 3:4, 5 (KJV)

Kevin C. Kennedy was born on November 3, 1955 in Clarksville, TN. He grew up on the Kennedy Walking Horse Farm, one of the oldest farms in Clarksville and in possession of the Kennedy family since the 1900's. Kevin graduated from Clarksville High School in 1974, and by the end of the same year he attended Austin Peay State University where he graduated with honors with a Bachelor of Science degree in 1978. While working on his Bachelor's degree, he served as a legal intern at the Montgomery County District Attorney's Office. After receiving his Master's degree in 1979, Kevin went on to teach American History classes at Austin Peay State University. Concluding his education to become a lawyer, he received his Juris Doctorate degree from the Nashville School of Law, ranking first in his class in the field of evidence, in 1983. In 1984, Kevin was admitted to practice law and became a member of the Tennessee Bar Association. In 1989, he was admitted to practice law before the U.S. Supreme Court. Shortly after receiving his license, Kevin joined the Bagwell, Bagwell & Parker Law firm as an associate attorney.

While Kevin's education was important to him, he also knew that God would play a big role in his life. He had the desire to be a God fearing and successful man, and accepted Christ into his life at the age of 8. His mother believed strongly in the Lord, and therefore taught him to read the Bible, pray, and tithe which he still practices to this day. He starts his day reading a chapter in the Bible to "conquer whatever comes my way that day", as Kevin would say. He believes firmly that without God he would be nothing, and that Christ is in the center of everything he does. Kevin truly trusts in the Lord with all his heart.

What would a man like Kevin be without a family? With the help of the Lord he was blessed with a beautiful wife named Rhonda Fulkerson, and three amazing children, Kevin Chambliss Jr., Kenneth Laurence, and Katelin Ruth. This wonderful family of his was, in Kevin's eyes, a gift from God, and he was honored to have them in his life.

With a family behind his back and praying to the Lord, Kevin went on to become a successful businessman. Growing up, Kevin knew he wanted to make a difference in other people's lives. He wanted to have a strong impact in his church and the community. He believed at a young age that he could become that successful businessman and anything that he would encounter in life using ambition, prayer, and conviction. This attitude about life gave him his first job at the age of 14 at Martin IGA. Kevin was ready to do whatever it took to be the man God called him to be with his family, school, community, and job. *"Commit to the Lord whatever you do, and he will establish your plans."* **Proverbs 16:3**

Being a successful lawyer was just one of Kevin's goals in life. While being raised on a horse farm, he knew early in life that he wanted to own his own horses and houses too. Owning his own horses was the prelude to owning his own houses. Kevin's determination and hard work paid off. By 1994 he managed to own one hundred eight horses at one time, and by 2010 he owned one hundred nine houses at one time. Additionally to those goals, Kevin already owned eleven businesses prior to owning those houses. Kevin learned that he cannot focus on just one business. Today, he owns three businesses.

God didn't just bless Kevin with a great family, and business sense, but allowed him also to have some profound people in his life. He has been blessed with ministers, close business associates, and also trained over 100 laywers in his career. It has been a blessing to see his prayers come to pass when asking God to surround him with the right people.

With knowing so many people in every aspect of his life, Kevin strongly believes that it is important for a business to surround themselves with a good team. He learned this philosophy from his business ventures. God says in his own words *"as iron sharpens iron, so one man sharpens another"* **Proverbs 27:17**. As a person begins to build his business, he must begin to build his team. Kevin always emphasizes "on how much you have to think about the team." It also has been said that "you will never do anything great in life without help." To Kevin, it seems that many business professionals fail to understand this concept - they can hear it and acknowledge it, but they do not really implement it into their business model. It would help them reap the full benefits of utilizing teamwork. When the concept of teamwork is deeply rooted within the employer and his organization, they will all move forward in an affirmative direction. Every decision they make will be centered on the good of the team.

Kevin has had the privilege to do life-long studies of different successful individuals. He discovered that there has always been a team. Thomas Edison was asked once why he kept a team of so many assistants and he responded, "If I could solve all of the problems myself I would." He knew that it would take a team to be successful.

While the success of a business is established by having a great team, it is also important to have a connection with the employer. Kevin believes that this is a part of having a successful business, as well as having a great team. The connection between employer and employee can also be found in nature. In the horse business, a horse "hook-up" is known as the moment the rider and the horse make an outstanding connection with one another. It's as if their minds link-up and they are on the same level. The time they have spent together has paid off and they completely trust one another. A great example of a horse "hook-up" was between General "Stonewall" Jackson and his horse Little Sorrel. His horse was aware of the General's aversion to his troop's praise and would gallop away upon hearing the troops cheer. Kevin believes that there is a similar moment between the employer and the employee. This moment arises in the business world when the employee fully buys into the employer's philosophy and strategy, and trusts him to lead everyone to newer and greater success. The "hook-up" cannot be forced, it must come naturally. Once this bond is formed, it is difficult to break.

Although having a successful business with a great relationship between the employer and employee, and being part of a team, there are still two fundamental parts for a relationship to work. To Kevin, respect and trust are important and the key to having a good relationship. A person cannot lack either and expect to have a healthy relationship with a employee or a horse. For example, a rider respects the power and ability of a horse to make a jump, but if there is no trust between both, then there will be a big chance that one, or both, will hesitate at a crucial moment. In that moment they both will fall. Respect and trust are necessary to develop a successful employer/employee relationship, and must be earned by both to have a successful flourishing business.

While Kevin always knew that he wanted to be successful in everything he does, he developed ten steps to succeed early in his career. God says in his words, *"But the fruit of the Spirit is love, joy, peace, forbearance, kindness, goodness, faithfulness, gentleness and self-control. Against such things there is no law."* **Galatians 5:22-23**.

Those are Kevin's steps for success:
1. Motivate yourself
2. Be a leader
3. Use your time wisely
4. Make a difference
5. Set goals and make priorities
6. Be honest in your relationship
7. Listen to others and make your own decisions
8. Constantly evaluate your situation
9. Read the Bible
10. Pray and trust in the Lord

These steps can be helpful in becoming a better person and to find a healthy balance in life.

With everything Kevin experienced in life, he knew that everyone has a purpose in life and everyone has to figure out that purpose. As Kevin would say, "think about what your passions are, what makes you happy, and what will make an impact." Also Confucius said once, "if you find a job you love, you will never work a day in your life." Kevin believes that God put a passion inside everyone, and God will make a way for everyone to walk it out. A person has to be focused and determined against all odds in their lives, to be the best person one can be in what Christ has called them to do.

One has to create opportunities for oneself. Waiting and sitting around for those opportunities to happen, a person will more likely miss the calling because one has to do their part.

Kevin believes that "in our pursuit for purpose and destiny we have to keep an open mind." A great man once said, "Let your mind escape into the jungle." The mind is a magnificent treasure, filled with adventures, and looking for answers to endless

155

questions. The mind is the key to infinite possibilities, ready at any moment to be unlocked. It is consumed by breathtaking ideas and untapped potential that can change the world. The mind is a beautiful creative tool when given the proper guidance and instruction.

In Kevin's eyes, God has given everyone a glorious life to live and the beauty of life is what everyone has been given. The ability to achieve anything that a person sets their mind to reach is powerful. The only limits a person has are created in their own mind. The worst crime one can commit when trying to succeed is not to believe in himself. Life can be what the person wants it to be and to realize that is to keep an open mind and to absorb all of the information that is coming through. One has to know that they can be a visionary; guiding people around everyone to success. Thomas Edison would not have been able to invent the light bulb if he did not keep an open mind. He failed over 10,000 times before he reached the vision he had in mind, and he would have never had the glory if he lost the ability to have an open mind to the possibility of succeeding in the purpose God put inside of him.

In God's word he says, *"Where there is no vision, the people perish: but he that keepeth the law, happy is he"* Proverbs **29:18**. God put a vision and a purpose in everyone. God desires for his people to be successful in the gifts and calling that he has put inside everyone. Kevin knew that he wanted to become successful, so he loved sharing the knowledge God gave him with others he met. Kevin was once asked what he would say to a believer and his response was: "The answer to any of your problems you are facing is Jesus. Because when there is no way, God will make a way". Kevin can testify to this in his life, and he has seen it in all of his businesses.

Failure was no option for Kevin, and he believes that his purpose is to share the knowledge God has given him to others. He loves Jesus and is not ashamed to say it. He would be nothing without God and believes that there never would have been success if he hadn't put Him first in everything he did and still does. Kevin shares a little secret he has learned over the years: "The wisest man sometimes makes no decision at all. He lets the problem run its course". Kevin used to worry about money and other issues to such an extent that it stressed him out and affected his life in a negative way. He learned over time that the best way to deal with his stress was to have faith in God. Kevin noticed when he put his faith in God, his problems began to solve themselves. Stressing over little things in life will only end up digging yourself an early grave. Give the stress and problems to the Lord. Talk to God in prayer daily, He will speak to you and give guidance. His answer will be the solution to the problem. Sit back and enjoy the ride of life. God says, *"For I know the plans I have for you, to prosper you and not to harm you"* **Jeremiah 29:11.**

Kevin has been a successful business man for many years. He has been on the bottom and on the top. He knew that he would not be anything without God. This is why Kevin praises in the midst of everything. God has put a purpose inside every person, and with some help everyone can become the best person they are meant to be. In Kevin's words: "Read your Bible, pray, tithe, and set goals for yourself. Be committed to the things that God has given you. Be the person who gets tasks done quickly and efficiently. Separate yourself from the ones who are not meant to go to the levels God will take you. Stick out like a white rose in a bed of red roses. Live up to your potential and be humble in all you do". God said, *"Let nothing be done through strife or vainglory, but in lowliness of mind, let each esteem others than themselves. Look not every man on his own things, but every man also on the things of others."* **Phillipians 2:3-4.**

Kevin would like to leave some inspirational passages of scripture to encourage everyone's souls. He has found them encouraging and applies them to the tablets of his heart.

Psalms 23 (KJV)
The Lord is my shepherd; I shall not want. 2) He maketh me to lie down in green pastures: he leadeth me beside the still waters. 3)

157

He restoreth my soul: he leadeth me in the paths of righteousness for his name's sake. 4) Yea, though I walk through the valley of the shadow of death, I will fear no evil: for thou art with me; thy rod and thy staff they comfort me. 5) Thou preparest a table before me in the presence of mine enemies: thou anointest my head with oil; my cup runneth over. 6) Surely goodness and mercy shall follow me all the days of my life: and I will dwell in the house of the Lord forever.

Psalms 91:7 (KJV)
A thousand shall fall at thy side, and ten thousand at thy right hand; but it shall not come nigh thee.

Psalms 121:1-2 (KJV)
I will lift up mine eyes unto the hills, from whence cometh my help.
My help cometh from the Lord, which made heaven and earth.

Contact: www.kennedylawfirmpllc.com

Magnificent Man

Lelan Statom

Love the Lord your God with all your heart and with all your soul and with all your mind. This is the first and greatest commandment. And the second is like it: Love your neighbor as yourself. All the Law and the Prophets hang on these two commandments. Matthew 22:36-40

If more people followed these first two great commandments, especially those who say they are Christians, our world would be a much better place. Note, God didn't put any quantifications on which neighbors to love.

I'm blessed! My journey to this point in my life has had its ups and downs, but through it all God has guided me to the place I am today. 2015 marks my 22nd year with WTVF-The News Channel 5 Network. Two months after I got to Nashville, I got

159

married. I had proposed while I was still working at WCYB-TV in Bristol, VA. Dr. Yolanda Statom and I have been blessed with two beautiful children. Our daughter, Kayela, is a student at UT-Knoxville. It's the place where Yolanda & I met. Our son, Taylor, is a middle school student.

Due to the nature of my job, a lot of people know about my family and I now, but how did I get to where I'm at in my life. To help you out, let me take you back a few years. Okay, quite a few years! To start from the very beginning, I'm the oldest of three children. My sister, Melaine Statom, and I were born in Chicago; we moved to Dyersburg, TN when I was five. My mom and dad were both from West Tennessee. My dad, William A. Statom, married my mom, Bernice Travis, after high school. After they divorced, he stayed in the Windy City. He became a minister with the Church of God in Christ. Now, he and his wife, Grace, help run the Pilar of Truth churches in the Chicagoland area. Momma returned home to Dyersburg, remarried and later gave birth to my brother, Corey Hickerson.

We didn't have a lot of money. For a few years, that meant living in the projects & eating government food. I remember those black & white labeled cans & food boxes. I love Cream of Wheat; so, the Farina that came in those food boxes wasn't bad; neither was the government cheese, but I still get a bad taste in my mouth anytime I think about instant milk. I know in reality it was not long, but it seemed like it took me over an hour to eat any cereal that had that instant milk, but I don't ever recall us going without, even if that meant having the left overs from dinner for breakfast. My mom laid a good foundation for me and my siblings, and I hope and pray that my wife and I are now doing that for our children.

In high school, I was a very active 4-H'er, and through that program, I knew I wanted to go to The University of Tennessee-Knoxville. As I noted earlier, there wasn't a lot of money in our family, but I was determined to go to college. Pell Grants, TN Students Assistant Corps, and college loans helped me greatly. I also worked, beginning with cutting the lawn at my home church, Salters Chapel African Methodist Episcopal in middle school. In high school, I worked at the Piggly Wiggly and a couple of other grocery stores in the same building. In college, I worked in the food court, was a Resident Advisor and served as Athletic Director at a 4-H Camp in Milan, TN. Those jobs served to give me good work ethic, but loans helped get me through UT.

There were points in my life after I graduated from UTK that I didn't think I would ever get those loans paid, especially when my first TV job paid $12,235. Fortunately, Ford Motor at the time had a program for college grads; so, that helped me get a brand new Ford Escort. In the early part of my career in TV, some of us had a saying that we wanted to have a job where the pay at least matched our age, meaning that I wanted to make at least 22-thousand per year since I was 22 when I graduated UTK.

During my senior year at UTK, I met a beautiful young lady, Yolanda Taylor, who would later become my wife...years later. We met because her best friend had a crush on me. They were freshmen students at Hess Hall dorm where I was a resident advisor. Our first meetings were designed to set-up her friend and myself. We all became great friends as I returned to Knoxville after college to work at two TV stations, but I had a crush on Yolanda that never really went anywhere until I got a job at the NBC station in Bristol, VA.

Fast forward a few years to 1992, I was still working in Bristol when I proposed. The next Monday, I got a call from Ron Howes at News Channel 5 Nashville. They asked me to send in a resume tape, and 4 months later I was offered a job. That made 1993 an even bigger year. My first day at NC5 was May 10, 1993. Two months later, Yolanda and I got married; then, I finished the Broadcast Meteorology Program at Mississippi State University in August.

Two decades later, I can say how blessed I am on this journey that God has laid out for me and my family. I have been blessed with a host of opportunities at WTVF, and my wife has had several great career moves with Metro Nashville Schools including a very recent appointment as Assistant Principal as well as being an adjunct professor at Trevecca Nazarene University. We have been blessed with two beautiful children. The oldest is a student at UTK, and the youngest is in middle school.

I grew up in the church and was active at Salter's Chapel A.M.E.C. in Dyersburg, and I think that foundation served me very well on this journey. One of the things I remember hearing often was that God works on his timetable and not ours, and that has been a blessing for me.

After graduating college, I didn't get that job in front of the TV camera immediately. As I noted earlier, I took a job with a small salary to get my foot in the door. It wasn't what I wanted, but it was God's plan. Over the course of my nearly 3 decade career in television news, I have had the opportunity to do a host of jobs. I have been a photojournalist, assignment editor, video tape editor, teleprompter operator, producer, reporter, anchor, meteorologist & talk show co-host, but that was God's way of making sure I'm appreciative of all the jobs.

I'll end this with the way I began it. Blessed….we're so very blessed!

Contact: lelan.statom@newschannel5.com
Facebook/Twitter: NC5_LelanStatom

Magnificent Man

Leroy Hyter Jr.

A LESSON IN TRUST

"Trust in the Lord with all of thine heart; and lean not unto thine own understanding. In all thy ways acknowledge Him, and He shall direct thy paths." Proverbs 3:5-6

My Dream

I was born in Detroit, Michigan in the late 50's, right at the birth of the Motown era. Music was everywhere so it wasn't strange that I grew up dreaming of being a musician. After experiencing a certain level of success, while pursuing my musical career in Detroit, I was blessed to experience the majority of my success when I moved to New York City in December of 1987. As fortunate as I was to have had the wonderful opportunities awarded me during my stay in New York, those opportunities and successes didn't come about without first learning a valuable lesson in trust.

A Lack of Trust

I was in my thirties before I got the revelation that God's plan and direction for my life was the most blessed and prosperous plan and path to follow. Many times while thinking back on that period in my life, I have asked myself the question, why didn't I seek God for His direction and guidance before then? Why was it that I felt more comfortable taking an authoritative role over my own destiny and path through life? It wasn't that I didn't know God or believe in Him. It wasn't that I wasn't aware of the fact that He had created me and blessed me with all of my gifts and talents. Today, I can honestly say, as I write this message, that it was simply a matter of trust; I didn't trust God with my life. I felt, during the early years of my life, that my life would be lived out more in agreement with my own personal desires, if I controlled and directed it myself, without God's personal input. To put it plainly, I didn't trust that He had my best interest at heart.

Though it sounds strange to hear me say that today, at that time in my life, I couldn't think of any better or safer way to live. But how many of us know that during that period of self-rule, I was being totally deceived by the enemy. I was naïve to think that I had a better plan for my life than the God who created me. I was totally self-seeking and self-centered in my approach to life, as well as in my relationship with God and it was because of my lack of humility and surrender that I found myself living completely outside of the will of God for my life. I thank God that I finally did learn to place my total trust and reliance in Him.

Experiencing Life with God

What was it that helped to bring me to a place of trusting and submitting my life to God? What was it that humbled my instinctive nature to be head and ruler over my own personal affairs? There is one experience in particular that played a major role in initially teaching me the benefits of surrendering the affairs of my life over to God, an encounter with the Spirit of God that changed my life forever. I like to think of it as my own personal road to Damascus encounter or my burning bush experience, for I too, much like the Apostle Paul and Moses, through this experience, came to better know and trust in God. Let me briefly share this experience with you.

A Dream Come True

In December of 1987 I was offered a recording contract with one of the most successful production companies in the music industry and it was because of this wonderful opportunity that I decided to move from my hometown of Detroit to New York City. To make a long story short, unfortunately tragedy struck the day I arrived. After relocating to the Big City I was sadly informed by the vice president of the company that my recording contract was no longer. Legal matters had caused the deal to be dropped unexpectedly. Needless to say I was devastated, for this was the opportunity I had spent my whole musical career preparing and believing for, a dream come true, to receive a recording deal with a major record label and now in one day it had all unraveled before my very eyes.

A close friend had been kind enough to offer me a place to stay for the first week I was in New York. I was faced with deciding whether to go back home to Detroit, find someone else who would let me stay with them, or be homeless in the streets of New York City. Prior to leaving Detroit, I had vowed that regardless of whatever happened, going back home was totally out of the question. So that left me in a very serious and uncertain predicament of trying to survive in New York with very limited means to support myself. Faced with these overwhelming obstacles I soon began to feel that my life was beginning to sink into an extreme state of darkness.

There was a slight entrance of light though in the midst of this dark situation, for before the week ended I was blessed to receive some good news. Through the help of one of my friends back home in Detroit; I was invited to live, rent free, at least until

I could get on my feet, with one of their close friends, who stayed an hour outside of the city on Long Island. As excited and thankful as I was to have a place to stay, I knew that this was only a temporary fix and that it was crucial that I find some work as soon as possible.

Looking For Work

So every day I would collect my demo tapes and resume and hit the streets of New York looking for work. Days would pass and then weeks and much to my disappointment I had no success. As my savings began to dwindle, I also began to have problems with the man I was staying with. My life seemed as if it was being totally destroyed. My dream had been dismantled, I was running out of money, I couldn't find any work and now I wasn't getting along with my landlord. I desperately tried everything within my own power to resurrect this dying situation, but everything I tried quickly failed.

The Solution

Then one night I received a call from a close friend. This was the same friend that was responsible for helping me find a place to stay. Upon hearing of my troubles she immediately took me to the Word of God. Well to be honest, what she had to say was the last thing I wanted to hear. Yet regardless of my opposition she went on to minister to me.

She told me that God always allows challenging circumstances for a reason and that my situation was no different. She promised that only good would come from my sufferings if I put my trust in God and Him alone. This situation, as difficult as it may appear to be, she said, was awarding me the opportunity to get to know God better and to experience His faithfulness. She then went on to challenge me to spend more time seeking after God, through my prayer and fellowship time, and spending less time focusing on my problems, She urged me to take the time to

166

read the Word of God and to allow God's truths to be an anchor and a light in the midst of my present storm.

I was extremely upset by what she had to say, because I felt that she was being overly judgmental towards me, for during this time in my life, though my relationship with God was quite immature, I strongly believed that I had one, even if terms like personally seeking God and fellowshipping with God were foreign to me and even though I actually felt that reading the Bible was only appropriate for ministers or religious fanatics. I knew I had a strong love for God, but unfortunately for me, what I didn't know was the fact that I possessed very little knowledge about Him. Much to her disappointment, I repeatedly told her how I felt, yet not to be moved from her position of faith, even after hearing my angry responses, she challenged me all the more to take this opportunity to seek God and to trust in Him with all of my heart.

Learning to Seek God

When I hung up the phone with her that night, though I was extremely upset, I knew in my spirit, not only that she was right, but that I also desired to accept her challenge. So the following day, after I shared my new feelings and outlook with her, she decided to send me a copy of a daily devotional called "The Daily Word", to help me in my study of the Bible. The first day it arrived, I immediately read the message for that day, on my train ride into the city, which was entitled "Let Go and Let God." In this particular devotion was the written testimony of a young lady who went through a horrible situation in her life and when she finally realized that within her own strength she could do nothing to successfully overcome it, she let go of her care and anxiety of the problem facing her, and surrendered it all over to God. The story concluded by stating that when she finally let go and let God her challenges were supernaturally resolved, for God blessed her by resurrecting the deadness of her situation and transforming it into a new and glorious life.

My Surrender

After reading this inspiring testimony I took a good look at my own life, and how overwhelmingly devastating my circumstance had been for me; all that had been lost, and all that I had tried to do within my own wisdom and ability to fix the problems facing me, and I could see that my life, while in my hands, was spiraling out of control. Then as I sat there, flipping through the pages of this short testimonial, while riding the Long Island Railroad, I finally came to the realization that within my own power I too could do nothing about my present situation and right then and there I made a decision to do like the woman in the story, to "Let Go and Let God." At that moment, from the depths of my heart, and for the first time in my life, I was willing to surrender the reigns of my life over to God, for I truly felt that I had nothing more to lose and everything to gain. Needless to say I spent the rest of my train ride stress and worry free,

A Supernatural Lunch Date

Well as always, once I arrived in the city I walked the streets looking for work and as always I was met with the constant rejection of my potential employers. That afternoon, though, I had a lunch appointment with a friend at a restaurant named 20/20 owned by pop stars Ashford and Simpson. As I entered that restaurant I was met with a surprise, I noticed a beautiful grand piano set up ever so gracefully on the stage. This was shocking to me because the last time I visited this restaurant they didn't have a piano. I immediately asked the hostess about the piano and she went on to inform me that it had just been delivered to the restaurant that morning. What immediately came to my mind was my prayer and decision to let go and let God. The fact that the piano was delivered on the very day I walked through the door caused me to think, "...was this simply by coincidence?" I thought to myself, "...or was God working on something here on my behalf?" But not wanting to be too overly spiritual I quickly pushed that thought aside.

Not long after taking my seat and while my friend and I were enjoying our lunch, a young man, who I later learned to be the manager of 20/20, approached the table to speak with my friend. While they were conversing, the same young man, who I had never met or been introduced to, turned and with a surprising look on his face, asked me if I was Leroy Hyter. When I responded by saying yes, he went on to tell me that he was a big fan of my music and that actually my CD of solo piano music was the music they played in the restaurant during the dinner hours. We both stood there puzzled and surprised by this unusual occurrence as he went on to ask me, "Where did you come from and what are you doing in New York?" When I told him that I had just recently relocated from Detroit and was looking for work, with much excitement he responded, "Well we just received delivery of our piano today, so if you need work, you can work for us!" I was both humbled and shocked upon hearing that statement, and because of the overall miraculous nature of the whole experience, I quickly discovered the simple truth, that letting go and letting God is the only true way to live a successful life. This was how I received the first of many jobs in New York City and I never again desired to take the leadership role in my life or career.

Success Almost Leads To Failure

After learning that valuable lesson in trusting God, my career began to blossom. It wasn't long before opportunities just began to pour in and none of them were jobs that I had personally sought after. Whether it was working as Musical Director for pop singer Freddie Jackson, performing as a musician for the Cosby Show or in a film with Barbara Streisand, God just supernaturally brought all of this work before me.

In the midst of my success though, I'm sad to say I began to change. Where I once loved to seek God in prayer, I found myself feeling as though I just didn't have time any more for that. It wasn't long before I had totally fallen out of fellowship with

God. Then soon following all I had achieved was lost just as quickly and supernaturally as it had first occurred. Just before I lost everything I had renewed my relationship with God. Though I was broken once again, I was more at peace in my poverty than I had ever been in my success, due to the fact that I was back with my heavenly Father.

Then God said something to me that changed my life. He said that He actually never created me to be the next Quincy Jones, or any of the great entertainers that I grew up admiring. He said He created me to be the next Apostle Paul, the next Peter, the next teacher and minister of God's Word. At this point in my life I was broken and fully ready to do anything God required of me. Then God asked me to do something else. He said, "give me your dreams." This day for the first time I was finally ready to surrender them all to Him. So I did as He requested.

Then He said something that amazed me. He said, "Now take them back. Those are dreams that I Myself have given you. My intention was never to take them from you, I simply wanted you to allow Me the opportunity to personally lead you to how your dreams are to be fulfilled." A few weeks later I answered the call to the ministry, I left New York City and set out on the pursuit of God's path and plan for my life. Today I am a licensed and ordained Minister serving as Minister of Music at Faith Life Church in Antioch TN and have discovered that there is nothing more fulfilling and rewarding than surrendering the whole of your life and dreams to God.

Contact: lhyterjr@yahoo.com
www.leroyhyter.com

Malcolm O. Munro

Endeavor to Persevere

For I know the plans I have for you," declares the LORD, "plans to prosper you and not to harm you, plans to give you hope and a future. Jeremiah 29:11

Have you noticed that life sometimes clogs up your dreams, goals, and aspirations? The challenges come from financial worries, family issues, health problems, and just plain old boredom and complacence. Whatever the case, the result is a feeling of depression and a lack of motivation. Sometimes you feel lethargic and other times jittery and hyperactive. Either way, the feeling is disturbing, and if not addressed, will soon affect your relationships and your own peace of mind. In these moments, a clog has occurred in your life and needs something to come along and create a breakthrough.

I've experienced many of these "clogs" in my life. You'll read about them in the next few pages. For many years it seemed as though I had no direction and that God had somehow forgotten about me. Fortunately, that's changed.

Right now you could say I'm "living the dream." I have a consulting, training, and coaching practice that's very profitable and, best of all, gives me the flexibility to work the schedule I want. I get to teach workshops in fun places like New York City, San Francisco, Shanghai, London, and Munich. I've written several books, appeared on the radio and in *The Washington Post* and *Men's Fitness* magazine, and spoken to large audiences in a number of interesting industries. I have the privilege of working regularly with groups of military folks who are transitioning out of the service and into their second careers as civilians. Most of all, I don't dread Monday mornings and never live from vacation to vacation.

Does that sound like a typical statement from some rich motivational speaker? Probably, except that I'm not a rich motivational speaker. Sure I have enough money to be happy and yes, I am actually a motivational speaker, but beyond that, I'm just a regular guy who enjoys football, wrestling, UFC, hot wings, working out, and church on Sunday morning.

It wasn't always like this. For much of my life, I was a lot like the average American. I had a job and career I hated and lots of dreams that seemed a little too big and far off to be real. That part of my story begins in 1982 while sitting in my high school Civics class watching each Friday (which was designated as "career day") as representatives from colleges came in to present to us soon-to-be-graduating seniors.

I wanted no part of college, having just spent four years in a tough, college-prep school. My parents had no college education and seemed to be happy so I figured I'd just find a job after graduation. I didn't really know what I wanted to do, but that changed one day when somehow a trade school managed to sneak into the class to present. It was a representative from the Southern California College of Medical and Dental Careers in Anaheim, CA. They were talking about careers in dental laboratory technology, which is the process of building dental appliances like dentures and crowns. It looked a lot like building

172

plastic models, which was my all time favorite hobby. I made up my mind that day to apply. The news only got better when I learned of a scholarship program they had if you won an essay contest. I wrote a couple of paragraphs and lo and behold, won the contest! My tuition was free. I started the six-month program just two weeks after graduation and did really well, specializing in removable prosthetics.

My first experience in the "real" world was a four-week externship in a rundown dental lab in Orange, CA working for the ultimate cheapskate dentist. He paid me $10.00 per day and I worked 12 hours straight with no lunch break. This was in 1982, long before the push for standard infection control processes. Because of this, he could turn out a set of dentures in one day for select patients, most of whom were too old and senile to know the difference between quality and safety. This dude was a slave driver! My dream career suddenly looked like a nightmare. When the externship mercifully ended, he told me I wasn't a good fit and would not be hired. This was no disappointment, but I did find the market for dental lab techs was pretty saturated. Most labs in Southern California wanted techs with at least five years of experience. I applied for every job I could find and had only two interviews and no offers.

Frustrated, I went back to the school and asked my instructors for advice. All of them were retired military folks who recommended I join the Navy and become a lab tech there, get my five years of experience, then get out and get back in the field. It sounded good to me so I went to a recruiter, took the ASVAB test, and was qualified. The recruiter told me I'd have to come in as a dental chairside assistant but that I was certain to get the advanced lab school since I did it as a civilian. With that promise, I signed the papers, went to the processing center in downtown Los Angeles to undergo a physical exam and sign more papers. At the end of the day I was sworn into the Naval Reserve and placed in the Delayed Entry Program, which meant I'd be hanging around for about nine months before having to report for Basic Training. During this time, I took a job stocking shelves at a grocery store and began the mental preparation for my new and exciting career in the Navy.

Finally, on December 5, 1983 I left for Basic Training in San Diego, CA. Boot camp wasn't nearly as tough as I expected, but the 12 weeks certainly dragged by even though they were filled with activities. I learned how to properly fold my clothes, make my bed, work with others, and respect authority. We marched endless miles, spent hours in classes, and experienced first-hand why tear gas can dispel an angry mob. When my time there ended, I was sent just a few miles down the road to Naval Station San Diego to the Naval School of Dental Assisting and Technology. School was a bit stressful but my spirits were high thinking of how wonderful it would be to get past the chairside assisting classes and move back into the lab! Sadly, the convening dates for the start of lab school and my graduation date were off by three months. I was told I'd have to go "to the fleet" for three years and reapply to the lab school. This wasn't what I bargained for. As far as I was concerned, dental assisting was a terrible and disgusting job. Plus now I'd be forced to work with dentists, which after my experience at the lab in Orange, was not an appealing thought. The only bright spot was my set of orders to NAVCOMMSTA Harold E. Holt in Exmouth, Western Australia.

I graduated from assisting school in June of 1984 and left for Australia four weeks later. My first job was working for a dentist who resembled, in both look and demeanor, my very first dentist boss! His first words to me were: "Munro, you need to get over to the gym and get weighed. I know you're over bodyfat and weight." His chairside manner wasn't much better. Thankfully, he transferred about six months later and the next guy was a big improvement. During this time, I flew back to the states and married my high school sweetheart. She flew back with me and we moved into base housing. Life was much better now and I actually settled into a routine that was fairly comfortable. The job was tolerable, but interestingly enough I began to lose my interest in getting back into the lab. Still, I didn't quite know what to do, but had no intention of going back to school.

In 1987, we returned to the states on leave for a well-deserved break. I was helping my dad clean out the attic in my old house when I found a box of my old term papers written during my senior year. I couldn't believe it was my writing. It was almost as if it was someone else's work. I didn't even remember writing many of them but they were all excellent! It made me realize how far I had sunk intellectually and academically. I decided, right there in that dusty and dirty attic, to go back to school.

When we returned from leave, I enrolled in my first college class at the University of Maryland extension. It was Physics 100. Now I'm pretty bad in math and science, but I managed to gut out an "A" and was pretty proud! I then took Algebra, Economics, and my favorite class, Intro to Writing. During this period, my new boss, Dr. Greg Nelson, took me under his wing and encouraged me to go to dental school. He was so confident in my abilities that he let me fill one of his teeth! I had a new goal and was going full speed at it.

We transferred to Naval Hospital Long Beach in January 1989 where I found myself back in direct patient care as an oral surgery assistant. I started back into school, but the pressure of moving back and a very stressful job derailed me. I began to rethink a career in dentistry but didn't know what to replace it with. Some of my co-workers were enrolled in a degree program at the Southern Illinois University extension for a Bachelor of Science in Health Care Management. It was a great arrangement, as I could take my upper division stuff on weekends and get the lower division work done during the week at a community college. I threw myself into the program and quickly made progress.

Unfortunately, the work and school blitz took its toll on my marriage and family and soon I found myself going through a divorce and moving in with my grandparents. Regardless, I kept pushing ahead, and two years later, I was leaving California for the island of Guam with my new wife. Guam was a great tour career-wise. I finished my degree and set out to get a commission as an officer in the Medical Service Corps. I was probably the most "squared away" I'd ever been in my career and actually thought I'd do my 20 and retire as a Naval Officer.

We transferred back to the states in December 1994 for orders to Naval Dental Center Northwest in Washington State. I was taking over as clinic manager at the Bangor Submarine Base. This was my first real experience in management and it was challenging. Now I had to manage a staff of 23 and deal with about 12 dentists. I also kept applying for the commissioning program. The competition was very tough for this program and most of those selected had graduate degrees, so I signed up to work on my Master's Degree in the evening. I didn't really care what the degree was in so long as it didn't have a lot of math in it. The only one I could find was a Master of Arts in Organizational Leadership from Chapman University. I didn't really know what the program entailed; it just looked like an easy degree. I applied for the commissioning program again in 1996 and was rejected. After this, my third rejection, I again had second thoughts on my career choice. Every endeavor to that point started well, but quickly ran out of steam. I was in my mid 30's and still didn't know what to do with my life. What was interesting though was that the further I progressed in my college program, the more interested I became in the content. It got me thinking about a possible career as an organizational development consultant. I also started doing some work in a collateral capacity on training in the Navy's Total Quality Leadership program. Training seemed to come quite natural to me and it was fun! Best of all, people really enjoyed my workshops.

When I finished my degree in 1997, I got a part time job teaching courses at a local college. I was also getting more involved in the command strategic planning process and doing workshops for audiences far more senior than I. I got into the habit of reading everything related to training and development I could get my hands on. I still thought the Navy would be my career, but now I knew what I really wanted to do. There were some limitations, but I overlooked them until our command's IG inspection in 1998.

IG inspections are really tough. You'll endure months of preparation for this weeklong event. This year though, our strategic plan was to be scrutinized as well. We put a lot of time into it, and I felt good as a lot of my sweat was in there too. Shortly before the inspection, the Executive Officer came to me and told me he had a very important job for me. The IG was going to be briefed on the strategic plan and he needed me to be right there with him. I was so excited! This was my moment to shine. Fifteen long years of planning and trying to figure out what to do with my life were all leading to this big moment. There was only one problem. My important role was to be the guy who advanced the PowerPoint slides while the Executive Officer gave the briefing.

I was heartbroken. I knew then that my Naval Career was for all intents and purposes, over. No matter what I did to advance myself, I'd never be taken seriously. That day I decided to leave when my enlistment was up. There was an early retirement program in place and I was selected for it. In January 1999, I transitioned out of the Navy and moved with my family to Millington, TN.

My career transition was pretty easy. I landed my first job doing supervisory training for a large medical practice group in Memphis. I learned a lot and had fun teaching workshops for a whole new audience. I also taught part time in the Management Program at Crichton College.

We transferred in 2000 to the DC area and settled in Germantown, MD where I took a position as Director of Training for a trade association. The position was ok, but a little slow for my tastes so I left and took a job at a big hospital doing all the management education. That was a great job in a great environment. I could have stayed there forever but there were few opportunities for advancement and I had much bigger goals in mind. I ended up going back to my old position at the association, but it was a promotion and gave me some flexibility. It also enabled me to network with and be mentored by some great business owners that were association members. I started my business in 2003 while working there and by the time 2005 came around, I was able to fire my boss and for the first time work for myself. The breakthrough I needed all along finally came and with it a whole new set of great opportunities.

Since that time, life has been a whirlwind. Through networking and hard work, I've built a strong training, coaching, and consulting practice which allows me to do what I love full time. I feel for the first time an alignment with my purpose. I don't dread work or my career, and get tons of satisfaction from what I get to do and from the people I do it with.

This is the life I want for all of you. More importantly, it's the life God wants for you. My life verse from Jeremiah says it all:

For I know the plans I have for you," declares the LORD, "plans to prosper you and not to harm you, plans to give you hope and a future.

Life is truly a gift and you are equipped with unique knowledge, skills, and abilities in which to live it with. God has made sure of that. Take some time to reconnect with Him and rededicate the years you have left to His control. Don't miss out on the life you were designed to live.

I want you to have the best ride possible. If you're in a situation where you need a breakthrough, be sure to take the principles in the following pages very seriously.

Malcolm O. Munro is the President of **Hired Guns Consulting, LLC.** He is a nationally-recognized author, speaker, consultant and coach who works with companies and organizations in all industries nationally and internationally.

Contact: *www.HiredGunsConsulting.com*

Marvin L. Winans Jr.

Trust in the Lord with all thine heart and lean not to thine own understanding, in all thine ways acknowledge Him and He will direct thy paths. Prov. 3:5-6.

Growing up

I was born on December 28th, 1979, in Detroit, Michigan to my wonderful parents Marvin and Vickie Winans. I remember living in Gale Gardens in Melvindale, MI. My early memories begin around age three with my family including my brother Mario and cousins. I also remember my dad and uncles, more famously, known as the Winans, rehearsing in our apartment clubhouse.

I remember good food and good times and playing at the swimming pool. I remember my mother doing hair in the kitchen. I loved going into our refrigerator at the age of 3 and making ham and cheese rolls with just a piece of ham and cheese. I shared a bedroom with my brother. I also remember in the middle of the night, going into my parents' bedroom and asking if I could sleep with them. I am sure they got sick of me doing that because I was a wild sleeper. Many mornings I woke up with my head at the bottom of their bed and my feet in their faces.

Growing up I had a huge family that not only included eleven aunts and uncles on my mom's side, and nine aunts and uncles on my dad's side, but also, two very big church families. My family's home church was Shalom Temple, pastored by Jesse E. Stacks in Detroit, MI. But we would often visit my mother's childhood church, the International Gospel Center, pastored by Apostle Charles O. Miles, in Ecorse, MI.

Music has always been a part of my life. My dad had a Casio piano in the early days then later upgraded to baby grand pianos that he played and wrote songs on. I spent a lot of time in studios because my parents would be in the studio recording. At the time, I didn't like the studio because I knew we would be there forever. The only thing I really enjoyed about the studios was the couches, because I knew I'd be able to sleep. There was one studio in particular I did like because it had an arcade game. I also didn't mind going if I knew my cousins would be there. Overall, I just wasn't a studio fan.

As early as 5 years of age, I was traveling on the road with my mom and singing with her. These are times I will never forget. All I remember is hearing her introduce little ol' me and then walking out on stage with a mic in my hand in front of possibly a thousand people. The song that we had practiced so many times at home was *"Everything Is Going To Be Alright."* I will never forget the way it felt singing the first lines of my verse *"Don't let your problems get you down."*

182

I grew up in and around a pretty famous musical family, but did not truly grasp the concept of what was going on. Some of my favorite times were watching the Winans Family, especially my dad, perform at their annual Christmas concert at the Fox Theatre in Detroit. My dad was so good. The way he moved and performed on stage was mesmerizing. The Christmas concerts were always a blast.

I remember at the age of 7 riding with my mom and dad in the car and hearing my dad talk about having a date. I thought to myself, "Oh no this is horrible." I did not realize he was talking about a concert date and not a date with another woman. I did know my parents had some problems in their marriage though.

At different points you can tell when someone is upset and or when someone leaves the house. You can feel it. Yes, there were some uncomfortable times, and times it seemed that maybe they would be splitting up. At that time, they stuck through it and stayed together; even renewing their vows by having a big wedding ceremony when I was 10 years old.

Through the years I remember my brother Mario gradually becoming an incredible musician. He was a very good drummer. My parents bought him a drum set and he would play in the basement. Later he began really getting into drum machines and four track recorders and maturing into a producer. At this time I still wasn't into music. What I really enjoyed was basketball and after my dad, my next childhood hero was Isiah Thomas of the Detroit Pistons. I loved the Pistons and I loved basketball. I thought one day I would be in the NBA.

My Encounter with God

At age 7, I would go with my family and visit Bishop Norman L. Wagner's church. He was the pastor and later would become the Presiding Bishop of the Pentecostal Assemblies of the World (PAW) in Youngstown, OH. We would travel there back and forth in those days. It was here that I first gave my life to

Christ. I remember getting saved and going down to the altar. I was playing in the balcony with my friends, when Bishop Wagner, or Uncle Norman as I called him, presented the good news of Jesus Christ to us all.

Next thing I knew, I was leaving the balcony and walking down the center aisle with tears in my eyes. I made it to the altar and fell to my knees and publicly for the rest of my life gave my heart to God. My life changed at that day. They would baptize there every Sunday. I remember going in the back of the church, changing my clothes, then being ushered up the steps to the pool to be baptized. When I did, I came out of the water I began to utter words I never uttered before. I later realized that I received the gift of speaking in tongues. I knew this was real because I wasn't making this up. Something came over me. God totally filled me, and at this point I knew something was different, even at this age, I knew that something was different. I saw my friends after the service but felt I could not play the same way I did before. I felt like I had to protect His Spirit within me. Yes, it was totally different. I will never forget it. This was the most important time of my life.

At the age of 10, I started to dabble on the piano, but hadn't quite got bitten by the music bug. I thought things were going good. Around this time my dad started his own church called Perfecting Church, and I enjoyed watching it grow. But I guess things were not going too well for my parents. They soon separated and later divorced. If it had not been for my relationship with God, and Him teaching me His truth, I am not sure how I would have responded. I held on to Him, more than I ever had in my life. Those times truly made me.

Then it happened. At age 15, out of nowhere there was this strong desire that came over me for music and the studio. I remember being in high school looking in a magazine at a mixing board and for some strange reason wanting to turn those knobs. I found myself wanting to learn more about music and everything about it. I also had the burning desire to have my own singing group. I started a group with one of my cousins Michael Winans Jr., and two of my friends, Karl Jackson, and Lance Bennett. The name of our group was called One Way.

One day I got a call from my cousin Carvin who told me that my Aunt Debbie had a vision of my cousins Carvin Jr, Juan, Mike, and myself singing in a group together. We were all the sons of the original Winans. It made sense, but I was committed to One Way. I toiled over it but eventually felt like God was leading me to do this new group. So Winans Phase II was born. We began having rehearsals at my Uncle Carvin's house, who was also our manager. He got us a record deal pretty quickly with Epic and Myrrh records. We signed. I had also just graduated from high school and had been accepted to Michigan State University but elected to start my career versus pursue college. We did the whole group thing and this was the beginning of Winans Phase II. We recorded an album, traveled, shot music videos, and were blessed to work with top producers. There were lots of great experiences for us, like being featured on the Oprah Winfrey show and others. Wow, I was now in the same business that I saw my family in growing up. This is when God gave me a vision for M2 Entertainment.

My biggest passion has always been business. I really enjoy it. I have always loved singing and music. I realized, however, once I started producing myself, that there's no point if no one ever hears it. So my mindset shifted to make sure that the things that we produced as a company would get out there and be heard. It is one thing to have artists of your own that you produce music for, but another thing getting their music out there through distribution and marketing. When I was young, I remember asking questions about business as early as 6 or 7 years old. I would ask anyone I could about it. I even remember asking a cab driver how I could get into the cab business! LOL!

I always knew God wanted me to have a voice to speak to people and entertainment and media is a vehicle where you can have that voice. I knew then that was how God wanted me to use my voice and that is what I am doing now. It isn't always easy doing what God wants you to do, but we all have to trust Him and go wherever He wants us to go. You don't want to start out with God and quit. *"It is vain to start out with God and not be willing to finish."* You have to be willing to go all the way with God. His path is not conventional. If you trust in your own way and not in His way at some point you will give up because you will not understand His Way. God's ways are above ours. That's why it is important to die to this flesh. You have to give it up. You cannot be in the middle.

Humbleness before God

When you submit yourself to God, you allow Him to do what He wants to do in your life; which is to keep you. We must be humble. The Lord will show us ourselves. One thing I know is that our righteousness is as *filthy rags* and there is nothing one can do to earn the grace of God. The most important thing for me is keeping that mindset. There are times I have gone through financial difficulty on my own; and then God tells me that I cannot ask anyone to help me. I have been broke, and God still won't allow me to ask Mom or Dad to help me. However, because I am submitted to God I am learning His ways, He is teaching me humility. I have had that happen to me many times in my life and it's not always easy because things will not always happen the way we expect them; especially when God is having you do something different. God hasn't always given me the opportunity to do whatever I want to do music or entertainment wise. I cannot take the easy route to make money. It's about God's will for my life and to continually trust Him for what He wants for my life. *It has to be real life submission* and giving up of myself to follow Him. It's a very clear path. I know personally that if it wasn't for God I would be nothing and that will never change. Through marriage or life in general, it can hurt, but you must know that God is bigger than you. *If I do it on my own then I am not trusting in Him*. I have to trust God. That is where the humility comes in.

186

Be Yourself

Having a relationship with God keeps me focused on what I am supposed to do. The most successful artists have been people who know who they are as an individual. Their success is based on them knowing who they are in Christ and what they are called to do. My dad is good because he knows who he is and what he can do; so is my mom. My father is very intact and in tune with who he is as an artist. That is how he taught me to be. If I ever have any success it is based on the fact that I have expanded *myself*. This leaves no room for competing. I am going to be who I am regardless. My song, my style, and voice will be what it is. You may want success, but not at the point where you should be concerned about the way another man is doing it. My father is good because he is great at being himself. Donnie McClurkin is great because he is being Donnie McClurkin. Fred Hammond is great because he is being Fred Hammond.

Fatherhood

I am so in love with my children. I have a three year old son named *Marvin Winans III.* We actually call him 3 and I have an 8 month old daughter named *Miranda Lark Winans*. It is a beautiful thing. It is amazing. My amazing wife *Monique Winans* and I had been married for 12 years but for the first 8 and a half years, we had no children. We thought we would have children earlier and tried for at least 5 of those years. Being a person that trusts God's will, I don't ask for much. But one day feeling desperate, I asked God for a son and a month later, my wife was pregnant. It was an awesome experience. It really taught me the strength of God's love. As a father, I wouldn't let anyone do anything to harm my child, so I am in awe of how God gave up His Son for us. His love is serious. *He did this for me and for billions of others who may never even say thank you or let alone love Him back.* Having children taught me God's love.

Parenting is so interesting. I love it. I know I will have a great relationship with my children. My wife is the best wife and mother I can imagine. We have so much fun as we work to build this family together. We have such a great relationship. I am so blessed.

Words of Encouragement

Overall, I believe God is blessing me to provide opportunities for others to do what God has called them to do. I believe I am called to steward millions of dollars for His Kingdom in entertainment and media. I also believe I am called to pastor, and will be in full time ministry by the age of 40. I am trusting God for everything.

For someone who has not accepted Christ, remember *the fear of God is the beginning of wisdom and to know Him is to love Him.* I want to encourage anyone reading my chapter, to get into a relationship with God. It will change your perspective of anything and everything. What happened to me at 7 years old changed my perspective. The first thing is to have the faith and take *a submission* plunge by saying to God that you are going to trust Him with your *life.* For those who know Christ, and may be in a tough situation, remember to live is Christ and to die is gain.

Our reward is summed up in our relationship with Christ. As a son, you have everything He has promised you. God is not a liar and not a man to lie. *You may be in some tough times but keep your eyes on Him.* Just being a son of God keeps you from not worrying. Take each day at a time and seek God first according to Mathew 6:33.

The tough times may come in life and you may worry when will it happen; *but in the silent times, remember to be thankful* for who Christ is in your life. He will come through for you. Take one day at a time and don't give thought for tomorrow but let your focus be on God. Be thankful for who He is, and trust for everything. At the end the day, what God said is going to be true for you in your life and that is the common thread. *God's word works. It never changes.* Allow the Word of God to continually impact your life.

Contact: info@m2-ent.com
www.m2-ent.com
Twitter: @MARVINWINANSJR
Instagram: @MARVINWINANSJR

Maurice Johnson

Blessed is the man that walketh not in the counsel of the ungodly, nor standeth in the way of sinners, nor sits in the seat of the scornful. But his delight is in the law of the Lord; and in his law doth he meditate day and night. And he shall be like a tree planted by the rivers of water, that bringeth forth his fruit in his season; his leaf also shall not wither; and whatsoever he doeth shall prosper. Psalms 1: 1-3

Life's journey began when I was born in Valhalla, New York. I was raised in Newburgh, New York by way of Clarksville, Tennessee, a God fearing gentleman, who was always outgoing. The main objectives for me were to please God and to give a smile to every person I encountered throughout the day. I always knew my life was going in different directions than others. I found myself doing a bit here and there just to occupy my time to fit in with others. I later turned to running track where I had the opportunity to run in the Junior Olympics in New Orleans, Louisiana. Being Mr. Popular in high school all the way up to college, I would do various activities such as being involved in television network stations, serving as class president, winning prom king, and winning awards based on my ambition and determination. All that took a bold level of confidence. I was that go to guy for everything, I would literally put others before me at the top of my priority list, never really having time for myself, because I was so active.

Growing up in the church where I played the drums and the saxophone. I knew I had a special call on my life that only God could get out of me. But instead, I dealt with voices of society and myself. As a result, I suffered academically, physically, mentally, and emotionally. I felt myself slowing down, and then facing an identity crisis with myself. Deep within in my heart I knew the word of God, I knew how to pray, but at the same time, I really wasn't trying to do either of them at the moment. Most importantly, I lost focus on what I enjoyed doing the most, which was school. I scored tremendously low on the ACT. From that point on, I just knew my life was over. I couldn't get in to any of my desired colleges and began to think very low of myself.

People knew me as the smart, intelligent, outgoing Maurice, so I wanted to keep that image of myself. It was very hard hearing and seeing people get into the schools they always dreamed of attending. I was really happy for them, but on the inside, I was saddened. I prayed asking God to just at least let me go to some school. I really didn't care at all where. I just wanted to be accepted in a college somewhere. The opportunity opened for me to go to Western Kentucky University. I was extremely excited. I was so excited that without me being watchful on who I linked up with, I got connected to some wrong influences.

Within my first year there, I turned to heavy drinking, partied heavy, and even did some things I said I would never do with other people. Also to mention, I barely went to class on a daily basis, I stopped going to church, and I stopped seeking God the way I always knew I should. Yet, God reminded me of this scripture, Ez. 7:25 "Destruction cometh and they shall seek peace, and there shall be none." Not really caring about what was going on around me, things begin to shift. My finances for school dropped and my grants were no longer available for me to use anymore. So, I had to start over and go back home to re-focus some things. I was angry with myself. But I certainly knew this had to happen to get my attention back to what I knew is right. Regretting the way things happened, I prayed and asked God to help me in areas where I needed help. Suddenly, he opened up the door for me to have a chance at managing a gospel-recording artist at the young age of 18. Not only did he open that door, but also he allowed me to have my own management company called Devoted Management, which also handled the needs of artists in the music industry. During that time, I had the opportunity of meeting some of the top producers, music artists, and even traveling the states. While doing that, I still missed the mark spiritually.

In the year of 2014, I moved out of my parents' house for a couple of months. Then shortly after, I moved back in with my family. When I went back, I just knew something wasn't right in the atmosphere. I could just feel negative vibes floating around, and I felt unloved. Later that day my Godmother calls me over to her house to talk, and out of nowhere she warns me saying, "be careful". I starred at her wondering where she got that information from, then brushed it off. Then later, my father and I got into a fistfight over some things he felt I should have done around the house. He had been bottling up feelings for the past couple years of why I was so foreign to him and made it a point to finally attack me at the right time. My father would always tell me to do what he never did as a child growing up, and I did that plus more. And it all resulted into jealousy, he was so jealous of me and couldn't understand who I was and where I was going in

God, because of many different things he didn't get to do at a young age. We never got along.

After the big fight, my dad kicked me out of his home. I had no place to go. My dad, my mother, and my Sister all packed my belongings into my truck. I wasn't caught by surprise, because my family and I had never been close as people saw us to be. Growing up, I was like a fatherless and motherless child. Yes, we all once lived under one roof, but they never really parted into me what I needed spiritually and mentally. I cannot remember one thing my parents deposited into my life that really stood out to me. I was alone, as time went by, I found myself growing apart from my family daily. I was homeless, for a while. I went from sleeping in my truck for a couple days, to sleeping from couch to couch, and even staying from hotel to hotel that I didn't have the funds to pay for. Things were happening so fast, I couldn't catch a grip on life, so I fell into a deep depression. I couldn't even rub two pennies together, because I had no money at all to even try to get up on my feet to provide for myself. Debts begin to pile up, and bills needed to be paid. I had absolutely nothing to my name. I had nothing to eat. I was constantly shedding weight, and I hid from people who I knew were going to ask what was going on with me.

Family members would call me, not to check on me, but to only be nosey and spread rumors among other family members. Praying and hoping they would discern that I was in need, I was still left with empty promises. Feeling hopeless and worthless, I didn't want to wake in the morning because I had already felt as if things were not going to change. Never would have thought both of my parents and my family would throw me in the fire and leave me there to burn the way that they did. I was extremely hurt to the point where I didn't want to live anymore. My mother, I always thought we had a common understanding but in reality we didn't even know each other, when everything went down between my father and I, she didn't take up for me as I thought she would. She went days without calling me, didn't even check if I had food or even a place to stay. It just blew my mind away because before things happen. I would share exciting news about church or general information I would be interacted with, she would always blow me off, never receiving anything I had to tell her. We barely spoke to each other. Life immediately flashed before my eyes. I didn't know what to do while sleeping in my car on the side of the road feeling lonely and hoping someone cared about me. Moments after, God really stood in where family slacked off. God immediately snatched me up out of my sleep and begin to speak to me clearly. I was charged to get myself together and be made whole again.

From that point forward, I knew that God had something great in store. Jeremiah 29:11 "For I know the thoughts that I think toward you, saith the Lord, thoughts of peace, and not of evil, to give you an expected end". That very moment God downloaded specific instruction on how to get out of my situation. My journey wasn't easy, but he yet reminded me when I surrender and to God yes, that yes came with a sacrifice of life. Needless to say that during the moments spent with Him, I have grown and matured spiritually in my walk with Christ. Everything that I experienced was necessary in my growth walk, and I begin to see things in a different prospective. Many times I didn't like what was going on around me but everything I experienced was all a part of the process of me breaking and burning off something in order for me to go higher. A lot of times we can be our own hindrance of fully getting all what God really has for us, because we can't let go. I am grateful for the mighty man God has pruned me to be. I will never be the same, and I will never go back! I am free!

You must remember, never get weary in your process. There is always a process and a sacrifice before God. When God is calling you to go higher, expect the hand of God to be with you, also expect the hand of the enemy to come strong against you. But the mere fact of the matter is that you must be still and let God be who He says He is. Everything you go through in life is not always the devil. Trials happen to us so that God may be glorified and you may become stronger in Him than you have ever been. In order to get what you need, remember simply to eliminate the distractions that cause you lose your focus. Don't qualify things into your new season that God never intended to go. You've got to drop the old to pick up the new. Get in the rhythm of champions! Bring out the inner warrior in you! Be Blessed!

Contact: Mauricejohnson99@yahoo.com
www.facebook.com/ MauriceJohnson

Pastor Anthony Daley

Success Is In Every Step- #liveonpurpose

Looking Back to Lean Forward

Most of us have found ourselves in unexpected places. We are standing today where we never dreamed we would be or planned to be. Life kept happening and as it passed with each day, minor decisions we made shaped our way, and here we are now with the consequences of those choices. Those decisions were made largely through the effects of our past. Life is lived in reference to yesterday's experiences. Those experiences shape dreams, define possibilities, and paint the self-image in which we view ourselves. When we ask young children what they want to be when they grow up, the answers are limitless. Whatever they see before them, occupations that people admire, views of the night sky that draw the curiosity are their future. If we ask the same question of that child who is now thirty, we will get a completely different answer. Life's current circumstances communicate limitations. In our view, its experiences have revealed our inabilities.

Have you ever been around someone who is acting in a way that annoys you? Maybe it is someone who seems to act more important than those around him, as if he's got it all figured. But you know the difficult life he lived prior to his success, so you might be tempted to tell him, "You need to remember where you came from." For myself, knowing where I came from helps keep my present place in right perspective. I am fortunate to have an amazing wife to remind me of this from time to time.

I have now been married to Julia for twenty-six years. She is an awesome wife, mother, and companion. She has been my soul mate since I was fourteen years old. We have two great kids, Devin and Lauren, who are both college graduates, married, and living strong lives with vision and purpose. We are pastoring a church that makes a difference to thousands of people around the world. I have been a pastor at The Tabernacle since 2003. As leaders in this ministry, we have planted churches both at home and abroad. We have been fortunate enough to travel around the world, experiencing cultures and seeing landscapes that I never considered possible or even desired to reach. We have created relationships from India to Africa that continue to define our role and create responsibilities that bring hope and expectation for the future.

At forty-five, I feel we are just getting started. My outlook seems to get clearer with each passing day. I communicate vision to those around us with passion and intention as never before. Without comparing my life to anyone else's, I love my life. The value I place on my life today and the possibilities of tomorrow are not hindered by my past. Instead, I am empowered by it. The good and the bad share equal value in making me who I am today.

Looking back on where my life began, I would have never thought I would have the life I have now. I was born in

Middletown, Ohio, and raised in the Oneida district called The Ghetto. The name is fitting for the physical landscape and people's mentality. My father left when I was two years old, leaving my mother with three children. She was not yet twenty years old. She remarried soon after only to see that marriage end when I was about eleven. She set out to raise what had grown to four children.

Being raised by a single mom has its own difficulties, most of which I did not realize when I was younger. She worked hard to support us, but her absence meant freedom to run, and run we did. Unlike today's children, we did not stay hidden in our bedrooms. The neighborhood was our playground and in the ghetto, there were plenty of things to occupy our time.

I found myself smoking marijuana at a young age. Standing at the bus stop heading to middle school getting high, chasing girls through the neighborhood, and just hanging out with my friends seemed like a great life. Mom was not able to buy many things because we were poor, but so were most people in the neighborhood. When everyone around you looks and lives like you do, it makes the world you live in appear normal. The perspective condones your behavior and influences your dreams. Exposure creates vision. For vision to be cultivated properly, the scenery has to change, and change it did.

Unable to find peace, needing family support, and longing for a new beginning, my mother decided to move us all to Tennessee. My grandparents had bought a farm in a small rural community called Indian Mound. We loaded all the material things we had, which was not much, and the five of us headed for the country. But leaving the ghetto was the last thing I wanted to do. Complaining and being difficult became the norm for my sister and me. We hated Tennessee, especially Indian Mound. Mom rented a trailer in the middle of nowhere. There were no bus stops and no friends living next door anymore. We caught the school bus at 6:00 in the morning for an hour and half ride to school. If you were going to ride a bike, there was no neighborhood to do it in. Playing outside meant hanging out with my younger siblings, and my sister and I were certainly not doing that. We resented our mother for pulling us out of the ghetto and bringing us to this hick town of Indian Mound.

There are some things in life that we do not get to choose. We do not choose the family we are born into or the town we are raised in. There will always be people in our lives that make decisions that impact us. Often times these decisions are made without our consent or consideration. When this happens, we have to adjust and make the best out if it. We were being forced to adjust to a new way of living.

Adjustments are one of the most difficult parts of our lives, but they can create new experiences and relationships that create within us ideas that broaden the scope of the world around us. We are creatures of habit and habits only instigate more of the same experiences. We had to adjust and we did. In the process, we found that outside the logistical hurtles, there were opportunities. After all, girls and drugs are everywhere.

My mom found Christ through the divorce. Before she made a commitment to Jesus, we did not have many church experiences. In fact, the only memory I have of church is getting on a Sunday school bus because my sister had heard that a local church was having a contest where whoever brought the most guests to church would win a new bicycle. Like I said, we were poor, and a new bike was golden. My sister persuaded our mom to go one Sunday, and she said yes. Everything in our lives changed that Sunday. We were still poor. We still lived in a very small, rundown trailer, and we still lived in the middle of nowhere. This newfound faith in our mother became a new way of living for the whole family, so even though we were not concerned about church, we all went anyway. A new environment with different values does not always produce immediate results, but as the years passed, the seed grew and so did our perspective of the world we lived in.

Church is where I met my wife Julia. She was twelve, and I was fourteen. I didn't have any intentions for going to church beyond spending time with this beautiful girl. Even though I did not realize it then, I can see clearly now that God was using my nature to get me into position for the future. Most people do not realize that what took place yesterday has value, a currency, to purchase a successful future—even the difficult moments!

I should have been paying more attention to the preacher instead of my Julia, but I was not. As a result, she got pregnant at sixteen and we got married. Talk about adjustment, now here was one. I was forced to father without knowing what one looked like. I watched my friend's fathers and imagined what my life would have been like if my dad had been there. These were my only resources. I had to grow up fast. We made numerous parenting mistakes, but I can say we made it. No one is ever ready, whether they are eighteen or thirty, to become parents. Some things we have to learn through the journey, and my being a husband and father would be a life-changing journey.

The next ten years nearly resulted in divorce and me having to pay child support, but Julia and I have an incredible love for one another. I now know that love has a language, and I was losing my ability to speak it. My casual drinking and marijuana use gained priority in my new life. I had no mother to correct me, and no demand to go to church. I was working, making my own money, so I got to make my own decisions. My newfound freedom was misunderstood and misappropriated. Most of us look at freedom as the ability to do what we want, when we want, as often as we want, and as long as we want. But that is not so!

A few years ago, I read a book titled *True Freedom* by Steve Frye, in which he discusses a study in an American university, concerning people and their response to boundaries. Researchers went to a local elementary school and removed the fence that surrounded the playground area, then monitored the behavior of the children at recess time. When the children came out, researchers assumed they would run beyond the former boundaries, but instead of running farther away from the building, they stayed closer to it, grouping with other students into large groups. After a period of time, they reinstalled the fence and continued to monitor the students' behavior. They discovered that the children used the entire playground, and only grouped together in smaller groups. Researchers concluded when the boundaries were easily identified, the students felt more security and true freedom.

At this point in my life, I did not have clear boundaries and my life began to spiral out of control. My alcohol and drug abuse escalated until one night on July 21, 1998. I was high on crack cocaine, sneaking into my own home at 3:00 am. I had allowed ten years of poverty, my unwillingness to submit to authority, and my struggle with father issues bring me to a place of utter brokenness. That night, while lying in my bed, I decided to make a decision to change my heart. I reached with a childlike hope for a better future than I knew my past had been. I got down on my knees and prayed. Something happened to me that goes beyond words. Rather than allowing my crisis to be my conflict, I allowed the hope of a better life to become my fight. That night everything changed when I surrendered to a life of faith in Christ. I allowed the character of Christ to become my new boundaries. I lost myself in the stories from the Bible and began to learn lessons from other people's stories. I used their freedom within the boundaries they had allowed Christ to establish in them help me have proper vision for my future.

On the day my son got married, I tried to find something meaningful to say. He did not need the sex talk, the job, money, and responsibility talk. We had had them all, so I told him, "There is a place a man comes to in his life when he realizes that what he is leaving behind is more important than what he is pursuing, and the younger a person is when he discovers this, the more successful his life will turn out."

I have finally found that leaving something behind is what makes life worth living. I can see the future much clearer today because I know where I am now and the value my past has had in getting me here. I realize that where I am would have not been possible if I had not been where I was in the past. This encourages me even with the adversities that exist now; I know that tomorrow will be greater than yesterday was.

Life is the consequence of collaborative events, compiling themselves into a place and opportunity that continually develops and grows us. We had no way of knowing that the tragedy of abandonment, the emotional ride of divorce, and the lifestyle of poverty would be so powerful in shaping our lives, into something of value that would one day make an impact on the world.

I am certain that this man who was born into dysfunction, moved as a consequence of the choices of others, who lived without restraint and boundaries has now been positioned for a future that will leave a legacy behind.

Do not look back on your yesterday and allow it to define your future. Allow it to empower you to live with purpose, for leaving something behind that speaks about who you once were here on earth.

Contact: thetab.adaley@gmail.com
www.thetabernacle.us

Pastor David D. Allen

"I knew you before you were formed within your mother's womb; before you were born I sanctified you and appointed you as my spokesman to the world."

"O Lord God," I said, "I can't do that! I'm far too young! I'm only a youth!" Jeremiah 1:5-6 (TLB)

It was early Sunday morning, May 16, 1971 at Memorial Hospital, Clarksville Tennessee that David D. Allen was birthed into the world. Born to Joe & Nancy Allen, I would be the third of eventually four children. My parents were certainly proud of the new addition to the family. My parents brought me home and things couldn't have been better. My oldest sister Annette was six years old and my brother Joe was four years old and Regina would come a couple of years later. The name David means ''Beloved,'' this certainly depicted how they felt about their little boy. As I hear the song around the Christmas season ''Mary did you know" I often want to change the name and ask Nancy did you know. God had a plan for my life that was not made known until much later. Satan has always tried to interfere with God's plan. As we look back on it, we can now see that Satan would make the effort to take my life at an early age.

When I was only 6 months old, I became very ill. My parents took me to the children's clinic where I had begun to fade in and out and was lethargic. My father described my condition as "limp as a dishrag". I was rushed across the street to the same hospital that I had just left 6 months prior. I was immediately examined by the doctors who ran numerous tests on me. After hours of testing, the doctor came out to share with my parents the diagnosis. He explained to my parents that I was suffering from spinal meningitis. This condition is an infection of the fluid and membranes around the brain and spinal cord. Once the infection starts, it can spread rapidly throughout the body. He reiterated that I was a very sick child and grimly shared with them that the chances of me pulling through were slim and if I did survive I could have severe brain damage. He stated that the next few days would be critical.

After speaking with the physician, my parents were allowed to see me briefly, but were not prepared for what they would witness. I was in the intensive care unit with tubes coming out of my head, side and stomach. They stared at me in disbelief. This couldn't be my baby boy who was so healthy at birth and seemed to be just fine a few days ago. They were overcome with grief. The agony of watching their baby in such a helpless way was almost unbearable. As family and friends crowded the waiting area, prayers were being offered up on my behalf. There is a saying that says into each life some rain must fall. Well it seemed that a typhoon had hit our family. Upon consulting with the doctors again, my parents were advised that it was just a waiting game. They stated that they would monitor me closely and that it was a touch and go situation.

As the family patiently waited, minutes turned into hours and hours into days. After the first day there was no change. I was just as unresponsive as when I was admitted. My parents and my pastor Alvin O. Oldham continued to lift me up in prayer. By the second day my condition still hadn't improved, but my parents have always been strong in the faith and they never gave up on God. They realized that God had the power to turn my situation around. The Psalmist says weeping may endure for a night but joy comes in the morning. That third day brought about a wonderful change. When my parents came in to check on me, my eyes were open. I was moving around full of life. God had moved in a mighty way. The family began to praise God for opening my eyes and allowing me to move around. God had showed up and showed out. The doctors were pleased to see that I had showed signs of recovery. The fever had broken and I began to get stronger each day.

God uses modern medicine and doctors to heal us, but we must be careful to not give God's glory to man. It was "Jehovah-Rapha" God our healer that made the difference. The doctors shared with my family that they didn't see any short-term brain damage, but they cautiously stated that they didn't know what the long term effects would be. Years later I would hear my daddy sing "Prayer will fix it." He would sing and the spirit would move in his heart and he would get happy. I can't help but to wonder if he didn't have a flash back to my sickness and their prayers.

I had a happy childhood. My parents raised me in the church. They taught us Christian values. Things such as put God first in your life and everything else will fall into place. I was educated in the Clarksville Montgomery County School System. I was never an honor student and graduated high school with a 3.0 grade point average. One thing I remember in high school was a teacher told me that I wasn't college material. I didn't think much of it then, but in retrospect this is something that lingered in my subconscious. I thought a good educator would always push and encourage students to succeed. I'm reminded in Paul's letter to the church at Philippi, Chapter 4 verse 13 ''I can do all things through Christ who strengthens me'' I would encourage every person young and old to never let people determine your destiny. Put God first and don't allow anyone to punctuate your life by placing periods were God has scripted comma.

In 1992, I married my high school sweetheart. Tonya Nichole Graves. She is the love of my life. Full of beauty and this woman was truly God sent. I was the first of my siblings to be united in holy matrimony. I've learned over the years that marriage takes a lot of hard work. Everyone dreams of a big wedding with all the trimmings. It doesn't take long for one to realize that marriage is not what you read about in a novel, watch on television, or see in the movies on the big screen. Every marriage is different and there are no textbook solutions for all of the many problems that life throws at you. God ordained the family and the church. Satan has been on his job to destroy both ever since. In over 22 years of marriage I can truly say God has been on our side. As a relatively young man, I want to share with those who are single and looking forward to marriage to pray and ask God to send you a mate who loves Him first. I've discovered that when a person really loves God with their heart then the rest will fall into place.

In May 1995, God gave us a wonderful gift. This gift was Tatyana Nikhole Grace Allen. This was certainly a big adjustment. For almost three years Tonya and I only had to concentrate on ourselves. This required a major adjustment in our marriage. I recall being excited and yet nervous when we received the news. What kind of father would I be? Am I really ready to father a child? It seemed like only a few years ago that I was carefree. I realized that being a father required sacrifice. Was I willing to sacrifice my time and treasures for the sake of my child? I remember talking to my mother about it one day and she said to me, David, just let the Lord lead you.

Certainly, the year of 1995 was a life changing year for me in so many ways. In September 1995, I was called by God into the ministry. On October 1, 1995 at the Concord Missionary Baptist Church under the pastorate of the late Alvin O. Oldham,I preached my first sermon. Although it's been over 19 years ago, I can remember it like it was yesterday. The text was Luke 15:11-32 and the subject "A good man in a bad fix." God was doing a great thing in my life and I felt honored to be a part of His program for the work of kingdom building. My pastor encouraged me to go and further my education. He said to me, David, you don't have to go to school to be what God called you to be. He stated that I'm still a preacher if I never step foot in a Bible college. Then he shared something with me that was passed down to him. He said that education to the preacher is what shoe polish is to a shoe. A shoe is still a shoe without polish but the polish helps it shine. Indeed I wanted to shine for the Lord.

Shortly afterwards, I enrolled in The Clarksville School of Religion. I had a yearning to learn as much as I could. After completing the required courses I enrolled in American Baptist College. It was tough being a married man with a child working full time and going to school full time. I would burn the candle at both ends at times, but God gave me the strength to endure. It required sacrifice. While my friends were hanging out I was writing papers. I studied hard and although I had taken some other college classes before, I was never a full time college student. Each semester David D. Allen was written on the Deans List. I enjoyed reading, writing, and learning.

In May of 2000, I was blessed to walk across that stage receiving my Bachelor of Arts degree with a dual major of Theology and business management (Magna Cum Laude). God blessed me to be listed in the Who's Who Among College Students In American Universities & Colleges 2000. I went on to earn my Masters in Theology (Summa Cum Laude) and my Doctorate Degree in Theology (Summa Cum Laude) from Slidell Baptist Seminary. I ran into that teacher years later that said I was not college material and we talked and I had to share with her what I was able to accomplish with God's help.

209

I want to share with someone reading this chapter that God is able to do exceedingly abundantly more than we ever think or ask. I was a non-traditional student that didn't go to college right after high school. I had to make sacrifices, but God allowed me to reach a level that I couldn't even dream of. I would encourage every young person to go to some college, tech school or trade school. The world is a very demanding place and education is what separates you from your peers. Also for those that think they're too old. I want to encourage you to sign up for a night class or online classes because you're never too old to learn.

God continued to show me favor and in April 2002 God called me through the membership to lead the Mount Olive Missionary Baptist Church located at 608 Main Street, Clarksville Tennessee. When I was an associate minister, I shadowed my pastor, taught Sunday school, and was the minister of education at Concord. A few years after, I was called to preach when my pastor had a stroke. For two years, I preached some Sundays and was assigned by him to conduct the pulpit. I would often be seen filling his water glass or carrying his Bible. I'm reminded of the scripture that says if you're faithful over a few things God will make you ruler of many. I believe that God was preparing me to pastor from the start. God expects us to be faithful in whatever task he has assigned us to do. I have discovered that some people view pastoring as a position of power and prestige. I say from experience that pastoring is a call to serve.

In July of 2004, God blessed us with another child, Daelyn Denae Allen. When I think about how God has blessed me, one of the many things I'm thankful for is that he has allowed me to baptize both of my children.

If at first you don't succeed, try and try again. God placed in my spirit a desire to serve people. I want my life to be a life of service first unto God as I serve His people. In May of 2000, I made an unsuccessful bid for city council. I was defeated by 83 votes. This was a bitter pill for me to swallow. I didn't give up and in 2004, I ran again. Once again, I was unsuccessful in my bid for the office. On the surface it seemed that I had wasted a lot of time. The time spent was not wasted. I met a lot of wonderful people and I also learned a great deal about campaigning. This knowledge would prove to be valuable as I made my third attempt. In 2008, I was elected to the city council by an overwhelming majority.

I want to encourage some person reading this who has met what seems to be defeat in one area or another in your life. Don't give up! A blessing delayed is not always a blessing denied. One memorable moment in my life was reading the front page of the local newspaper and seeing the headlines that had a picture of Barak Obama and the words yes we can. On that same front page were the election results of the local city races. David D. Allen and Senator Barak Obama, we were both victorious. I was reelected in 2012 in which I presently still serve. Often times we complain about our city, state, and country. You can make a difference by voting and even running for those offices in which decisions are made that affect us. I thank God that he has let me live a life of service.

I have to say that God has smiled on me. For ten years I served as the president of the Pastors' Conference for the Cumberland River South Kentucky Middle Tennessee Baptist District Association. Faithfully I served under two different moderators. In August 2014, I was elected as the moderator of our great district which consists of some thirty three different churches. To God be the glory.

There are times that I felt like Jeremiah as it pertains to leading God's people. I was the youngest pastor in our district when I was elected to serve as president of the conference. I am still the youngest pastor now serving as moderator. I say that to inspire our youth. You may think that you are too young to make a difference but God can use you.

God has certainly been good to me. I wear many hats. God's called Preacher, Husband, Father, Pastor, Moderator, and

Councilman. The unique thing about all of the hats I wear is that it's gives me another opportunity to serve people. I always wanted my life to be one of service. Each day God blesses me to see another day, I realize that in the words of Mahalia Jackson ''If I can help somebody as I travel along the way, then my living shall not be in vain.''

Contact: dr.dallen1700@gmail.com

Pastor Delbert Brown

If the Lord had not been on our side— let Israel say—
If the Lord had not been on our side when men attacked us,
Psalm 124:1–2

"Because the Lord was on my side"

In spite of my birth situation, the season in which God allowed me to be born, and the struggles that came with the civil rights movement in the fifties, a time when colored people struggled with the unkind acts from some white people because the color of our skin. As an adult I can look back and see clearly that the Lord was on my side. I could not have made it without His guiding hand on my life.

"Because the Lord was on my side He gave me a Godly mother"

In 1955, I was born to a single twenty year old colored girl. During this time it was very difficult for my mother. The odds were against her because she was single, colored, and the mother of three children. I learned through watching my mother's struggles in life how real God was to our family.

I watched my mother suffer the loss of my baby sister and the burning down of our house, during the Jim Crow time. Jim Crow were laws that segregated black and white Americans. It was through these hardships, that I learned listen to my mother praying. It was while listening to her that I learned to trust God in prayer. These hard times taught me to pray to God. I learned that it's not the words you say when you are praying. It's knowing who you are praying to in your time of need.

When I listened to my mother pray. She would pray as if God was in the room with her. She prayed with such power and belief that God was going to do what He said He was going to do. The way my mother prayed made me believe that God is real.

My mother struggled working three jobs during this era. She would also pick up small jobs like cooking, ironing, and washing clothes. As a child I did not understand why my mother would fall asleep while we were talking and playing around her feet. I later understood that she had given her all, all day long. My mother always took time to care for her children. Looking back I realize how easily my mother could have given up. Yet in spite of what was going on in her life she always poured into her children. She taught us to pray, what I call "Mom's Prayer:"

"Now I lay me down to sleep. I pray to God my soul to keep. If I should die before I awake. I pray my soul to take."
God bless my mother, brother, sister, and Paw Paw.

"Because the Lord was on my side He gave me a Godly grandfather "

I am who I am because of my biological father and mother as it relates to my DNA. However I did not grow up around my father. A few months after I was born my father joined the United States Marine Corps. He would come home to visit in the summer time. I received letters that helped me know him when I became a man. In the absence of my father God gave me an amazing grandfather that loved and watched over me.

214

My mother gave me her maiden name "Brown." My biological father and I discussed me changing my name to "Heaggans" when I started my own family. I'm grateful for my father, but I grew up being a "Brown." My grandfather K.C Brown, taught me everything I needed to know to be a functional adult. It was only right for me to keep my mother's maiden name "Brown." My father understood my decision to keep the Brown last name.

It was my grandfather, K.C. Brown, who taught me how to cut grass, plow a garden, and the difference between a watermelon and tomato seed. He also taught me that there is a price to pay for taking short cuts. One of many great lessons was taught in the cotton field in Sand Town Bottoms in Morrilton, Arkansas.

My grandfather took my brother, cousins, and me with him to learn how to pull cotton. Pulling cotton is when the cotton bowls open and you pull the cotton bowl with the cotton. After pulling the cotton you put it in a cotton sack.

My brother, cousins, and I decided to not only pull the bowls. We pulled a few stalks and hid them in bottom of the bags because we were being paid by the pound. We did not realize when we were taking this short cut that our grandfather, K.C. Brown, would be the one emptying our sacks. My sack was the first one to be emptied. My grandfather took the first stalk out of my bag and looked straight at me. I knew by the look on his face that he was not happy. I got one of the worst whippings in my life for choosing to take a short cut and lie about the weight of cotton in my sack.

I thank God for my grandfather not allowing me to take a short cut. I learned in that moment short cuts cause great pain. I thank God for giving me K.C. Brown in the absence of my father K.C. Brown was a great example of a Godly man.

"Because the Lord was on my side he gave me a community to help rear me"

The Lord gave me a community of men that shaped my values. I grew up in the west end of the city I'm from. Looking back I see now more than ever, our communities need what I had all around me growing up. **MEN!** I thank God for Mr. Otis Kindle, Mr. Minus Kindle, Mr. Frank Anderson, Mr. Dock Robinson, Mr. Clearance Hersey, and many more that I did not mention. These men shaped me as young boy.

These men taught me what it meant to be a leader in my home, community, and church. They also gave me hope in spite of the social, economic, and political struggles that were taking place and yet to come during that time. God used all these men to show me how to handle adversity with integrity.

In 1967, the school system in our city integrated blacks and whites. The Lord used a white teacher to reach out to me and give my mom hope in a time that seemed hopeless to the black community. The school counselor, Ms. Fiser, informed my mother of the pit falls associated with integrating the schools. Ms. Fiser told her that the students would be at a disadvantage no matter if they got good grades. The black students were not exposed to the material necessary to allow blacks to compete with the white children.

My mother immediately became proactive with my education. She enrolled me in summer school at Reynolds Elementary across town. Reynolds Elementary was funded by the Rockefeller family. This was the first time in my academic life that I was able to write my first and last name in the front of a new book. I thank God for his ever present help in my hour of need.

"Because the Lord was on my side through it all"

I thank my mother for affording me the opportunity to go to a great school. I did well in school. I was the first male in the K.C. Brown family to graduate high school and go onto college. My goal was to be a business man. I wanted to get my liquor license and get rich quick. The Lord has a way of revealing himself in such a way that His will and plan for your life can become a great burden. Our will, dreams, and goals will change when we know and understand he has a calling on your life. I would try to do things my way and I would hear my mother praying. No matter where I would turn I would hear my granddaddy say there are no short cuts to success. Every time I tried to out run the calling that God had for my life the burden would become heavy. I could hear the community of men that are yet in my life say trust the Lord and keep the hope alive. I finally let go and let God have reign in my life. My desire to have a liquor license turned into a desire for a preaching license. God was patient with my will until I was willing to accept his will.

I have learned so much on this journey. The one thing that I have learned is that you cannot out give God. He gave me my mother and my mother gave me physical life. My granddaddy gave me a fatherly example; my community gave me hope.

My greatest desire is to reproduce the spirit of giving in the lives of those the Lord has, and will allow me to touch with my life. To borrow a quote from the late Dr. Caesar Clark, he states that "there is a weness about all of us," Weness implies that none of us have arrived where we are without help. If you are struggling to find out what it is the Lord would have you to be in this life. My recommendation is that you start by putting God first. God gave me an amazing mother, granddaddy, and community to shape me into the servant of God I am today. I'm thankful to God and each person that poured into my life over the years. God is no respecter of persons. He knows the plans that He has for you and that is to prosper you and not harm you. If you are running from your calling like I was at one time, stop, because

God will not fail you.

The moral of the story is God uses the least of us when we are available to Him. No matter what it feels like, what it sounds like, or what it looks like. This one thing I know is that the Lord is on my side. I can testify from my childhood into adulthood the greatness of God.

- Reverend Delbert R. Brown a native of Arkansas. Married to the former Lorraine Johnson of West Columbia, South Carolina. We have three children and ten grandchildren
- Acknowledged his call into the ministry in 1989, Lawton, OK. Ordained in 1992, Kruezburg, Germany
- Associate of Art degree, Central Texas College
- Associate of Science & Bachelor of Science, University of Maryland
- An advanced degree, Bachelor of Theology Th.B. with Honors (Magna Cum Laude) from American Baptist College of American Baptist Theological Seminary.
- A Who's Who among Students in America University and Colleges
- Pastor, Concord Missionary Baptist Church, Clarksville TN
- 1st Vice President of the Missionary Baptist State Convention of Tennessee
- Dean, Clarksville Baptist School of Religion
- Chair of the Orthodoxy Committee, National Baptist Convention of America Inc. International
- Finance Committee Member National Baptist Convention of America Inc. International

Previous Service

- Moderator of Cumberland River South Kentucky Middle Tennessee Baptist District Association
- President of the Missionary Baptist State Convention of Tennessee Congress of Christian Workers
- Pastor's Conference Board of the National Baptist Convention of America Incorporated
- President of the Pastor Conference for the Cumberland River South Kentucky Middle Tennessee Baptist District Association
- Established and Pastored a mission church in Bahrain Saudi, Arabia
- Pastor, Kreuzburg Community Chapel, Kreuzburg, Germany
- Pastor, Ogburn Chapel Missionary Baptist Church, Clarksville, TN
- Member of the Education Board, National Baptist Convention of America
- Committee Chair on Education for the Clarksville Branch of the NAACP
- President, N.I.A. Board of Directors
- Power Board Secretary for the Clarksville Department of Electricity
- Member for City of Clarksville Storm Water Drainage Committee
- Retired veteran of twenty years' service with the United States Army
- Awards and decorations include the Army Commendation Medal (six oak leaf cluster), Meritorious Service Medal (third oak leaf cluster), and the Bronze Star for service to this country during the Persian Gulf War

Contact: Pastorconcordmbc@gmail.com
      Twitter: drb@ministry
      Soundcloud: drb ministry

Pastor Franklin Jackson

"Give where you live"

"Talk is cheap, but commitment is costly"

Trust in the Lord with all thine heart, and lean not unto thine own understanding. In all thy ways acknowledge him, and he shall direct thy paths. (Proverb 3: 5-6).

INTRODUCTION

Growing up in the islands as a child with parents separated and struggling to make it, I was often left with my grandfather and different aunts. I often reflect back to how frequently I flew on airplanes and moved from one family member to the next. As a child, I came to the understanding that God was looking out for me. I also thought that there was something better around the corner. However when I arrived, there seemed to be another corner to go around each time.

I was also very observant as a child. I paid attention to the physical movement of things and questioned how they worked. For example, I enjoyed watching my father drive his standard shift car. I took notice of his hands and feet and realized that his left foot had to push on a pedal before his hand could shift the gear in the car at around the age of 5 or 6. Needless to say I drove the car on my 7th birthday.

During my childhood, I was exposed to many different Christian denominations. My mother did not attend church to my knowledge, but my aunts did so I was a little of Anglican, Catholic, Wesleyan Holiness, Baptist, and today thank God my mother is Seventh Day Adventist, and I am Church of God in Christ. I contributed this to my aunts, who as a child drug me to church no matter what church it was. My grandfather was an important part of my upbringing and his name was Eleazar Williams. His first name was the name of Aaron's sons in the Old Testament, and he always used to say these words to me "Hail thy hilo thy hilfit" interpreted, "I came, I saw, I conquered" I had no idea whether it is Greek, Hebrew, or Latin. And I still don't know to this day. My mother was the youngest of her four sisters and I was her only child even though I do have other brothers and a sister on my father's side. In between staying with her sisters, I would occasionally get to spend time with my mother.

When I turned sixteen, I went to a boarding school in Edison New Jersey. At nineteen, I realized that a black man in Edison New Jersey or New Brunswick, did not stand a chance with just a high school education. I also wanted more out of life than I was allowed as black man where I was living. As a result, I decided to join the military after listening to some of the World War 11 veterans who were instructors at the school. I even listened to some that were Viet Nam veterans that explained that even though it was rough and some did not received a hero's welcome; it was still rewarding, and they would do it again. When I inquired "Why?" Mr. Rhymer, affectionately called "Sarge" explained that he endured hardships and struggles because of his color, but that he was enjoying the fruit of his labor from being retired. After that, I told myself "self!" I think the Army just might be for me, but I was advised by Sarge who said, "The only way of making it through without any problems is to do as you are told and *&#$@@ do as you are told" and you will be ok."

I joined the Army on my 20th birthday and was scared out of my mind. I thought to myself, boy! You just listened to the good parts and never asked about the bad parts. I tried to see if I could delay going to boot camp because I was the only child and had never been away from home. Although I had siblings on my father's side, they allowed me to delay training for a few months by assisting the hometown recruiter which was one of the best jobs I ever had.

I often used to think about the next chapter in my life as a teenager, and used to wonder what would become of me in the next year, two years, or even the next ten years and I realized that I could not see that far in the future. So, I used to look at the setting of the sun a lot because it seemed as though where the sun was setting always was bright, wonderful, and would cheer me up. Whenever I reflected on my childhood, it seemed bleak. I was lacking everything on my own with no family close by and I wouldn't be remembered by anyone. So I thanked God for the sun that sets with that bright illumination of hope for me.

Today, I can truly say joining the military was the best thing that I have ever done. It gave me a new focus, helped me find myself, and I learned a lot from others more experienced than I. Unfortunately, I began seeing the other side of the military resulting in negative experiences that impacted my outlook.

During my first duty station in Mannheim Germany right after training, I began to feel extremely lonely around Thanksgiving and Christmas holidays. I spent a total of seven years in Germany and was able to speak the language and would eventually meet my wife there. After having our first child, my priorities shifted from being about me to putting my family first. I had to get my mind and body to think, act, and look like a family man. I ditched the brand new Maxima for a mini-van and a stroller.

When the second child came, I wanted be more prepared and realized that there was something missing in my life. I knew about Jesus and recognized it was His grace and mercy that kept me alive. Jesus used these circumstances to draw me back to His fold and continued to pour out blessings on my family.

Initially it was a struggle for my wife to get me back in church. Each Sunday, she would dress our daughter for church as ask if I wanted to attend. Although, I would say "no", deep inside I wanted to say "yes." I had made a vow to God that "I only want to get married once" and I want to be a father. I began to question how I could be a husband and a father while my family went to church without me every Sunday. Making matters worse, I would ask my wife to bring me a six-pack of beer that I would mix with my mountain dew soda to quench my thirst after a half a day of basketball.

After a while, I realized that I should do better as a father and husband so I began attending church with my family. One Sunday morning after running away from God, He caught me at a Sunday morning worship service and let me have it by using the preacher to reach me. It seemed like the preacher was speaking directly at me and in my mind I was saying, "Man you don't know me or anything about me!" I even tried to hide behind other people in the pews in front of me, but he was a moving preacher, so his eyes always seemed to catch mine which frustrated me because I thought he was singling me out of all the people in the church.

My final attempt to break his gaze was to slouch down in my seat. Breathing a sigh of relief I thought I was safe until I saw the preacher coming down the center of the isles as he began alter call. I decided to sneak out, but as I got up to leave it was as if I was in a trance as I walked towards to alter instead of the exit. Tears of joy began to run down my face as I gave my life to

Christ!! From that day forward, God saved me and I have not been the same.

God has been good to my family and I. I know that on that day the Devil said, "We lost out on that one." He knows that I was serious about it, and I believe that God knows it too. There is a song that said "I can see clearly now the rain is gone. I can see all obstacles in my way." It is so true, after Christ reclaimed me, everything became so clear that even when the Devil disguises himself in sheep's clothing, I still was able to see him and call him out. Sometimes I just laugh at him, and say to myself "He is on his job." I know better, so just keep on going. I came to the conclusion that I can do nothing without God. and the bible did not have to tell me, so I experienced it for myself, and now I use Proverbs 3:5 & 6 which states;(5) Trust in the Lord with all thine heart; and lean not unto thine own understanding. (6) In all thy ways acknowledge him, and he shall direct thy paths.

I realize that I must trust Him (God) and I can't do it without a personal relationship with Him, after all that He has done for me by making me a millionaire and taking all of it back, then starting me over with a purpose to forget about myself and concentrate on His work. It is my heart that said "I'll go if I have to go by myself" knowing if I start going, God will send help, and my God has been sending help ever since. He has lifted me, elevated me, opened doors, and finally, called me into the vineyard to work even the more as a Pastor, a servant, and the founder of THE HOUSE OF GOD CHURCH, in Clarksville, Tennessee. To God be the Glory forever and ever Amen.

Contact: elderjackson506@gmail.com

Pastor Horace Bracey

KJV – The LORD is my light and my salvation; whom shall I fear?
the LORD is the strength of my life; of whom shall I be afraid?
Psalms 27:1

Introduction

My name is Horace Bracey, I was born in Columbia, South Carolina to Houston and Magnolia Bracey. In, April 2002 I married my best friend LaVon Cooper (Bracey). I am a father of two sons Emmanuel and Gabriel and two daughters Alexis and Magnolia. I am an Associate Pastor at God's Sanctuary Church. God has called me to go into the hedges and highways to gather the people to come to Him. The heart-beat of God is His souls. I oversee the street ministry as we go out every month to share the Gospel and love of Jesus Christ. I have been blessed to travel on mission trips to Kenya, Tanzania, Nigeria and Honduras. It is my prayer to be a true representative of Christ in the church, local community and abroad.

A Motherless Child

There is something so beautiful about the relationship between a mother and her son. I read a poem once that said *"The bond between mother and son is a special one. It remains unchanged by time and distance. It is the purest love-unconditional and true. It is understanding of any situation and forgiving of any mistake..."* They say every mother loves their son and every son is a mommy's boy even if they won't admit it. At least that's what I have been told. My mother, Magnolia Bracey, passed away when I was six months old. My mother's sister, Aunt Eartha, told me her last moments and words were "I want to hold my baby." When my mother died I was too young to understand the great sacrifice and loss. My mother had rheumatic fever and the doctor told her she should not have a child. When my mother discovered she was pregnant the doctors gave her two choices. She could abort the baby and live or risk death. She choose ME. I only had her on this earth for six months but she was the greatest MOTHER. She had to be Heaven sent to lay down her life for me. That's love.

As I reflect, I see that God's hand was already on me. God will never leave you or forsake you. God put mothers all around me. First He sent my father's mother, Randy Bracey, to raise me as her own. I called her momma. I didn't know any other mother but her. She raised me in the church and when needed she gave tough love. In my teens God called her home. When it seemed like I was all alone that's when God sent spiritual mothers in my life to steer me to God. Mothers in Zion, Mother Cochran, Mother Covington and Pastor Olla Parker. Pastor Olla Parker is my aunt but more than just family I always watched her life. She is a trailblazer that God used to teach me the things of God. God never left Magnolia's baby motherless.

Life in the Fast Lane

At the age of 17, I began to run with the wrong crowd. I no longer wanted to go to church. My life took a great turn for the worst. I began to sell drugs on a small scale and the money was easy. That's how the devil deceived me. The bible says in 1 Timothy 6:10 "the love of money is the root of all evil." The money seemed to give me power and respect but it was all a deception. Before I knew it, I had moved up in the drug ring. I had workers and runners and began trafficking drugs from state to state. I was in and out of jail all my young adult years. God was trying to wake me up from my spiritual slumber, but pride made me think I could buy my way out of anything. Just like with Paul, God knows how to get our attention. My heart was tender to God. When ministers would come in town I would take up an offering from the drug dealers to help them on their mission for God. My soul was convicted but I didn't know how to get out. I owned houses, cars, jewels and an unknown amount of money. Still I had a void in my soul. Money and things are nothing when you can't sleep at night or feel the presence of God. The police were watching my every move. Rival drug dealers wanted me dead. Something had to change.

The Call

"Many are called but few are chosen." Matthew 22:14. To be chosen by God comes with a great price. Your life is not your own. So I was doing any and everything I thought I was bad enough to do when God invaded my life. I had just been released from being locked up. A friend wanted to celebrate by going to the club. That's why it's important to surround yourself with men of faith and integrity. I went to the club and started drinking and smoking pot. The music was loud, lights were flashing and people were dancing. Suddenly, I heard a voice shouting "GET OUT OF THIS CLUB!" I looked at my friend and asked "what did you say?" I knew it wasn't my friend's voice but the fear of hearing that voice shook me to my very soul. My friend had no idea what I was talking about. He wanted to know if I was alright and said I looked like I had seen a ghost. I tried to drown out the voice that I heard by drinking and talking really loud. Unexpectedly, the voice spoke again "GET OUT!" I couldn't shake it…the voice got louder. Quickly I left the club. I drove to a hotel to meet my girlfriend. "This is going to be a good night," I thought. After entering the room I tried to relax and forget about the voice. I turned the TV on and news reporter's voice changed and sounded like the voice in the club saying "GET OUT!" I poured my beer out and flushed the marijuana down the toilet. While I was flushing the drugs my girlfriend said "let's smoke one." However, when I turned the skin on her face began to peel before my eyes. Somehow I knew it was sin on her and me. The Bible talks about how God will open your spiritual eyes and enlighten your heart. That's what I experienced that night. I told her I will pray for you. She was afraid that I had got some bad drugs. I emptied my pockets of all money and the key to my truck and began to walk out the door. She tried to hold me in the room but I heard the voice again. I told her "I must go, God is calling me." She stepped aside and I left walking down the street calling on the name of Jesus.

While walking down the street an unmarked police vehicle pulled up beside me to see if I was alright. I began to preach and tell them that Jesus is coming soon. They thought I was high and put me in the back of the car. Once in the car I fell asleep. When I woke up, I was in the psychiatric ward. God had my attention. They kept me and began to medicate me because I kept calling on the name of Jesus. But the medication had no effect on the presence of God over me. I called his name louder and continued to preach to the staff and patients. God had opened my eyes and I saw evil spirits on some of the workers as they mocked me. "You need to call Him louder than that....you have really lost it now!" After spending six months there it was time to go before the release board. The panel of judges asked me so many questions... "Do you feel like hurting yourself or hurting others...what are you going to do if we release you today." I told them "I have an aunt in Tennessee who is a pastor. I will go there and do what God wants me to do." God used a lady on the board to stay behind to speak to me. The glory of the Lord was all over her. She spoke into my life "Horace you're not crazy. God has His hand on your life. And when you get out, do everything that God put in your heart to do for Him. The world thinks you're crazy but I know you're not." And that's what I did.

When I was released I called my aunt and pastor in Tennessee and began to seek the Lord like never before. I accepted my call into the ministry and was moving forward with my life. The presence of God was strong and His voice was very clear. One night I had a dream that two Marshalls came to Tennessee with a warrant for my arrest. In the dream they took me and stood me against a wall facing them. Then one of the Marshalls pulled out his gun and shot two times. I saw the bullets coming towards me. But before the bullets hit me they fell to the ground. This was very disturbing to me. I woke up and told my aunt the dream.

Within a week's time they were knocking at my door. My aunt answered the door and told me two bounty hunters were sent from South Carolina looking for me. They took me in custody and transported me back to South Carolina for previous charges. Once back in South Carolina my aunt tried to put her house up to bail me out. However they did not accept her offer. So I contacted my former attorney to see what my options were. He told me they wanted to give me forty-five years. On the other hand I could pay him a retainer fee of over $200,000 and he would get my sentence reduced to twenty years. I knew there was no way I could come up with that kind of money. I knew the word of God says, "Be not deceived; God is not mocked: for whatsoever a man soweth, that shall he also reap Galatians 6:7." I had to pay for the sins I committed in the past. Thus, I prepared my heart and mind to go into prison preaching the gospel and winning souls. After a month they gave me a speedy trial date. It was said they knew I didn't have a lawyer and wanted to get me off the streets. Fear tried to enter my heart but that's when God gave me a word. Psalms 27:1 KJV – The LORD is my light and my salvation; whom shall I fear? The LORD is the strength of my life; of whom shall I be afraid?

On the day of my trial, I was sitting in a holding tank, shackled and waiting. There were five other men with me. While reading my bible I out blurted "I can't go to prison I have too much work to do for the Lord!" Some of the other inmates became nervous while others mocked me. "Man are you crazy. You have seven felonies pending against you and you think you're not going to do time. Correctional Officer you need to come get him he has losing it." I was beginning to think I was losing it and didn't know where that outburst came from but now I know it was God. The day seemed to drag on forever and they never called my name. Court was over at five o'clock so I guess I would have to play the waiting game again the next morning.

The next morning at breakfast I didn't want to eat anything but the Word of God. As the hour passed I noticed no one came to get me for court. Then lunch time came and I continued to fast. At that point a Correctional Officer came and called my name. I thought it was strange because I have never seen this officer before. Having been in and out of jail, I knew all the officers. He was short with a stern voice. He called my name again, "Horace Bracey....All The Way," which means you're getting out. I hesitated for a moment, "Do you have the right man?" He said "Is your name Horace Bracey...I have papers saying for you to go."

I gathered my things in a daze waiting for the moment for them to say we made a mistake. The officer open the door to the cell and I began to walk down a long hallway and asked him "Who paid for me to get out?" He said all he knew is that he has papers saying I should go home. We arrived at the desk and the lady was filing something. When she looked up she only saw me. I turned to show her an officer brought me here....he was gone. Within seconds he was gone.

I asked where was the officer that walked me up here. She named all the officers on duty but that wasn't the person that walked me down to her desk. I knew it was an angel that opened up the jail just like Paul and Silas. I never had an attorney and I never stood before a judge. God cleaned my slate and my record is clean. God is doing great things in my life. From the beginning

232

the devil didn't want me here. But, when God has a plan for your life not even you can stop it. I just want to take time to pray with each of you reading this, please repeat after me "Lord Jesus, I come to you as a sinner repenting of all my sins. Come into my heart. Be my Lord, my Master and my Savior. Deliver me from all unrighteousness…that I might serve You with all my heart, my mind and my soul. Fill me with your precious Holy Spirit. I am washed, I am cleaned and I am saved. In Jesus Precious Name. Amen." You have a new beginning today. God Bless!

Contact: lavon.bracey@yahoo.com

Pastor Jimmy Terry

I am crucified with Christ: nevertheless I live; yet not I, but Christ liveth in me: and the life which I now live in the flesh I live by the faith of the Son of God, who loved me, and gave Himself for me. Galatians 2:20

Background:

My name is Jimmy Terry Sr., Pastor of the Tabernacle Baptist Church. My journey began July 22, 1937, in Tuscaloosa, Alabama (Roll Tide). I was abandoned at 3 months old. But God had a plan for my life. It was my devoted Aunt Lucy who raised me. There were two things my Aunt Lucy taught me, and I still share her words of wisdom wherever I go. These two have remained with me. 1. Son, if you stay with Jesus you can make it. 2. Son, when you grow up both you and your wife work together to have something. She was right. I attended Castle Hill Elementary and Druid High in Tuscaloosa. I stayed with my Aunt Lucy until the age of 17, and then moved to Dayton, Ohio.

From Dayton Ohio, I joined the United States Navy, and served honorably for 4 years. I was stationed for three years and six months aboard the USS Saratoga (Plank Owner). I was later honorably discharged. I moved back to Dayton, Ohio until 1979, and from there moved to Clarksville Tennessee, where I have remained until this day. I have been blessed to live in the great state of Tennessee. I married Servella Lee Broomfield. She is my best friend. We have four children, Vaughn, Jimmy Jr., Loretta, and Shana.

My Story:

My conversion to Christ came July 22, 1958, while stationed on the USS Saratoga. At age 13, I gave my life to Christ because of my Aunt Lucy. She told me to get off that mourning bench, and out of obedience to her I did so. On my birth date of July 22, I was in the middle of the Atlantic Ocean, when the Holy Spirit led me out on the sponsor deck and dealt with me; this is where my conversion took place. Since that day, I have put forth every effort to serve my Lord and Savior Jesus Christ. I have failed at many things, but this is one thing I don't want to fail in which is my calling. I have been consciously striving to please Him ever since.

My call to preach was in 1970 at the Mt. Olive Baptist Church in Dayton, Ohio, and my first church I pastored was Harvest Grove Baptist Church in 1973 in Dayton, Ohio. I was blessed to attend the American Baptist Theological Seminary and graduated in 1977. God eventually led me to the City of Clarksville to pastor the Mt. Olive Baptist Church, where I served faithfully for two years before organizing the Tabernacle Baptist Church in 1982.

No one gets to be who they are on their own. It's takes people supporting and cheering them on for them to be successful. Thank God for the people who have invested in me. I put forth every effort to be mindful of them and never to be an embarrassment to them, but most of all not to be an

236

embarrassment to my Savior who died for me on Calvary.

There are three things that I am very passionate about. First, leading people to Christ. Second, Christian education, and third, Black History Month.

1. Leading People to Christ

The scripture says, For God so loved the world that He gave His only begotten Son, that whosoever believeth in Him should not perish but have everlasting life. John 3:16.

I believe that whoever will be willing to call on the name of my Lord and Savior Jesus Christ will be saved. Salvation and getting to heaven should be our number one goal. *For what shall it profit a man, if he shall gain the whole world, and lose his own soul?* Mark 8:36.

Salvation and getting people saved and on their way to heaven matters to me. I preach it not only in the pulpit but also my community. I wear a button on my suit jacket that goes with me everywhere I go and it simply says '**Trust Jesus, Jesus Only**'. I believe in soul winning. I love winning souls for Jesus. If you are not saved (you ought to be), or if you have not asked God into your life, now is the time.

Get in a good Bible believing church where the word of God is preached. Read the Bible. The B-I-B-L-E. It is God's **Biblical Instruction Before Leaving This Earth.**

2. Christian education is very important to me.

I am an advocate for Christian education. I believe that early Christian education is the foundation for life's success. God gave me a vision to build a Christian school. When you read the Bible closely it is God's command that Christians teach their children under a Christian umbrella. Please read Deuteronomy chapter 6.

As Founder of the Tabernacle Baptist Church, my heart's desire was that the church body would embrace the vision of a Christian School. Through the vision, future generations of leaders would be cultivated and inspired to achieve academic excellence though solid Christian doctrine.

In September 1999, the vision came to fruition. Tabernacle Christian School opened its doors with 16 students, three teachers, and an administrator. The school supported pre-kindergarten through third grade. TCS's first edifice was a small house donated by Mr. and Mrs. Rigoberto Rivera. The houses original location was University Blvd. here in Clarksville, TN. As the pastor, I enlisted the assistance of Mr. Carlos Lewis & Sons to move the building to its present location. Mr. Carlos Lewis & Sons did a great job. The church family and community painted, did carpentry work, solicited the public for donations, and they supported the school with fervent prayers and financial support, the Tabernacle Christian School and Christian education in general.

3. Black History Month

When I first came to Clarksville, I saw no movement for a Black History Month. God moved in my spirit to lead the African American Community to have a celebrated opening and a celebrated closing. Dr. Carter G. Woodson, the father of Black History Month, was instrumental in helping us to get to Black History Month. Let us get busy and make it relevant for generations to come. Start now in your community. Let us put together a greater effort to show unity with all of our brothers and sisters in America. **We Can Do This!**

As an American citizen, as an African American preacher, visionary, and founder of a church and a Christian school, I realize America has gone through some rough times. There is work to be done. We are fortunate to look to the White House and see change that has taken place. It makes me happy to see our President and his wife in the White House. We must continue to move forward. As Black people, we must stop making excuses for not moving forward. God has given us an entire month in February. But what are we doing for 28 or 29 days? Instead of complaining about what we don't have, we should come together to build something, own buildings, and schools. Have a place for our youth to go without being in a dangerous environment.

I challenge every African American, to fully embrace Black History Month. I am speaking to all of America; but even more so to African Americans. This may not be what you want to read, but I simply believe that **Black History Month is a vast wasteland**. That is why I shared my notes about this very subject in the back of this book about my love and support for Black History Month. I wanted to share with you in hopes that it will ignite positive change and growth. Our future begins with all of us. Together we can achieve great things when we work together. Again, I will refer you to the back of this book.

Giving God the Glory

Among many honors that God has bestowed upon me in life, I am blessed to name a few. I was selected as one of the Founding Directors of Legends Bank in Clarksville, TN. I was the first African American Pastor to serve as President of the Pastor's Conference for the Tennessee Baptist Convention. Then there was the time I led my community to give greater honor to its home town hero, Miss Wilma G. Rudolph, who was the 1960 Olympic Champion. I was a part of the vision to honor her with a road named in her honor as well as a life size statue. I was also instrumental in the naming of the Dr. Martin Luther King Jr. Parkway.

Today, I currently serve as one of the Trustees of the Baptist Memorial Hospital in Memphis, TN, which has hospitals in Tennessee, Arkansas, and Mississippi. By the leading of the Holy Spirit, God led me to lead the community to read and recite the Gospel of John by Memory. By the leading of the Holy Spirit, He led me to present a greater awareness to my city about

239

Christmas and Easter. In 2014, I led the community to purchase 10,000 yard signs at $3 each to display that Christmas is all about Jesus. When you look at America, Christmas and Easter are not really embraced as I think it should be. To God be the glory! As of this writing, all of the signs have been paid for in full, and we are now gearing up for the Easter campaign (That Easter is all about Jesus).

Past Participations

I have been the Chairman of the 2006 fundraising campaign for the Clarksville/ Montgomery County American Red Cross Chapter, as well as a member of the NAACP. I have served on the Board of the Customs House Museum in Clarksville, TN. With all that God has given me to do, I count it an honor to have served my community honorably.

Last but not least, I encourage you to dream up ways in which you can make America, your state, your community, a better place to live.

I would like to close with this poem written by Edgar Guest.

Can't

Can't is the worst word that's written or spoken;
Doing more harm here than slander and lies;
On it is many a strong spirit broken,
And with it many a good purpose dies.
It springs from the lips of the thoughtless each morning
And robs us of courage we need through the day:
It rings in our ears like a timely sent warning
And laughs when we falter and fall by the way.

Can't is the father of feeble endeavor,
The parent of terror and halfhearted work;
It weakens the efforts of artisans clever,
And makes of the toiler an indolent shirk.

It poisons the soul of the man with a vision,
It stifles in infancy many a plan;
It greets honest toiling with open derision
And mocks at the hopes and the dreams of a man.

Can't is a word none should speak without blushing;
To utter it should be a symbol of shame;
Ambition and courage it daily is crushing;
It blights a man's purpose and shortens his aim.
Despise it with all of your hatred of error;
Refuse it the lodgment it seeks in your brain;
Arm against it as a creature ot terror,
And all that you dream of you someday shall gain.

Can't is the word that is for to ambition,
An enemy ambushed to shatter your will;
Its prey is forever the man with a mission
And bows but to courage and patience and skill.
Hate it, with hatred that's deep and undying,
For once it is welcomed 'twill break any man;
Whatever the goal you are seeking, keep trying
and answer this demon by saying: "*I can.*"

~Edgar A. Guest~

Contact: visiontb@bellsouth.net

Magnificent Man

Pastor Joseph Morgan

Now unto him that is able to do exceeding abundantly above all

that we ask or think, according to the power that worketh in us.

Ephesians 3:20

As I look back over my life, I have come to realize that via pulpit, television and radio I have ministered over 5,000 sermons. Keep in mind - a sermon is more than just words from a pulpit; it is a life-coaching event that becomes the impetus for change in a person's life. When you consider this from the enemy's perspective, I am a threat to the kingdom of darkness. It's not surprising that Satan has attacked me repeatedly. Those of us who make a significant difference in someone else's life will have to deal with adversity. Adversity and challenge will always be connected to great doors of opportunity (1 Corinthians 16:9); it just goes with the territory!

Early in my life, I knew I had a calling and mandate from God. There wasn't a specific grand event or a-ha moment. God did not audibly speak to me; I just knew! You know how it goes - sometimes you just know.

It was the desire of my father that I become a voice for God. My dad told me, on more than one occasion, that when I was born, he prayed and said, "God...make him a preacher." I remember my grandmother, Mama Lena, grabbing my cheek and telling me I was going to preach. I also remember looking into her face and thinking, "No, I'm not. I have other plans for my life."

As many who are called tend to do, I ran from the call on my life. I didn't want to be a preacher! I wanted to be a rock star in a rock and roll band. I was into loud music and the fast life; I loved motorcycles, fast cars and electric guitars. I was mesmerized by my Dad's 1960's Gibson Les Paul. Playing that electric guitar was my driving passion. While I sat in school, I would sneak and study chord charts for songs by the Beatles, Rolling Stones, Paul Revere and The Raiders, Eric Clapton, The Animals and other favorite bands. When I got home from school, I couldn't wait to get my hands on Dad's guitar. I would play until late in the evening when Mother would say, "Put the guitar up – you have to go to school tomorrow." Obediently, I put it away, but later, I would sneak it back out after my parents were in bed. With the guitar unplugged, I played late into the night, thinking to myself, *this is what I'm destined to do*. I was preparing for my future.

Around the age of 16, I began to pursue music seriously. I responded to an ad and auditioned for the band, "Phyve of a Kind." They felt I was a perfect fit so I joined the band that very day to sing and play guitar. I was excited to be living my dream and the lifestyle of a musician. Staying out of trouble was quite a challenge. Unlike most rural towns, ours rocked! My best friend and I both had 67 Pontiac GTOs and we would go out on the town in his car one night, mine the next.

Our band traveled often, performing at bars, high schools, penthouse parties and other rock concerts. I loved being on stage; the flash of the strobe lights, the haze of the smoke machine, and the throngs of screaming fans were addictive. Like many legends of that time, Jimmy Hendrix, Janice Joplin, Jim Morrison and The Doors, we were surrounded by the heavy drinking and drug use that was common in the music scene. I lost some friends to drug overdoses, but I was enraptured by the era and the lifestyle.

I could never escape God's call on my life. I heard His voice speak to me regardless of where I went or what I was doing. Though I shoved it aside, He never failed to remind me of His mandate. I was convicted of the wrong choices I made but I continued to neglect my primary calling.

Though I pursued a different lifestyle than my parents, I continued to attend church as long as I lived with them. It was a rule of our household. Although I didn't recognize it then, looking back, that wasn't a bad thing. We may not know as much as we thought we knew in our youthful years. By the way, parents, don't leave your children with so many options: have some rules for your home. The choices you make for your children affect their destiny; teenagers don't always know what they need to be doing even though they think they do!

In my own teenage years, it was time to make a choice. I remember driving home late one night from band practice when I heard the voice of God clearly say, **"You're on a dead end street going nowhere."** At that point, I realized I had truly been neglecting my calling. I was headed down the wrong road in my life and needed to make a U-turn.

When I arrived home, I walked in the house, picked up the phone, and called my band mates to tell them I could no longer be a part of our group. Even then, I knew enough about God to know that when He gives you a mandate, the last thing you want is to become a Jonah. Rather than continuing to run from God's calling the way Jonah did, I knew I didn't want to be swallowed

245

up by something bigger than I was. Pursuing an ambition is not as important as perfecting a God mandate.

I would be remiss if I did not stop here and tell you the impact that a young lady had on my life at this point. The timing was perfect, the middle of my so-called glory days, I found myself at a crossroads in my life. I was at a concert at a church in a small town in Mississippi singing with a gospel group one night when a girl named Yolanda Delmas walked in and immediately captured my attention. After the concert, we talked and got acquainted. Though the conversation was brief, she definitely made an impression on me. Little did I realize the spark created that night would later turn into a flame.

Yolanda lived on the Mississippi Gulf Coast while I lived in Baton Rouge about two or three hours away. Because of the distance, our interactions were limited but I never forgot her. About a year after the concert, I was at a buddy's house working on my GTO when my Dad drove up to tell me I had received a phone call from Yolanda. Clearly, he was happy to deliver the message because he knew she would be a positive influence on my life. I immediately remembered the night I first met Yolanda and the impression she made upon my heart. I was thrilled to hear that she called!

The next day, I called Yolanda who told me that she had been at a recording studio with my aunt when my aunt shared that I was struggling spiritually and asked if she would call me. (I believe it was God working in my life the day that my aunt and Yolanda were brought together in that recording studio.) During our conversation, Yolanda encouraged me and preached to me a bit. I admitted to both her and myself that I did desire to do more for God. I gladly accepted Yolanda's invitation to visit her church but when I came to town we went on a date instead and we continued dating steadily. As soon as we started dating, we instantly connected. Right away, we recognized that our life goals, vision and purpose were compatible.

I moved to Houston to attend Bible college a couple months after we started dating but every weekend, I made the 6.5 hour trip to the coast to see her. Seven months after we met, we were married; that was over 40 years ago!

The Apostle Paul stated that it is possible to be unequally yoked together. Life is so much easier when you're married to someone who shares your mandate. Like me, Yolanda had a strong calling on her life. From a very young age, she was involved in ministry, singing and even traveling with her pastors. After we married and I finished Bible college, we began working as itinerant evangelists for six years.

Did you know *success* is referenced 11 times in the Bible? In Joshua 1:8, God told Joshua He would make his way prosperous and give him good success. To be truly successful in life, you need other people to help make it possible. In an ideal partnership you both share common visions, interests and goals. Gratefully, I have been blessed to have married my soul mate who shares my passions and desires. For me, success is about living with expectancy, about keeping life simple and about maintaining a fresh perspective. It is possible to forfeit success in the pursuit of it, getting bogged down in the process so much that you don't enjoy life's journey. Real success is not about material things since it's possible to have things and be totally unhappy. Remember, if Satan cannot keep you from being successful, he will try to steal the joy of it; take some time to savor your success.

Just as Jesus gave Peter the keys to the Kingdom, you must have the right keys to live a maximized life. A major key to success is having passion for what you do; passion fuels your mandate. Did you know that 80% of the fuel used to launch a rocket ship is expended at the launch? Think of that: only 20% is required to journey through space and back to Earth. Getting started always seems the most difficult part while momentum requires less energy.

Speaking of momentum, another challenge we must face is overcoming inertia – the loss of power or energy, sluggishness or inactivity. To overcome inertia, seek a cause greater than yourself. As Galatians 6:9 reminds us: it is possible to become weary while doing the right thing, so take caution not to lose heart. In order to not lose heart you must be invested in your calling. Investment creates ownership. For example, you would never wash and wax a rental car because there's no significant investment or ownership there. Ownership keeps us at our post of duty while others walk away.

To continue my story, while we were in our early twenties, we spent several years traveling with two small children. With another baby on the way, Yolanda began to express her desire to settle down. At Christmas time, a district official of our denomination called and asked if I would like to be considered for an available pastorate position. Thinking I would not be selected, and out of sensitivity to Yolanda's feelings, I agreed to be considered.

A few days later, the official called us back and said that overwhelmingly the people of the church voted for me to be the pastor. (Only one person voted against me.) Now I was angry. I didn't want a church. I wanted to see the world, make music and go places. I was happy traveling to a new town every week pulling our Airstream trailer behind us. Yolanda's feelings were different; she was excited we would finally be settling down.

At only 24 years old, I wondered if I were ready to be a pastor. When people ask how I did it at such an early age, I reply - *they needed me, and I needed them.*

On the way to church that first Sunday, I said to Yolanda, "I'll stay six months, and then I'm resigning." Thankfully, I had a change of heart and began to appreciate my new role. Six months became six years. We have many great memories of that first church – great friends, great food and great growth. As I look back, I see that God really began to develop us there.

From there, we felt the need to pioneer a new church. We moved to Baton Rouge, Louisiana and began a church in a small rented building. Soon after, we had a growing and dynamic church and built a beautiful building on some nice acreage. While great things were happening, we ultimately felt ourselves called to Tennessee and the greater Nashville area.

My Mom and Dad sold their home to move with us and be a part of founding our new church in Nashville. We moved them to Nashville and returned to Baton Rouge to finish up some business. They moved into their new home on Thursday, and we made the journey back to Baton Rouge on Saturday. Monday morning, the phone rang with a sad turn of events. My mother called to tell me Dad had a stroke. Yolanda and I grabbed the kids and jumped on a plane back to Nashville.

Sadly, my dad required brain surgery which would only give him a 50/50 chance of survival. Without surgery, he would certainly die. Dad had the surgery but never totally recovered; nine months later, he went home to be with the Lord.

At this particular point, we had people telling us, "You're out of the will of God! This would have never happened if you had stayed in Baton Rouge." While at the hospital visiting Dad, God confirmed His will. We ministered to hurting people in the waiting room and the nurses who took care of my father. Later, those people would become the first members of our new church and even bring us food and take care of us when my dad died.

After Dad's death, it was difficult for me. I stood at the door of our home on one cold gray winter day and looked out at this strange place I didn't feel I belonged. I asked myself, *what have I done coming here?*

Our commitment to God's calling in our lives paid off at that point. We were stable and resolute and recognized that adversity is always connected with any worthy mandate. I want to encourage any of you reading right now who might feel trapped or hopeless that circumstances do not *dictate* who you are; they *reveal* who you are. When your cause is greater than any of the fires you encounter, you succeed. Do not allow the storms of life to steer you away from your purpose: maintain your course. Then, you can say, as the Apostle Paul said, "I have finished the course."

My favorite scripture is Ephesians 3:20: "Now unto him that is able to do exceeding abundantly above all that we ask or think, according to the power that worketh in us." In other words, God's capacity to abundantly bless us is directly related to using our gifts for His will. When we function within the primary gift God has called us to, our potential to live a rich abundant life is much greater.

Today, Yolanda and I are very active and involved in ministry, but we are ever mindful of retaining our peace and joy. What have we done if we've made some notable achievement in life and are miserable at the apex of it? The epitome of life is not so much the achievement of reaching some worthy goal, but, more importantly, what state those goals leave us in. The phenomenon of the burning bush experience on the backside of the desert with Moses was not so much that the bush was on fire but that it could not be consumed by the fire! Don't allow the fire of any experience to consume you; instead, let it catapult you!

Yolanda and I now serve as founding co-pastors of Celebration of Life Church, a thriving multi-cultural, multi-racial church in Hendersonville, Tennessee. God has extended many wonderful opportunities to us through the years including appearing on, hosting, and being interviewed for a variety of Christian programs. Through the books we've authored and the mediums of television, radio and internet, God has given us a platform to minister to millions of people.

In case you're wondering, my passion for guitar remains strong. Yolanda and I have composed and released multiple music projects. We both speak at conferences throughout the country, sharing our testimony and encouraging others to live life to the fullest. I have more passion for God than ever before – living for God just keeps getting better and better!

Consider this final thought: as I have experienced firsthand, it is imperative to realize that your capacity to deal with adversity ushers you closer to your mandate and God's destiny for your life.

Joseph Morgan
Senior Pastor
Celebration of Life Church
Hendersonville, Tennessee

Contact: pastor@celebrationoflife.com
jymorgan.com
facebook.com/pastorjosephmorgan
Twitter: @josephmorgan22
Instagram: josephmorgan77

Magnificent Man

Pastor Luis Reyes

For the one whom God has sent speaks the words of God, for God gives the Spirit without limit. John 3:34

I was born in the suburbs of Puerto Rico where drugs and violence on the streets was the normal. In my earliest years I was raised in the projects. When I was eight years old my family and I moved into the countryside into another poor neighborhood. Our surroundings were no different. Drugs, alcohol and violence continued to flood the streets on a daily basis.

My family was a basic Catholic family. My mother mostly stayed at home with us kids. My father worked as a mechanic. Our house was always full of neighborhood children. We weren't a rich family, but the neighborhood knew where to go if they were hungry. Poverty was all around us. It was normal to see children outside playing without shoes, seeing drunkards on the streets, people hungry, and homeless.

Although we were not steeped into Catholic tradition, I was raised in the Catholic religion. I had a love for sports, namely basketball, and my father was involved in coaching community teams. My peers wanted me to play on their team.

As I neared my middle school years I began paying attention to what my peers and teachers were saying about God. I was Catholic and they were Protestant. I was in the minority and I felt it. My peers were prejudiced against my religion and made sure I knew it. My problem was, although I was labeled Catholic, I knew nothing of "my religion". I just knew that I was different

Although my peers mocked my beliefs, I was still well accepted because I was a basketball jock and that took precedence over anything I believed. As I went through my middle school years, the mocking of my religion worsened. My peers started rejecting me. They never rejected any of my ungodly actions. They rejected my religion. At this point I developed a bitterness toward Christians. Their rejection pushed me away from God and I began rebelling. I stopped participating in community activities. There was such a division of religions that my peers no longer wanted me playing ball with them.

I started becoming successful in basketball at school. I became a successful student. I had good grades and friends who liked me for my ball skills. On the outside my life was good but I was miserable within. I was fighting to survive against their religion. I attended a public school but it seemed that everyone around me claimed Christianity. They lived what seemed a moral life. I didn't share their values and I continued to feel the rejection.

In high school I made a decision to never be a part of Christianity because I didn't want to act like my peers. They didn't live the words that came from their mouth. What they professed didn't match their actions. They judged my religion but couldn't live theirs. If I was in a sinful situation they were always there following me right in. It made no sense to me.

As my basketball career strengthened, the people who rejected me now wanted me on their team. Churches began hosting basketball tournaments as fundraisers. They were eager to have me on their team. They wanted nothing more than my skills.

They had opportunity to witness to me and share their faith but what I got was, "This is what you must do to behave…and take those earrings out of your ears." They made sure I knew the "Christian language" in case an adult approached me. They didn't want me embarrassing them.

I began blending in with the Christian crowd. My peers knew the real me. They knew I didn't profess Christianity. They also knew I had become like them, blended in and an "okay Christian."

Although I went on to college to work on my basketball career, I came back on breaks to play in the Christian tournaments. I began recruiting some kids from the projects. I received news that these churches rejected these kids because they weren't Christian. That angered me! At this point I made the decision to make myself an enemy of every Christian I came in contact with. I even became their stumbling block, enticing them to fall into sin. I mocked them. It was my desire to make them feel how they made me feel.

In my first year of college I began dating Roselyn, my future wife. On one particular day we were at her great-aunt's house. I had been drinking. At this point drinking alcohol was a daily norm for me. I was sitting on her front porch and overheard her inside. She was looking through an old photo album. As she and her family were looking, all of a sudden she yelled, "Stop!" Everyone looked at her in anticipation. She pointed to a young man in the picture and asked who it was. Before anyone could look and answer, she spoke. She pointed and said, "That person is a pastor." Pastor? No one in their lineage was a "pastor". They were Catholic! Before anyone could see who she was pointing at, she spoke it two more times. "That guy is a pastor!"

Everyone had to see who this crazy old lady was pointing at. To everyone's shock it was somehow a picture of me! I had somehow gotten into their family album. Everyone began laughing loudly. They quickly called me into the house. I stood at the door with a beer in my hand looking at these people laughing and pointing at me. They were laughing at the "mistake" this old lady made. Then with all seriousness this lady looked at me and said, "You will see! You ARE a pastor." I looked at her surprised and asked, "Who me?" She said, "Yes! You will see." I shook my head no and told her she didn't know what she was saying. She sternly looked at me and said, "Let the Lord touch you and change you. You will see. That can you have in your hands, and everything else, you will drop it all to follow Christ."

At that point I didn't believe this old lady. But I didn't forget what she said either. I continued my life of sin. I continued my journey to make Christians miserable and fall. My whole purpose was to prove to myself that I couldn't find any Christian that lived what they professed. I never believed I could find a "real Christian." Up to this point there were only "okay Christians", those that professed it but didn't live it.

Roselyn and I married before I could finish college. I could have had a career in basketball but chose a different route. We moved to Florida where my first son was born. I continued to make poor choices. My life was in chaos but I couldn't see it that way because it looked like I had everything I wanted. After living there for 10 months we moved back to Puerto Rico, where I began making deliveries to retail businesses. From there I built my own business. In a worldly sense my life was successful. Inwardly I knew something was still missing.

For 8 years I rebelled against God and every Christian I came in contact with. In those 8 years I became a different man. All my peers knew me as Charlie. They said I looked like an artist, Charlie Zaa. I lived the life of a different man. Although I wasn't involved in drugs or murders, I was steeped into that street life. Drug lords had my back. I knew all that went down or was going to go down on the streets. As Charlie, I wreaked havoc on Christians everywhere I went. But in that season, I had lost who I really was.

One day I was doing my usual condemnation of Christians and one of my friends who wasn't a Christian said something that caught my attention and stuck with me. He looked at me and stopped me mid-sentence. He said, "Stop! Please, never mess with a child of God because when you do you are messing with God himself. I don't go to church or desire to be around them, but I have learned not to mess with them." This man wasn't a Christian but he did fear God. At that moment I realized that in the last 8 years I had lost all fear and respect of God. That day I began examining my life.

My wife began reading the Bible. She was flooded in her mind with question after question about God. Being raised a Catholic herself, she now had been introduced to a different belief system. The atmosphere at home was still not good though. Although I had begun examining my life, I wasn't ready to change. My drinking had gotten worse. I was an alcoholic.

My son played little league baseball and we had begun making friends with some of the parents. We spent a lot of time together. One lady was a Christian and testified often of the many great things God was doing in her life. She was a happy, lovely and sincere person. She was not like the other Christians. She continued to show love and testify of the greatness of her God. Every opportunity she got, she would invite us to church. I would always reply with, "One day I will go." One night I was drunk and she invited me to go to church the next day. In my drunken state I agreed to go. She said, "You are drunk and tomorrow you will not remember this." I told her I gave her my word that I would be there and when a man gives his word he must do it.

That next day I awoke and kept my word. I went and this time it was different. These Christians weren't judging me! They accepted me for how I was and poured love into me that I never felt before. This prompted me to try church. After all these years of playing basketball for churches, I finally went to church for the first time. Oh my! It didn't go well. The preacher shoved his sermon aside and told the congregation that God was taking him

257

in a different direction. For the next hour or so this man meddled in my life as if someone had told him everything I had ever done. I left there mad at my wife because I believed she had previously met with this preacher and told on me. But she hadn't. At the time I didn't know it but the Holy Spirit had spoken through this preacher to me.

I left angry and not ready to change. I went to church about once a month just to keep my wife off my back. Then we began going to some Sunday evening services. I actually started enjoying it but was still not ready to give up my worldly life.

One night I was at the baseball field with some friends. They were all in the bleachers drinking heavily. All of a sudden a weird feeling came over me. I thought maybe I was really drunk. I looked up to the sky and saw a lot of demons flying in the sky. That freaked me out! I got up and began walking across the field. My friends asked where I was going. I told them I was tired and needed to go home. I jumped the fence and got into my car. Just as I got in my car a fight broke out. Guns were firing and it was a mess. I left that night and never looked back.

I got home and said to my wife, "I think God spoke to me." That night changed me. I told God I wanted to change. I realized I was now living the life that I had been criticizing all these years. I was attending church but living a life of sin. But no more! I had such an urgency to change. I felt that in order to change we had to move away from my surroundings. I had in mind to move back to Florida.

I ended up moving to Tennessee. I came here knowing no one but wanted to pursue a life of transformation. I still dealt with rebellion and had trouble letting go of my worldly life. But I didn't give up pursuing God. I finally had that transformation I was longing for. I was no longer an "okay Christian". I was now a "transformed child of God".

God began doing amazing things in my life and in my family. As I grew in my knowledge of the Lord, God started putting me into place. He began using me to teach and disciple others. The more I submitted to Him, the more He used me. Now I am a pastor. Now I am teaching others how to go beyond being an "okay Christian" to becoming a true child of God. An "okay Christian" doesn't care if someone dies and goes to hell, they don't live what they profess and they don't stand for what they believe. And that my friend is NOT OKAY with God!

God has been faithful. I have seen it in every aspect of my life. He never left me alone. He has been my refuge and strength. I have seen the provision of God since the first moment I began serving Him, especially these past years.

One of the most significant times in my life that I saw the love, fidelity and provision of God in my life was when He asked me to quit my secular job and go into full time ministry. I had to fully trust and depend on Him. Today I can say this scripture: Psalm 37:25 *I was young and now I am old, yet I have never seen the righteous forsaken or their children begging bread.*

God called me and put in my heart His great love for souls and a passion to see the transformation in their lives. This is how Conversion Ministry was birthed. It's a ministry focused on evangelism, discipleship, and church planting; that people will be transformed through the power of the Holy Spirit.

Conversion Ministries was founded in July 2011 with a family that has the same passion for souls. Later on God added on two more families. We began meeting to pray and later began evangelizing. Quickly the ministry began growing. Through this, New Wineskin Church, a ministry under Conversion Ministries, was birthed in October 2011.

Today I am a pastor in New Wineskin Church, a multicultural church. At this point the services are spoken in both English and Spanish. But the cultures are expanding quickly and

God is stretching our horizons. This is another example of God's hand on my life, because of my primary language and English is not my strength. But when a heart is willing to follow and obey God, God will use the available vessel to glorify His name. 2 Corinthians 12:9-10 says that God's power is made perfect in my weakness. When I am weak, He is strong.

Do not conform to the pattern of this world, but be transformed by the renewing of your mind. Then you will be able to test and approve what God's will is – His good, pleasing and perfect will. Romans 12:2

To the Jews who had believed him, Jesus said, "If you hold to my teaching, you are really my disciples. Then you will know the truth, and the truth will set you free." John 8:31-3
The tongue has the power of life and death, and those who love it will eat its fruit. Proverbs 18:21

Contact: luis.reyes@conversionministries.com
conversionministries.com

Magnificent Man

Pastor Raymond Eaton

I Can Do All Things Through Christ Who Strengthens Me
Phil 4:13

Hello, my name is Raymond Eaton. I was born in Decatur, IL at St. Mary's Hospital, November 14, 1967 to Dr. Joe W. Eaton and my mom, Judith K. Eaton. Yes, I was raised a preacher's kid. Both of my Grandpas were preachers also. I have had great influences in my life.

I grew up with two sisters, Sonya and Teri, and one brother, Tim who has already gone to be with the Lord. We grew up a loving family. We never had a lot of material things. Doesn't it make you wonder why I became a preacher? At first I didn't, because of all that I had seen my Dad go through, but in due time the Lord got my attention. I was saved at the age of twelve and also surrendered to the ministry a short time thereafter.

I have not always lived the way I needed to, but God can always find a way to bring us back. Throughout my life, I can remember my grandparents as they influenced me in my life and my walk with the Lord. My Mom's parents, Raymond and Cleo

261

Bulla were special. Everyone tells me I am a lot like my Grandpa Raymond. This includes, for both of us, a sense of humor, and we are both stocky.

My Dad's parents, Sam and Olene Eaton, were special as well. Grandpa Eaton was a prayer warrior, preacher and a singer. He would shout at the drop of a hat. He had a good reason. He was hit by a drunk driver head on, and it crippled him. They said he wouldn't live, but he did. They said he wouldn't walk, but he did. I would say that is enough to shout about!

A preacher kid's life is probably one of the toughest ones to live, but God had His reason for putting me there. I was the baby of four kids, a little of an advantage at times, but other times a disadvantage. My parents would tell me that as a kid, I would grab the Bible, jump on the couch and start preaching and singing. Dad would set me on the pulpit at age 3, and we would sing a song. Our entire family sang. Growing up we were like any other kids, arguing and fussing, but we loved each other. Sometimes I miss those days. My brother and I fought, but we were close. We fished and hunted together, sang together, and yes, even cried together. I guess you would say we were and still are a close knit family. I can look back at my life and see many blessings and downfalls.

The Lord has given me the privilege to sing with groups like the Kingsmen, Four-Fold, Gold City, Mystery Men and the Blackwoods. I have sung to thousands of people all over America. The only two states I haven't been to are Alaska and Hawaii. I always had the most fun singing with my family.

The Harmonites, our family singing group, consisted of my Dad, Mom, and my brother. There is nothing like family harmony.

My wife Montrie Eaton and I have been married for soon to be twenty years. We have three wonderful sons. Jacob, nineteen and a freshman at Bethel University, Joshua, seventeen and a junior in high school and Nathan, 15, a freshman in high school. The Lord blessed me with a wonderful family.

My education consists of graduating from Victory Christian Academy in Paducah, KY, Bible Baptist College in Mattoon, IL, Union University in Jackson, TN, and Liberty University in Lynchburg, VA. The Lord also has let me work and pastor several churches in my early years of serving the Lord.

My wife and I were hurt in a church and we stopped attending for a while. I began coaching travel baseball. My son, Nathan, started playing at a young age and showed a lot of talent. We traveled all around playing baseball. He was inducted into the Babe Ruth Hall of Fame at age 10. At age 12, he was chosen within the top 25 individual players in the nation.

The devil kept us wrapped up. I tried making it right by doing chapel on Sundays at ball tournaments, but I knew it wasn't enough during these 3 years. I buried myself in baseball, trying to keep my mind off God and church. My Dad and Mom didn't quit praying. We even stopped being around them because of it. One thing about it, the devil will let you have fun for a little time, then God continues to remind you of what you need to be doing.

One night, September 11, 2012 at 2:00 a.m., the worst news that I have ever heard came ringing my doorbell. My sister and her husband, along with my niece, were at my door with tears running down their faces. They told me that my brother, Tim, was dead of a heart attack. I had just seen and visited with him that day. I vividly remember our last words to each other, "I love you."

The morning of September 12 was an emotional day for me and my family. Memories flooded my head. To be honest, I wasn't thinking as much on my brother's death. I was thinking of how it could have been me. You see, the Lord had been after me for 3 years telling me I needed to get back serving Him. I kept saying "no". This is what was running through my mind at the time of my brother's death. No, my brother didn't die because of me, but God used his death to grab my attention, and boy did He grab my attention. I kept thinking of my wife and kids and how it would be if I wasn't here. Then, I started thinking of all the blessings I missed not serving Him. Yes, there were heartaches and pain in serving God, but the good outweighed the bad. How many souls had I passed up by being away from God? Instead of my brother's death bringing me down, it was actually powering me up. God through His love and grace was strengthening me and preparing me to get back to His service.

My hesitation was my wife. She was mad at God, but little did I know, God was talking to her and softening her heart to be ready to support me in His service.

The night of my brother's visitation, we came back home and we were sitting in our driveway, when a conversation broke out that changed our lives. My wife and I along with the boys were all in agreement that I had to get back to preaching. The night of September 13, 2012, we started praying that the Lord would use us and where He opened the door we would go. In October, 2012, I went to work at a place where a preacher friend of mine was a supervisor. In January, 2013, his brother-in-law and Intern-Pastor of a church, was looking to leave his position. He contacted my preacher friend, and he gave him my name. It is funny sometimes how the Lord works. I had no clue what he was doing. Before too long, a fellow from the church called me and wanted to know if I could fill in at the pulpit for a couple of weeks. I said, "yes". The first time I walked in the building, I knew the Lord was going to put me there. My wife wasn't able to come because of work, so it was me and our boys.

There were about 25 in attendance that day, but it was a good service. The next time I preached, I was there with my whole family. As we were returning back home, my wife said, "well we better get some boxes, because we are going to be moving here." February 24, 2013 Russwood Baptist Church voted me in as their pastor. March 3, 2013 was my first Sunday as Pastor and the Lord has blessed us. We started with about 25 people and the Lord has blossomed it into running 100 or above. We have baptized 54, have had 47 salvations and around 100 additions. The Lord is still blessing!

Since our arrival, my Dad has become our Music Director. Our youngest son, Nathan, is his assistant. Our oldest son, Jacob, was saved and surrendered into the ministry. Even though the Pastor's life is a hard one, it sure feels good to be in God's will.

I am still currently at Russwood Baptist Church, Springville, TN, enjoying what God has given me to do. May God bless and I hope that my story helps someone that either needed to be saved or to make themselves right with the Lord.

Remember, God loves you as much as His own Son.

Contact: bigdaddy.re66@gmail.com

Pastor Shawn Scott

Never let loyalty and kindness leave you! Tie them around your neck as a reminder. Write them deep within your heart. Then you will find favor with both God and people, and you will earn a good reputation. Proverbs 3:3-4

I was born and raised in Clarksville, TN as the only boy among my siblings. My biological father hasn't been in my life since I was five years of age. After my biological father disappeared, my mother, Mary Alice Scott, married the biological father of my sisters, Kiya and Kawawn Scott.

At some point in my early childhood, we ended up in Leland, Mississippi. The only thing my conscious mind can remember about that time is how my stepfather, the only man in my life, abused me with springs from the storm door. This was the same man that casually snorted cocaine and smoked marijuana on a regular basis right in my

267

presence as if it were normal. At the age of six years old, I lived in fear for my life every time I made a mistake. If it wasn't me receiving the abuse, he was constantly abusing my mother, even for the most trivial things.

Somehow, we ended up migrating to the projects of Phoenix, Illinois. The only real fun moments that I can remember came from this time. Moments like riding on my banana seat bike and being able to play with my sisters: the things that normal children get to experience. In the vividness of my memory, the abuse from my stepfather never ceased towards my mother and I. His temper far exceeds any man I have ever met to this day coupled with a drug habit that drastically flooded out any good memory I could possibly have of him. At that time, we lived in an apartment with one room. My sisters and I slept in the living room. The roaches were so bad in the apartment that I dreaded going to sleep at night because I was afraid that the roaches would end up in my underclothes.

One night, I can remember my stepfather and my mom were fighting worse than I had ever seen. My mother hit him pretty good causing him to back off. I don't know if he just got tired, or if she "cold-cocked" him so bad that she made him rethink his actions and he chose to save his battle for another day. That night, I remember looking through the darkness of the one room apartment because the electricity had been turned off. I can also recall hearing my mother crying until morning. The next morning my mother acted as if she was going to the store with my sisters and I. My mom took us with her to the police station and had the police escort us back to the apartment and get what little belongings we had out of the apartment. Having no electricity required us to depend on the light from the policeman's flashlight. What an unbearable moment that was in my mind. I thought to myself, "When this is over my stepfather is really going to beat us down."

Today, I can look back at that time filled with so many distraught memories, and realize that God was still keeping us. We ended up going to Chicago for shelter and support. I can remember my mother wearing her huge bumblebee sunglasses covering her blue and black bruised eye. While being interviewed by some lady at the battered/abused shelter for women in Chicago, Illinois, all I kept saying to myself was "why us". I didn't know it at the time, but God was creating hope for other peoples' lives through my story. My mom, my two sisters, and I ended up being accepted into the shelter. This is where I can remember hearing the Christmas story for the first time referencing the baby in a manger known as Jesus. That Christmas in the shelter, I can remember singing carols with other families, even though we had no idea who they were. The fear of abuse was gone, replaced by an exciting anticipation of what tomorrow would bring.

Before long, my mother saved up enough funds for us to return to Clarksville, TN. I often ask myself, "Why didn't my mom just call her five brothers and have them come up to Phoenix and 'whoop' my stepfather at that time like nobody's business." I believe in the midst of my stepfather's shortcomings, my mother was trying to hold on to hope for that relationship for my two sisters. Upon returning to Clarksville, we moved in with my grandparents Henry and Inell Scott.

Up to this point in my life, I had no exposure to God other than the Christmas story. I remember the Dillard family that lived close by my grandparent's house. They invited my sisters and I over for Bible studies and were very nice. Despite their efforts, at this point in my life I still didn't have a firm grasp of who God was.

My family was really close at that time, thanks to my grandmother ensuring all the grandchildren visited on the weekends. Meeting family members that I had only seen photos of in my mom's album was amazing. When my mom obtained a factory job, life for my sisters and I began to improve. While my mom worked extensive hours, I had to stay at home and watch my sisters. As a single mother, mom did an outstanding job making sure her children were attending and excelling in school. Throughout middle school, I maintained an A/B average until the eighth grade. This was when I was introduced to alcohol and sex. During freshman year, I was introduced to drugs and gambling, which led to a secret life that I tried to keep hidden from my mom. Without a father or strong positive male influence, I turned to the streets.

As I began to identify myself as a hustler, my drug activity increased. A hustler, at that time, was the coolest title that a teenager in the streets in the 90's could obtain. It was cool and it was common in my sphere of influence to always have crack cocaine and marijuana in your possession. Everybody was either selling dope or smoking dope. It was basically dependent upon who was mentoring you. Most of the teenagers I hung out with were either feeding their parents the dope or their parents were selling the dope.

Life, driven by my own illicit desires during high school, made my ambitions become unrealistic at best. The consequences of life on the streets drove me to create defensive tactics so as to not be pushed over by robbers or aggressive crack smokers. As a result, I purchased an unlicensed gun for protection while I was out in streets. Still trying to appear "legit," I took the ASVAB to get into the Air Force, and passed it. At this point, I was in my junior year of high school.

The week after I had purchased the gun, I ended up getting pulled over, and the police for some reason made me get out of the truck. They checked the truck and found the gun and some marijuana. You can imagine what happened as a consequence of that incident. I was not eligible for the Air Force from that point forward. My senior year at Northeast I played football, and we had the most wins at that time since 1943. I was on house arrest because of the gun situation, but I still continued to indulge drug activity while my mom was at work. I created a habit to sell and smoke drugs with no boundaries in mind.

Always trying to appease my mom and make her proud of me, I enlisted into a delayed entry program for the US Navy through some written waivers. You know how we young people do the "young and dumb speech: I have learned from my mistakes" confession. I wasn't trying to go to college and I felt like the military would have been an easy way out. Of course, I have since learned that nothing worth having comes without a price.

Just two weeks after beginning Basic Training, a Naval Officer pulled me up in front of the entire group of sailors in the class. In a nut shell, he said, "this is what happens when your life is on drugs." And with that, they discharged me from the Navy. There was so much THC that showed up on my testing that the only way I could stay was to accept some drug rehabilitation. I refused, so I was discharged. You can probably imagine the look on my mother's face when I finally made it home: Disappointment!

Back home, with no direction, I ended up getting a factory job and enrolling at Austin Peay State University to major in computer science. I had to take some developmental classes at the APSU campus on Fort Campbell, KY. While the different approaches of trying to find my way through life were changing, my secret life of selling and using drugs was still the same. Four months after being discharged from the Navy, the consequences of those actions led to a gentleman trying to rob me. That situation resulted in taking his life in defense of my own.

Seven days after my nineteenth birthday, I was sitting in front of a judge telling me that I was charged with first degree murder and would be facing life in prison or the death penalty. Because there were no witnesses, no one knew that it was self-defense except for me. The state that I was charged in doesn't have a self-defense law. All I can remember when my mom came to visit me was "I don't want to know what happened and I am here for you." When I finally sat down with my lawyer he explained that the only chance we had at winning the case was to take it to trial. The only strategy we had was to tell the truth and explain why I was meeting the man.

My lawyer was able to get my bond lowered to a feasible amount so that my mom could bond me out. We ended up going to trial, and because of some mishandling of evidence the judge ordered a mistrial. Three months later the state charged me again with the same charge of first degree murder. The stress had pretty much overtaken my mental capacity at this point, and I ended up going deeper into the streets and using drugs from sun up until sun down. The second trial came up, and the state convicted me of involuntary manslaughter. This conviction carried five to ten years in prison. The state ended up giving me the max time of ten years. The judge basically looked me in the face and told me I was lucky and my conviction was to due to the nature of the case: "drug deal gone bad."

I looked at my Mom and told her to not cry because it would make me cry. Before the deputy took me out of the building, the widow of the man's life I took asked to talk to me. During our time together she asked me this one question: "Are you saved?" It didn't make sense to me at the time, but the love of God was reaching out to me through that widowed woman. She was praying that I would come to find Christ.

When my Mom came to visit me after I was convicted, she brought me a Bible. She said, "Shawn, you are my only son and I don't have any experience when it comes to situations like this." My mother gave me the Bible because her friends at work had mentioned that this would really help me. Well, I read that Bible from front to back. There was this old man that would bring little Bible courses every week to the jail and I would take them, complete them, and would turn the Bible courses back in to him. One afternoon when I was working out, I experienced a huge flash of light that caused me to sit down in awe. Wondering what just happened to me, I started to feel this sense of need more than I had ever felt in my life. That night the jailors came through and reminded all of the inmates that church service was that night.

Not knowing what to expect, but still expecting something, I went to that service. There, I saw an African American and a Caucasian man preaching passionately about Jesus Christ. With no hesitation whatsoever I gave my life to Christ. I didn't have any experience with what a Christian was supposed to look like, but my convictions started to heighten in my life causing me deal with my inner man. I asked God in my first prayer:

"What is my purpose? What am I good at? All I know is how to do is get my way in the streets and manipulate people with my conversation."

That night I had a dream of drawing people. Three weeks later I was drawing portrait pictures for money throughout the entire jail. My mom was able to stop sending me money and I was not without the rest of my incarcerated time.

Before long, I got a packet in the mail from the Appeals Court stating that my lawyer had taken my case for an appeal. When the other inmates saw it, they downplayed it like it wouldn't amount to anything. After all, everybody appeals their case if they are convicted. Thinking no more about it I eventually got transferred to the penitentiary. Nineteen months later someone brought me a newspaper that stated that, "Lashawndrick Scott's constitutional right has been violated due to "Double Jeopardy." I had been tried twice for the same offence. In awe, I called my lawyer and I could hear the office in an uproar of excitement because my case was overturned. Before I left the penitentiary, I had gangbangers and hustlers confess to me that they believed that God was with me and they believed I could do anything that I set myself to do in my life.

It turns out, they were right. God was with me the entire time, and He has created such an awesome turnaround story in me. I am excited to say that I am happily married to my wife Melodie Lenich Scott, who is the mother of my three boys Lashawndrick "Shawn" Demans Scott Jr., Hezekiah Hea'ven Scott and Lenox Legend Scott. I am also the father of a wonderful daughter that I had prior to my marriage: Ti'onna Michelle Scott. My wife and I have been in business as the owners of *Positive Images Barber Beauty & Nail Salon* for twelve years. In addition to our business, my wife and I are now Executive Pastors of the Clarksville campuses of the Tabernacle Ministries under the leadership of our Senior Pastors Anthony and Julia Daley.

"I can now look back on the journey that God brought me through, and I can see His hand keeping me safe and guiding me. Not necessarily guiding me to perfect circumstances, but bringing me to a place where I could depend only on Him. After all, that's what I was looking for anyway. I couldn't find the answer to my problems in drugs. I couldn't fight it in the Navy. I couldn't find it in the hustle, or in making my mother proud, or any of the other things that I tried. I had to find it in Jesus Christ. He had to bring me to my lowest, so that I could see Him,

so that I could find Him. Now that I have Him - I'm never letting go."

Contact: thetab.sscott@gmail.com

Quenton White, Esq

For as he thinketh in his heart, so is he ... Proverbs 23:7

For as long as I can remember, there are three things that have played prominent roles in my life, sports, politics and my relationship with God. Not necessarily in that order but over the years, each has brought both solace and contradiction. Through each, I have encountered some dynamic men who poured into me wisdom, curiosity and a sense of self-worth.

Being raised in rural Louisiana by a single parent was a source of inspiration. Inspiring because my mother was a stern, yet endearing woman with an abundance of wisdom and love, who nurtured a morality in my spirit that doing what's right would always bear rewards. Though I have failed on occasion, my compass for right and wrong has always been, "What would my mother do?"

In addition to my mother's inspiration, I am also shaped by the signs and times of life in the 60's and 70's. Those who were living then can appreciate the intense struggles associated with segregation and the fight for equality and power. I am shaped by its popular culture and the imprint of some impressive figures. Aretha, the Supremes, Marvin Gaye and the pride everyone shared when seeing the Jackson Five on the Ed Sullivan Show. Who could forget the impact of great sports figures, Willie Mays, Jim Brown or Bob Gibson? Or, Wilt Chamberlain? Lew Alcindor's transition to Kareem Abdul Jabbar? And, my favorite, Cassius Clay, aka Muhammad Ali. Lest we forget the James Brown anthem, "I don't want nobody to give me nothing, just open the door and I'll get it myself." All of that shaped my beliefs.

No one gets anywhere alone. We all have people who God sends into our lives to nurture us, if only for a season. It took a period of despair for me to realize that God was constantly at work in my life, sending people, opportunities and obstacles to further His will. Up to that point I had deceived myself in believing that I was super special while giving God superficial acknowledgement for bringing me from abject poverty to appointments in the administration of a U.S. President and the cabinet of a governor.

Thus, I am grateful for this opportunity to reflect on the events and people that have shaped my thoughts and guided my life. President Theodore Roosevelt said, *"The credit belongs to the man who is actually in the arena, who face is marred by dust and sweat and blood, who strives valiantly; who errs and comes short again and again; because there is not effort without error and shortcomings; but who does actually strive to do the deed; who knows the great enthusiasm, the great devotion, who spends himself in a worthy cause, who at best knows in the end the triumph of high achievement and who at the worst, if he fails, at least he fails while daring greatly. So that his place shall never be with those cold and timid souls who know neither victory nor defeat."* I have experienced the triumph of high achievement and appreciate great enthusiasms and great devotion. All leaders do. However, I have known failure too. Personal failures. Not by others standards but by my own standards. Unfortunately, I went through a phase in life where I let myself down. Simply put, I was blinded by my own success. I have had to learn that God chastises those He loves. Believing that He loves me, the humiliations and setbacks I have suffered were a small price to pay for my arrogance toward Him. Fortunately, He gave me a renewed vigor and enthusiasm to put Him first in all that I do.

I am who I am because of the pivotal characters who helped steer my course. Hebrews 11 speaks of the Hall of Fame of faithful servants who diligently trusted and served God. Well, I too have a Hall of Fame. Men who God placed in my path to support my journey.

Although I have an older brother, he is 16 years older and when I was growing up, he was already on his own. So my cousin Gabe adopted me as his little brother. Thus, becoming the first member of my Hall of Fame. He was one of the few people my mother would entrust me to hang out with. He taught me literally everything I know about women, dressing and sports. He was a person who had no enemies. Everybody loved him! Gabe pushed me to play basketball which led me to dream constantly of playing basketball professionally. When I got to high school, I was fortunate enough to be the starting point guard for the freshman team and starting point guard for the junior varsity as a sophomore. I literally ate, dranked and slept basketball. However, a life altering thing happened. In a game during late October of my sophomore year I was injured. The injury resulted in a torn achilles tendon. I was out for the season. Up to then my grades had been marginal. Having to sit out for the rest of the season enabled me to really focus on my academics. When I returned for my junior year, I began to have strife and conflict with my coach over playing time. Although I was set on being a high school superstar, it wasn't in God's plan. Although I played for the next two seasons, my role and level of play was diminished. I held a grudge against my coach for 20 years after

279

high school. However, God has revealed that had the injury not occurred, I would not have become the academic student I became, nor worthy of the course solid academics placed me on. Additionally, I wrongfully blamed a man for obliterating my dreams to play college sports. Not to mention, I am only 5'9"! I thank God for revealing that the pursuit of sports was not in His plans for me.

Besides God and my mother, my Uncle Harry has had the greatest influence on me. He shaped my perspectives on life and gave me a sense of purpose. He was a brick mason and had a small construction company. I spent many hot summer days working for him. He had a love for politics and was very knowledgeable. I truly believe that were he white he would have been a United States senator. Politics was as natural as drinking water to him. When I wasn't playing basketball I spent a lot of time with him watching the evening news or current events. He literally explained the entire Watergate scandal to me and by 1976 during the nation's bicentennial celebration, we spent countless hours discussing the history of this country. He shaped my political views. He always instilled in me that college was important and that he expected me to go to college and get into politics. He used to say, "You can be the first Black governor of Louisiana." Well, I guess there's still hope!

I am first-generation college in my immediate family. Although I had explored entry in other colleges. I knew that my family couldn't afford anything more than Southern University, so I was satisfied going there. Early on, I decided that I wanted to be a journalist. Largely because of this cool black sportscaster on television. I remember saying to my mother as we were watching a game once, "that's what I want to do" and, she said, "Son, you can do and be anything you want." That sportscaster was Bryant Gumbel!

During my 12th grade year we were visited by the Army ROTC program from Southern University. I had harbored a faint interest in going to West Point at one time but that didn't materialize. By the time going to college came around, I was not thinking of joining ROTC. However, a funny thing happened on the way to registration. As I was walking across campus, literally my second day on campus, I heard someone calling my name. I turned around to look and there was a man in a khaki Army uniform calling me. He said, "Quenton, do you remember me, I am Captain Coats." I visited your high school last spring. Are you planning on joining ROTC?" Then he began to tell me that he thought I would make a fine cadet. Then he said, I could get a scholarship that paid for tuition, books and paid $100 dollars per month. Well, he suddenly got my attention! Do you know how much $100 was in 1978? Suffice it to say, I joined ROTC. Captain Coats and I became pretty close during my freshman year in ROTC.

When I returned to college to begin my sophomore year, I headed to the ROTC department to say hello to Captain Coats. Much to my chagrin, I was informed that he had transferred and that I had a new faculty advisor named Captain Day. I asked, where is he? The secretary says he is in his office and went to get him. When he appeared he reached his hand to shake mine and introduced himself, "Hi, I'm Captain Day." All I can remember is being surprised at who I was looking at. Immediately, my reply was, "Oh, I thought you were Black." Over the years he has reminded me of that several times. But thanks to now Colonel (Retired) Day, I learned a lot about myself and life. I remember fondly our counseling sessions and his ability to help me see things from multiple perspectives. He knew of my political ambition and activism on campus and appreciated it. He often referred to me as "Ike" and constantly lectured me on principles of leadership beyond that of a typical ROTC curriculum, insisting that I delve further than required into the military leadership lives of Generals McArthur, Eisenhower, Patton, Bradley and Benjamin O. Davis and what shaped their paths.

When I was completing my junior year, I expressed to then Major Day, that I was having second thoughts about joining the Army because I wanted to go to law school. He told me I could defer my entry into the military and pursue a law degree. I was fortunate to be commissioned as an Army officer, serving almost five years on active duty after graduation from college and law school as an Army attorney or "JAG" as we are commonly known. Thank God, for Captain Day and his not having the immediate prejudices against me as I had toward him. I learned a lot from him. Thanks be to God.

During my time as a journalism student, the chairman of my department, Dr. Henry Wiggins, coincidently had been born in my hometown but moved as an infant. When he heard where I was from, he asked for a meeting. It was almost like Nathaniel's question of Philip in John 1:46, "Can anything good come out of Nazareth?" when questioning Jesus's worthiness. I was a pretty good journalism student and was making a name for myself in the journalism department. My initial thoughts were that he doubted my abilities. Little did I know that this meeting would lead to my becoming a lawyer. As a result of the impression I made on Dr. Wiggins, when an opportunity developed to assign a student as a press-aide in the office of the Governor of Louisiana he chose me. This opportunity enabled me to see the communications field from a different perspective. However, due to daily interactions with lobbyists and legislators as a result of being around the Capitol press office, my interest shifted to becoming a lawyer.

Following my tenure as an intern for the governor, God presented an opportunity for assignment in another state agency. This time it was the Louisiana Department of Labor. Thus, the two Als came into my life. Al Johnson and Al Davis. Next to my Uncle Harry, Al Johnson taught me more than I could get from any classroom. Al was a guy who made it his business to know every detail about everything. He was the hippest old white man I have ever known. Al commuted from New Orleans to Baton Rouge daily. Al was fluent in different languages and despite his New Orleans ties, had spent many of his formative years in Washington, DC. Al was press secretary to the Secretary of Labor and during my tenure there which lasted my senior year of college and first year of law school, he served two secretaries.

He challenged me so much and would drop assignments on me last minute just to see how I would handle it, always complimentary that he knew I could do it. He instilled the ultimate confidence in me. But then the day came and Al sprung the big assignment on me. Whenever, the secretary would give speeches Al usually wrote them. Typically, I along with the other staff would research the information he wanted, however on this day, he said, "Quenton this one is yours." I had to write the first draft of the Secretary's speech! Talking about a confidence boost and a "defecate in your pants" moment, all wrapped into one! Suffice it to say, I wrote that one and over the course of my tenure was able to write a few more. I guess I did a pretty good job.

The two Als were good friends. Both, white guys in their 60s. Al Davis, was General Counsel for the Department of Labor. Al Johnson would find ulterior reasons to send me to Al Davis's office. I really didn't pay attention to it, nor to the fact that Al Davis had law clerks in his office. At the time, it was generally understood that first year law students should not work but I kept my job for Al Johnson as a press-aide during my first year. One day Al Johnson stopped by my cubby and said, "if you're going to be a lawyer, why are you holding down someone else's spot who wants to be press-aide?" I immediately said to myself, "man, I didn't see that coming. Al's firing me!" He then said, "Go over to see Al Davis." I went to see Al immediately and when I entered his office, he said, "Hello Quenton, Al told me you would be here today and commenced to outlining my new duties as a law clerk. Space and time does not allow me to tell Al Davis stories, but like Al Johnson, Al Davis was a good man who merits inclusion in my Hall of Fame.

When I moved to Nashville I was fortunate to meet some great people. Two have been noteworthy in my accomplishments. I have been enriched by these relationships. Samuel Howard, a successful African-American business executive who has been a forerunner in the Nashville business community and I began a close relationship when I served as a non-profit executive of an organization where he was the chairman. I have often quipped that I received an MBA from the Sam Howard School of Business. Having been around him in so many aspects, it's hard not to glean winning formulas for success. Moreover, his resiliency during a period of severe adversity was an example I had to adopt during a similar time. The second person is Charles W. Bone. I don't quite remember when I met Charles, but he became a confidant and tremendous asset over the years. I admire how he is able to win friends, influence people and see big picture unlike any other.

As with any story of triumph and adversity, adversity hurts. I am not sure whether I like the "thrill of victory" more that I hate the "agony of defeat." I suffered a very embarrassing public setback that became a real Damascus Road experience. My actions caused embarrassment and humiliation to me and my family. It was a fall from grace. Days so dark, the only thing I could do was look up to God. This ordeal forced a much closer relationship with God. In its aftermath, God has shared with me that He recognized my good and that it was necessary to get my attention by altering the things that I coveted most. He promised restoration and I trust that He will keep His promise.

I don't know what the next chapter in my life will bring, I just know there are a few more to be written. I have learned to trust God in the dark. Who I am and what I am, has been shaped by the men who God sent to nurture me and steer my course. My Hall of Fame!

Time nor space permits me to speak of others who have helped make me worthy of mention in the 50 Magnificent Men Book, but I must mention Thomas "Rocky Man" Wilkins, an alcoholic I knew when growing up. Despite his obvious flaws, he had a passion for Christ and his sincere encouragement to not be like him is a testament that God can use even the least of these! Dr. Wesley Cornelius McClure, an educator of the finest order who I had the privilege of working under while in college. He instilled in me many leadership and gentleman qualities. Lastly, but certainly not least, Michael Moss, a renaissance man and college roommate who dreamed with me back in the 80's of having this great African American law firm that touted the best and brightest among our ranks and rivaled the majority powerhouses. As a peer, he taught me a lot about not settling for second best.

If I am magnificent, I am because of God's goodness and my Hall of Fame. I have come to a realization that God can do anything with you if you allow yourself to be used by Him. To God be the glory!

Contact: qwhite@whitelawgrp.com
www.whitelawgrp.com

Magnificent Man

Ralph S. Payne

"Train up a child: and when he is old, he will not depart from it."
Proverbs 22-6

I am Ralph Payne, husband, father, grandfather, great grandfather, gospel singer, and business owner. I was born and raised in Clarksville, Tennessee and have lived here most of my life. I have been a business owner since 1968 and presently, co-own with my wife, Laura Payne, Queen City College in Clarksville and Paris, Tennessee.

Gospel singing has been a part of my life since I was a youth. I remember singing in the church choir at First Church of Nazarene when I was 12 years old and continued until I went to college. I had always been interested in music in all forms playing bass drum in the band at Clarksville High School. I earned a music scholarship to Austin Peay State University to play bass drum, not only for my musical ability, but my flashy drum stick style as well. However, mom had a different idea for me. She wanted me to attend Trevecca Nazarene College to become a minister of music in a Nazarene church. I was brought up with Proverbs 22-6 *"Train up a child: and when he is old, he will not depart from it."* Needless to say, I did as I was told at that point. Trevecca and I parted ways after my freshman year. It seems as a freshman you weren't allowed to have a car or date, and you must follow curfew. Apparently, there was a curfew earlier than the all-night gospel singings I liked to attend at the War Memorial Auditorium. After, returning many times at 2, 3, and 4:00 in the morning, I had broken curfew and the other rules one too many times. It was the suggestion from Trevecca that I take a year off that sent me back home.

I joined the Tennessee National Guard, regular Army and fulfilled 8 years of guard duty. I continued to follow gospel music and attended a concert at Gum Springs Baptist Church in Clarksville to hear the Marksmen Quartet. After talking with J.P. Harrison and David Hooker about the soon to be open position for their bass singer, I auditioned and became a member of the quartet. I traveled with the original Marksmen Quartet that originated in Seoul, Korea, for 3 years. We traveled in the professional market of gospel music during those years. It was as a member of the quartet, that I met and married Jane Heflin and we had our first child, a daughter, Cathy. I was traveling fulltime with the quartet and ended up in Memphis. After working in cabinet making and living in Memphis for a short time, we moved back to Clarksville so that I could find a more permanent and long term career. Thus, the decision to attend barber school at Nashville Barber College. I graduated from Barber College in 1960 and continued to sing with the quartet as much as possible. My new barbering career began at Fort Campbell. I cut for the Military Club Systems barber shops. You could get a haircut for just 90 cents at that time. I worked there from 1961 - 1965.

During this time, the Vietnam War broke out and in 1965 a large majority of Fort Campbell soldiers were sent to the conflict. Once again, a change would be required to be able to support our family. You see, our second child, a son, Michael, had been born and the need to continue my barbering career led me to Nashville, Tennessee to work for Mr. C.C. Sanders, President of the International Barber's Union. While I was working there, the barber's union contracted with the National Department of Labor awarding us a grant to upgrade regular barbershops to men's styling shops. We were to train as many barbers in men's hairstyling as we could. I auditioned for the training position and was sent to Indianapolis to complete training as an instructor. I returned to Nashville and trained 280 barbers to become men's hairstylists in Tennessee. Once my contract was completed, I opened my first men's hairstyling shop with a friend and partner, Al Cravens. We were located on Music Row, three doors down from RCA Studios. Our customers were mostly Country Music Stars, musicians, and record producers.

Listening to and singing Gospel music continued to be a passion of mine. Upon returning to Nashville I renewed my friendship with Glen Carvel and Bill Lamb becoming the bass singer that formed the new Marksmen Quartet. We added Ron Lovvarn as piano player and Jimmy Haley as our first tenor. We were fortunate to perform countrywide and sang some of my favorite songs to this day. However, a career in music takes a toll on the family requiring many hours and days apart. Since I also was a business owner, the time involved to continue my music career was overwhelming. The decision was made to move our family to Clarksville to raise our children. With this decision, came the opportunity for me to open the first hairstyling shop at the Royal York Hotel in downtown Clarksville. After two years in the downtown area, a very good friend, Dr. Wilson, gave me the opportunity to buy a building next door to the former Big K on Riverside Dr. to expand the business from a two chair shop to six chairs. God blessed and business was good! "Hair" Men's Style Shop was born! I have worked with and trained many barbers that have become very successful shop owners.

Along with this good fortune, the next several years also proved to be challenging. We experienced many ups and downs.

After 23 years, our marriage ended in divorce. I no longer attended church and was not relying on my faith to lead me.

On October 3rd, 1983, a life-changing event occurred...a massive heart attack that took me out of the barbershop full-time. Doctor's orders were: no more cigarettes, less stress, and no more cutting hair behind a chair 80 hours a week. During the time of the hospitalization and March 6, 1984, Queen City Hair College was established. We opened the doors with 20 students and have educated more than I can count since then.

It wasn't until I met my current wife, Laura, that I let God back in my life. Along with Laura, came four children: Brandie, Eddie, Steve, and Anna. We attended church together and I began thinking about singing again. Laura and I were married on May 5, 1985. I became Pops to Laura's children, our children. Laura was instrumental in helping me to follow a more faithful path. Ronnie Page from the Sewanne River Boys called and asked me to join their gospel quartet as the bass singer. Once again, I was singing professionally. We were the showcase act at the Ozark Mountain Theatre in Eureka Springs, Arkansas. Every afternoon we performed at the theatre and then at night I was an actor in the Great Passion Play.

Following our contractual obligations, I returned to Clarksville and barbered for a year. Laura was the chief administrator of the cosmetology school. In the early nineties, we were presented with the opportunity to buy a business college in Greenville, Mississippi. We decided that I should go to Greenville to manage the new college. Along with this decision came a name change for our businesses from Queen City Hair College to just Queen City College. I lived in Greenville during the week and commuted to Clarksville every Friday night at 10:30 returning Sunday night to start the cycle all over again. This merry-go-round lasted about four years. This was too much for us all and we closed the business college but expanded our school in Clarksville to include a barber program. Adding this additional license doubled our business.

In 2005, we lost our daughter Anna and adopted her 10 year old son Aaron. As painful as some of our life experiences are, God sees us through and blesses us in ways we certainly were not expecting! Becoming a father "again" at the age of 67 is one of those unexpected blessings.

I continued to sing gospel music, singing semi-professional with other quartets. Governor Bredesen also appointed me to the Tennessee State Barber Board for the years 2011, 2012, and 2013. Our business continued to grow. God continued to bless us and we moved to our present location at 1594 Fort Campbell Blvd. We have been at this location now 20 years seeing enough growth so that we are taking a leap of faith by adding a branch location in Paris, Tennessee.

Although I have dedicated many hours to the operation and success of our businesses, I still find enjoyment in singing and being a part of gospel music. I don't travel as much as I used to, but you can find me every Sunday morning at Russwood Baptist Church singing an occasional solo and always in the choir. At 76, I haven't slowed much and have been very fortunate to have done everything I've ever wanted to, except retire. I don't see that happening anytime soon! I'm not complaining!

The other day a friend gave me a scripture that really stuck with me. This scripture in some ways pertains to my life as God has given me the opportunity to be a successful gospel singer and a successful business person with the help of my beautiful wife Laura.

Thou shalt also decree a thing, and it shall be established unto thee: and the light shall shine upon thy ways.

Job 22:28

Contact: QCC1594@aol.com

Richard "Reason" Garrett

"Before I formed you in the womb I knew you, before you were born I set you apart; I appointed you as a prophet to the nations."
~ Jeremiah 1:5

Before I was born, God told my father to name me Jeremiah and gave him a vision of us ministering together. My mom wanted her first born named after her husband so they settled on Richard Jeremiah Garrett. In the beginning, I was passionate about serving Christ and would witness every opportunity I had. If you coughed or sneezed around me, you were likely to be the recipient of me laying hands on you with fervent prayer for healing.

Growing up, my dad was serving active duty in the Army and pastoring while my mom was a reservist. Both loved me and demonstrated in their own way, but I felt loved most by my grandmother. I still remember the tragic night that she passed away as if it was yesterday. She was hooked up to breathing machines and feeding tubes as the alarm kept going off. My parents frantically calling 911 to get the ambulance to intervene. I drew upon every faith passage I could muster and believed with all my heart that God would heal her. As the emergency crew rushed into her room and closed the door, I just knew that she would be okay. That is until they left her room without the same sense of urgency with a sheet draped over her body. As reality set in that my prayer went unanswered, my faith began to crumble and resentment began to settle in for God.

Over the years I began to grow distant from God. I neither felt loved by Him nor my parents. The enemy had tricked my mind into believing that my parents didn't genuinely love me unconditionally. I felt as though they merely tolerated me because it was the Christian thing to do and as pastor pops had to lead by example. As for God, I questioned His credibility in going against His Word and taking the one person from who I felt loved me unconditionally. In my rebellion I caused my parents a whole lot of unnecessary grief and battled bouts of depression off and on for years.

Although my parents constantly disciplined, they were always in my corner. However, my mind was so warped that I didn't really appreciate it. I even began to resent gifts that they gave me because I viewed them as methods to control my life. It would seem like whenever I didn't do something exactly the way my dad felt it should be done, he would limit or take away something that he gave me. So I became determined to make my own way in life so that I could have the things that I wanted with no strings attached. There was only room for one captain to control my destiny and in my eyes I was smart and strong enough for the task.

By the time I reached high school, I was a semi accomplished thief. Having built my confidence stealing sports cards and fake jewelry from stores, I began boosting electronics and reselling them in school. Getting caught occasionally never deterred me. I just became determined to figure out a better way not to get caught the next time. I eventually graduated from stores to breaking into houses and stealing cars. After getting arrested at the age of 16 for grand theft auto, I decided to move from theft to selling drugs to make extra money on the side while still working two legit jobs.

Eventually the street lifestyle started to catch up with me and I got in too deep. With my future looking bleak, I went ahead and enlisted in the Marines for a fresh start. While I successfully changed my environment, I never changed who I was on the inside. It wasn't long before long before old habits resurfaced and I began to surround myself with individuals who shared my twisted ideals. We began with stealing gaming systems to resell then gradually moved into selling drugs. Then started robbing other drug dealers as we began to work alongside established gangs in the area. I even had hustles going using my BAH from being married to buy property then rent it to low income single mothers that I was cool with to have section 8 pay my rent while I lived there as well. My master plan was to use the drug money/robbery money with the section 8 rent and BAH to pay off the house quickly then purchase another home and repeat the process until I had at least 3 to 5 homes paid off.

On May 1, 2004 in Jacksonville, NC it all caught up to me. I was arrested and charged with possession with intent to distribute 7.3 ounces of marijuana. I stayed in county jail for 2 weeks until the Marines took over the charges and decided to make an example out of me. I was imprisoned in the Camp Lejuene Base Brig to await sentencing. During this time period, I continued to pull strings from the inside and traffic drugs. There were even guards who ended up failing urinalysis and sent to solitary confinement for collaborating with us.

Then came a day of reckoning for me. I frequently spent time in solitary confinement for violating various rules. One particular evening as I sat in solitary watching my world crumble, the depression I often felt growing up began to consume me. I had lost control of life on the outside to the point that my enterprise completely fell apart leaving me nothing to look

295

forward to once I was released. The only thing that I had to take the edge off was nutmeg and various pills we often traded. It was in my darkest hours while I was at rock bottom where I had no choice but to look up. I began to identify myself with the Prodigal son who squandered the resources given to him by his father. God showed me how I misused the gifts and talents that He gave me for my own self ambitious, then gave me a vision for how I could use them to benefit my community and build His Kingdom. The concept of the LEAP Organization was birthed inside of me but it would several years before I began striving to make the vision into a reality.

In the meanwhile, while I awaited my trial date I learned another valuable lesson. I remembered the impact getting that collect phone call from me in Onslow County Jail had on my mother who as result fell down a flight of stairs. Although a few members from the crew I started kept in contact, it was my family who visited me the most and did their best to pick up the pieces for me of life outside the walls. The lesson learned was that it's not just the inmate that does the time, but also his family and loved ones because a piece of them is locked away with him. My parents were struggling being able to hold their heads up in church because of the heavy heart they had from my predicament. My younger sister became determined to go into law school because the only way she felt she could help her big brother was to become a lawyer so that she could represent me someday.

From that day on, I became determined that if I didn't care enough about myself to make positive decisions then I would let my family be the reason. Upon being reintegrated into general population, I discontinued trafficking banned substances in the facility and was often questioned. Fellow inmates noticed that I seemed to always have a reason why not to continue negative activities resulting in me inheriting the nickname Reason.

As my trial date got closer the JAG prosecutor offered my defense attorney a deal. They wanted to sentence me to 3 years if I pled guilty and 2 years if I snitched on fellow Marines involved in my enterprises. According to military law, my sentence carried a maximum sentence of 8 years. With my faith in God renewed and our relationship growing stronger, I decided to lean not with my own understanding and trust in Him for direction. God told me that the truth would set me free so I declined both deals and advised my attorney that I wanted to give an unsworn statement prior to sentencing. During the trial, one would have thought I was a terrorist with the way the prosecutor described me as they expressed their desire for the judge to give me 6 years. With so much uncertainty of not having the protection of a pretrial agreement, I felt peace in knowing that God would not give me more than I could bear. After taking complete ownership of my actions and sharing my renewed faith in God and plans to redeem myself, I recited the following poem that I had written for trial:

Trapped in a game where there is no clear winner
Which only has two paths to take, that of the righteous and that of the sinner
With principalities waging war at every fork in the road
As my eyes scan each path for the shorter route to the goal
But finding out too late that taking the easy way out has put my life on hold.
What happened to all those friends who said they'd always be there?
Turns out the family you ran from were the only ones who cared
The money, cars, girls, and crib all gone in the blink of an eye
Leaving you worse than what you started with and all you can do is wonder how and why
But deep down knowing the truth of how things turned out this way
With nothing else to do or say
Your only choice being to give it up to God and pray
For His grace and mercy to make it another day'

The end result of the trial was the judge sentencing me 2 years confinement which was a blessing considering the circumstances. Had I had accepted the plea bargain the judge would have more than likely sentenced me to the max sentence so that if I got into any trouble while serving the rest of my time they could have pulled my plea bargain from me.

I spent the remainder of my sentence getting closer to God, witnessing to other inmates, and trafficking evangelistic reading material. I also learned a lot about real estate investing, wrote my first book, and started my business management degree with Penn Foster.

Upon being released in January of 2006, I attempted to apply all my lessons learned and walk the right path, but ran into difficulties finding employment as a convicted felon. The only job I could get was working 3 hours a day, 7 days a week for $7 an hour as a custodian on Ft Campbell, KY. I was okay with these humble beginnings until I discovered my girlfriend at the time was pregnant. I was barely making ends meet and was determined to be a provider for my new family so I began trafficking drugs and engaging in other criminal acts. Things began to look up for us, I was able to purchase a car and get a place for us to live, however I was constantly at war with myself on what I knew was right and what If felt I had to do for my family.

One day I called my parents' house to speak with my dad but my mom told me he was at Faith Outreach Church preparing to preach. After fulfilling an order, I felt the desire to see pops in action. I at least had the common sense to leave my firearm in the car, but brought several pills into the church. As my dad began wrapping up his sermon, I felt God pulling at my heart and before I knew it, I was walking down the isle towards the pulpit. In front of the congregation I gave my dad the pills inside of my shooters glove. While this was an impactful experience, it was just the beginning. From that day forward, I quit selling controlled substances and gave up claim to some of the product that I had fronted several colleagues. This placed me back into a predicament of working a dead end job that couldn't adequately support my family. As a result, I turned to home invasions and robbing other drugs dealers.

One fateful evening, a home invasion went wrong resulting in my colleague being shot 3 times. After taking him to the hospital, one of the guys with us got nervous when questioned by the detectives and shared more information than he should have. As a result, I was incarcerated for 2 weeks until his story conveniently changed and the charges were dropped. While in there, I came to realize that I was relying on my own strength to provide for my family and that it would require me to completely trust in God to be a provider. Another insight was that God's grace is for everyone, but his mercy is more selective. God's mercy for my stubbornness was running out and if I didn't change soon, I would be dead or facing serious time which would really place my unborn son in a bad situation.

Upon my release, my dad reached out to me to help with a basketball program at First Missionary Baptist Church to work with the police department to help at risk youth. Several months later, as I was walking around the track at the Emmanuel Family Life Center, I felt God telling me this was good ground to plant the ministry that he placed in my heart years ago. So I immediately shared the vision with Pastor Harris who embraced it with joy. He gave me keys to the facility and to start the Leap Organization. Through God placing key individuals like Pastor Tommy Vallejos to mentor me and connect me to various resources the vision became a reality.

Over the years God has continued to provide provision for the vision. Leap has gone from being a mentoring program with 8 kids that I funded from my own pocket to a 501c3 youth development program that has served well over 763 youth in Montgomery, Robertson, and Cheatham counties, that has received state, county, and city funding to assist us with instilling positive moral growth and sustainable life skills in youth. We have also acquired a 24,000 square foot facility that was formerly Daymar College and converted it into our youth development headquarters and small business incubator/entrepreneurial center.

Some of my other achievements were graduating with Honors from Austin Peay State University with a Bachelors' in Public Management, obtaining my real estate license, and being elected as the Clarksville Ward 1 City Councilman. I am also married to Laquvia Garrett and have 4 children; Chasidye, Jaylen, Charity, and Trevon.

As I reflect on my journey, I have undergone several highs and lows. Most of the lows were a result of poor decisions that I made when I lost sight of the lessons I had learned along the way and got too busy for God. Thankfully He never got too busy for me and often used circumstances to humble me from my false sense of self sufficiency. Even good things can be perverted and come between us and God, making true praise impossible. We are often not aware that we rely on something other than God until that something is taken from us.

God does have a perfect plan for our lives. We may look at the circumstances surrounding us and think we've been standing still forever in one painful spot. The more we pray and cry for God to help us, the more the circumstances seem to pile up. The turning point can't come until we begin to praise God for our situation instead of crying for Him to take it all away. What happens next is God's move, not ours. We as Christians need to remind ourselves frequently that God is in total control. It is easy to fall into the trap of thinking that we have the power to manipulate or change a situation simply by reciting a certain form of a prayer.

Shifting from our own strength to God's doesn't come easy to any of us. We may rely on Him in one area, but not in another or we trust Him more in some things than others. Turning ourselves over to Him completely is a lifetime process. We think we have done it, then out pops that old ego still trying to run the show. How do we get to the point where God is all our strength? As long as we use our own strength, God can't use His through us. Only when we surrender our strength to Him will we discover what David meant when he said, "Blessed is the man whose

300

strength is in You…" (Psalm 84:5 NKJV)

Our own strength is only a false illusion; still we cling to it and hate to give it up. If we want God to be our strength, we must be able to say to Him, "I surrender to You. From now on I want you to be my only strength." If you say that and then find yourself getting more and more tired, praise God; He is letting you wear out your own strength, and when it is all gone, you will be where you ought to be dependent on God for everything. At last you can say with David, "The Lord is my strength and my shield, my heart trusted in Him,, and I am helped; therefore my heart greatly rejoices, and with my song I will praise Him." (Psalm 28:7 NKJV)

Contact: richard@reason4clarksville.com
www.reason4clarksville.com
www.reason4homes.com
www.leaporg.net

Reverend Dr. Aaron Laron Chapman

I Can Do All Things through Christ Who Strengthens Me"
Phil 4:13

A Long Shot

The story of my inception unravels in the year 1981. In this year several peculiar events transpired; Roger Smith became the CEO of General Motors, the infamous Bob Marley died of cancer, the assassination attempt was made on Pope John Paul II's life, and on a lighter note the debut of the first IBM computer was displayed. 1981 was a year of highs and lows, smiles and tears, but one person's cry was predestined and rang in the corridors of a hospital that brought cheer to a family because of the birth of Aaron Laron Chapman.

I was born in the city affectionately labeled as the "Motor City" Detroit Michigan. Born as the youngest child among two brothers and two sisters to Reverend Joseph and Faye Chapman, the circumstances of my birth yet baffle me and others even until this very day. You see, there should have been a burial planned as well as a birthing the day I entered into this world. My parents were informed when they discovered my conception that it would be life threatening to my mother. She was told that at the rhythm of 98% surety she would not survive the delivery (which means I was lethal, but not in a good way). But just like my selfless and loving mother she continued in her pregnancy with me. During the pregnancy there was a lot of prayer and petitioning toward God by my father and mother because of what appeared to be a pending peril, but God answered in a powerful fashion.

Almost in a Hebraic formulae God answered with the type of answer he gave Abraham or Moses; God told my father that the child my mother was carrying was a boy and that my name was to be Aaron. This was before everyone had any access to foreknowledge of the child's gender, but my father believed God and did what he was instructed to do. The day of delivery arrived and with my mother's life on the line following the birth pains and procedures, my mother and I made it through it by the grace of God. My presence on this planet was a long shot because my mother could have made the decision not to have me.

As I grew older my father informed me of these events and I always wondered why did the "good Lord" as he would say it in his preeminent way name me Aaron. I would soon discover a piece of the puzzle when I entered into the fourth grade. I viewed myself as an easy going, humble, extravert who yet possessed a shy personality. *Don't ask my wife Valarie about the shy part, she could create several arguments against that!*

In the fourth grade we had a split class of 4th and 5th graders. The students were placed in reading sectors to check the fluency of our reading to see where we would be placed. Did I not mention I was very shy especially around one girl in particular named Bobbie Romans, my kindergarten sweet heart. It was my turn to read in my sector and Bobbie was front and center. I begin to get hot inside, the words in my head somehow would not transfer to my mouth with the fluency I knew I possessed. I stumbled, paused and whatever could have gone wrong did. I failed in the most miserable way! I was then misdiagnosed that I needed reading lab. In my mind I said wait a minute I'm just shy and I'm being penalized for that. I asked myself why am I in reading lab? This was painful to digest as a child yet providentially necessary.

I became angry after that failure and it gave me fervor, I became furious, but yet flooded with a fight and drive that I'd never felt. It was my personal mission to prove them wrong whoever it was that was in my way. I wanted to prove I could be above average not just that. I had my eye on greatness! If there was a defining moment in my life this was it; the baby that was lethal in the womb desired to become lethal in a positive way for the Lord.

It was in this moment every chance I could get I ran with the giants. I was the youngest student on the safety patrol for Courtis Elementary in the history of the school and eventually the captain in my final year. I played basketball and was selected as the captain of the team. I possess the longest standing basketball hot shot record, 64 points in a minute. I was the youngest Sunday school teacher at my home church. I decided whatever I desired I was willing to work at it and walk with God if even alone to get it. Life for me has always been a long shot, but it was a shot I was willing to take even if I failed to get there.

As I matured, my grades were above average and I developed a love for basketball. I learned from the game how to develop more humility which was connected to my life journey of fulfilling my God given capacity. I had to listen very attentively to my brothers Fred and Joe. My coach was my brother Joe. I wanted to be just like him because you see he invented swag. What drew me to him was his determination. He hated to lose and if he did, he found a way to win. I remember him making me dribble in the dark in our basement which taught me to dribble without looking at the ball. I remember running in the winter with a lead vest on. I remember rain, snow, or sleet we played and practiced basketball. This taught me how to become extremely disciplined physically, mentally and even spiritually. It wasn't just a game it, became a lifestyle for me. Even while all of this was going on, I always had looming in my head even up to the point of my freshman year of high school, why did God name me Aaron?

At the tender age of sixteen I discovered why as I attended revivals. While at Shady Grove Baptist Church, I heard the voice of God saying to me you don't belong down here, you belong up there. I shook it off because I knew I admired my father Reverend Joseph Chapman and my Pastor, Rev. Tellis Chapman. After hearing this voice off and on for two years it began to get stronger when I turned 18 years of age.

During my senior year I was aiming for and was on track to start in the position of point guard for Murray Wright High School. I was stronger than ever, could dunk at 5'9 and could not miss anywhere on the floor. I was quick and could pass extremely well. I just came off of averaging 40 points in a gym tournament and was going into summer practice and in a pickup game I broke my finger and God spoke to me saying "Now will you preach?" From that day the love I had for basketball was like a transferring of documents on a desk top, it left from basketball and begin transferring into preaching. One night during my pastor's anniversary, Bishop Edgar Vann preached a sermon entitled "I just want to make God happy" and that night I knew what I needed to do. I discovered why God lead my father who is a preacher to call his son Aaron. It was because I was raised up and torn, pushed, and stretched to become a sermonic soothing sound in a sinister society. Rev. Aaron Chapman was born and the transfer was complete. The Lord removed the love of basketball and made me a diehard fanatic of preaching.

There is absolutely nothing in this world that I want to be besides a preacher. I eat, sleep, drink, and dream preaching. I have a work out regiment almost to the level of a professional athlete to help me have the strength for preaching. I diet based on preaching, I read based on preaching, and I prepare myself for the cause of Christ.

This mindset at 18 drove me to obtain three degrees and stand on the holy hill of God's grace with an earned doctoral degree at 29 years of age.

If someone asked me what your life means, I want to be a signal of pregnant possibility. I want for people to view me as the symbol and sign of hard work. I want people to follow God diligently because of my devotion and integrity which I exhibit for him. I want some kid that's out there to prove people wrong and wipe out the clamoring nay saying voices that believe your conquering could never be a conscious reality. I am the faceless person that's in the crowd that doesn't mind praying and pushing his way toward the progressive pedestal of life needing no pity but just an opportunity from providence to show I will give him the praise when I get the prize in my palm.

Currently I am the professor at 7 seminaries and bible colleges. I am the author of three books. I have 150 mentees in preaching ministry. I have through the grace of God been the conduit for the inception of Dedicated to Christ Church in Ecorse and lead humbly as her Senior Pastor. I am a husband to the lovely intelligent Valarie Chapman and the proud parent of Aaron and Destiny Chapman. Yet, I am still hungry for more.

As Les Brown would say it, "I want my life to matter. I want to make my mark." I decided I would not follow another drummer's beat or someone else's path but the chorographer and craver of my destiny came from the hands of God. What a season for the people of God to do more; what a season for innovative ideas; what a season for life transforming deliberate action. Wherever your life is you can compare it to my life and where I started from. I was a long shot, but remember if I never took the shot I would not know how far God could bring me.

I humbly ask you the question, what is the difference between me and you? I am flesh and blood and I give you this challenge, what shots aren't you taking?

Contact: dedicatedchristchurch.com

Magnificent Man

Rick Joyner

"Anything Worth Doing, Is Worth Doing Right The First Time".

I grew up in inner-city Memphis, Tennessee. My father was a wood worker who made things like baseball bats, walking canes, police sticks, etc. In addition, he was a pastor who founded Jackson Avenue Missionary Baptist Church, a small storefront in the heart of our poor community. He was my savior. What I mean is, whenever I was in trouble and mom wanted to whip me, all I had to do was stay away from her long enough for dad to get home then run to his lap and he protected me. I remember him going out of the house sometimes with his NAACP badge on. The civil rights struggle was at its height and my dad was doing what he could to make a difference.

On August 26, 1969, everything changed. My father dropped dead of a heart attack at work. Even now it still seems surreal, but the fact of the matter was dad was gone. My mom was left to raise three children and to take care of her two sick parents who had moved in with us from Mississippi. I was only eight years old and really didn't understand everything that was happening, but I did know daddy was gone.

At that time mom only had a part time job at the neighborhood hardware store, which was in not nearly enough to support three children and two senior citizens. So mama started selling Avon, and did so for over 23 years. She was truly a phenomenal woman. In spite of all of her responsibilities, she still found time to help others in the neighborhood. On the first and third of every month, mom would load up her car with people from the community that did not have cars, and take them to take care of their business like paying their bills, grocery shopping etc.

I didn't realize for a long time how much mama gave up for us. When I was about 35 years old, it hit me. Mama never brought a lot of men around us, and she never remarried. She took us to church including Sunday School and B.T.U. She never complained and always remained the jokester. I remember helping her bag up her Avon orders, load them in the car, and go with her to make deliveries. When my brother got too old for the paper route it was passed down to me. As a paperboy I was able to win lots of prizes including trips to St. Louis and New Orleans. Mom always encouraged me that if I really wanted to do something, I could.

As the years went by I watched my grandparents wither away. I became very familiar with death and the pain that it brings. But I always had my music to comfort me. I began playing drums in the sixth grade and singing in the church choir around the same time. I simply loved music. I can remember the Christmas when mom bought me a GE green plastic record player. I was so happy, and even more so because she also included the Christmas albums by the Temptations and the Jackson 5. Those classics are still part of my collection today, only now they're on CD.

As I continued to excel in music into high school, the choir teacher got wind of the fact that I could sing a little and sought me out to audition for the choir. From there I went on to audition for the West Tennessee and the Allstate choruses, and made them both each year I tried out. Music was just in my DNA.

I was offered double scholarships in choir and band at several colleges, but chose to attend Memphis State University. That is where I started to lose my mind. While music was so much a part of me, I didn't want to live the life of a musician. My idea was to become a CPA, get married, and have two kids and a dog and the house with the white picket fence. Little did I know the battle had started to wage inside of me.

Eventually I started DJing in little juke joints around the city, and for parties on campus. The attention I would get started to feed my ego. DJing was a natural thing for me. The better I got, the more fun I would have. Drinking, drugs, and women became the menu every weekend. In the process I decided to take a broadcasting course at a vocational school. Again it was just a natural thing for me and after finishing, I started doing radio shows on the jazz station at Memphis State. People were listening to me and I started to get encouragement from some of the program directors at commercial stations in the city. Then I got my first real radio gig doing overnight weekends at Magic 101 FM. Life was so good, or so I thought.

After getting in radio was when the partying really started. The perks of being popular can be good, and they can also be very dangerous. Because of my gift I was able to excel in my career at a great pace. I worked for several stations in Memphis, then went on to Jackson, Tennessee, Nashville, St. Louis and back again. But everywhere I went my partying continued to escalate as well. I did not realize that I was headed down a path of self-destruction. I thought I knew it all. I thought I could handle it all. Eventually I got too big for my britches, and God had to put me in check.

I always knew that God had something for me to do, but I kept running from him for many years. You see, Satan had become my best friend and I kept putting God on the back burner. But I'm so thankful that one day I was able to look up and hear God's voice speaking to me. And once I finally accepted the fact that I had to be obedient, things really started to change for me.

311

When I became committed to utilizing the gifts that God had given me for his glory, I really started to understand more about life. I came to learn that all of the things that my mother did for us helped to shape us into the adults that we became. And even though I strayed away from her teachings, I was able to come back because of them.

I was so humbled when the American Gospel Quartet Convention named me "Favorite Network Personality of the Year" for 5 consecutive years. After that, I went on to receive numerous certificates of appreciation, plaques, and recognitions. In 2004, I was inducted into the National Broadcasters Hall of Fame in Akron, Ohio. In 2013, I was nominated for the Stellar Award for gospel announcer of the year. That year I did receive the Reach Award for Listener's Choice. Then last year, I was nominated for the Stellar Award again. And now for the third year in a row I am nominated for announcer of the year. I'm so thankful to even be considered and I thank God for all that He continues to do in my life.

For over five years now, I have had the distinct honor of working closely with the most recognizable and influential individual in gospel music; Amb. Dr. Bobby Jones. Each week I do research, song selections, write scripts and oversee the recording of Dr. Jones as he reads the scripts for the Bobby Jones Gospel Countdown. Working with such an iconic figure has certainly been enlightening to me. I've seen Dr. Jones do a full day of television tapings, then stay up late into the night watching film and editing. His work ethic has inspired me to do more. One of the other great attributes of Dr. Jones is his humbleness. I've been around many celebrities throughout my career, but none quite as down to earth as Dr. Jones. While he is a consummate professional at what he does, he is also a very kind person with a heart for people.

It can truthfully be said that Rick Joyner is a voice in more ways than one. Embodying the elements of class, wit, and compassion for humanity, Joyner tactfully makes a difference

312

wherever he goes. Known nationwide as an eloquent broadcaster, speaker and businessman, Joyner's broadcast career began in Memphis, TN (where he was reared) over 32 years ago. He attended Memphis State University, majoring in Broadcast Journalism, and later honing his skills by working for several Memphis radio stations including **K-97, WLOK,** and **Magic 101.**

Joyner has served in many capacities within the industry including **Music Director and Program Director** in Jackson and Nashville, Tennessee; St. Louis, Missouri and Tupelo, Mississippi to name a few. In Atlanta he served as **Music Director** and host of "The Praise Party" for **"The Light"** on the Sheridan Gospel Network for seven years, and in 2004 was named **Sr. V.P. of Urban and Traditional Acquisitions & Programming for Gospel Music Channel.**

Joyner has been lauded well for his accomplishments. As such, some honors include induction into the **National Broadcasters Hall of Fame,** as well as recipient of the **Favorite Network Personality of the Year** award four consecutive years. Additionally, in 2013 he was recipient of the **REACH AWARD for "Listener's Choice", presented by Central South Distribution.**

In 2003, Joyner became greatly involved in community service issues throughout the country by forming **The Rick Joyner Foundation.** This non-profit 501(c) (3) organization focuses on providing assistance to single-parent families and under-privileged children, as well as providing resources for those addicted to drugs and alcohol so that they may obtain the proper help.

Over the years, Joyner has become well versed in the **Financial Services** arena as well. His new found passion for educating people on how money really works allows him the opportunity to empower individuals and their families, thus potentially increasing the positive financial outcome for generations.

Currently, **The Rick Joyner Experience** is the **Morning Drive** show on **The Sheridan Gospel Network**, and Rick is working with **Gospel Music icon Dr. Bobby Jones** as Creative Writer, Director, and Producer of **The Bobby Jones Gospel Countdown**, America's #1 Syndicated Gospel Countdown Show.

Rick is frequently called upon to host a variety of functions including live seminars, workshops, recordings, concerts, listening parties, banquets, etc. His extensive knowledge, comedic style, and impeccable timing, along with the ability to hold an audience's attention, make him one of the most sought after in the industry.

October 22, 2014, my mama went home to be with the Lord. It was a day that I had dreaded for so many years. I didn't know how I would react or respond, but I'm grateful to God that He has kept me. When I received my first nomination for the Stellar Award, Mama went with me that year. And even though I didn't win the Stellar she celebrated with me for winning the Reach Award. She was my biggest fan and always encouraged me. I thank God for giving me the kind of mom He did. She was the greatest woman I've ever known. So as God continues to bless me, I remember every day that it's not about me. I'm just working on my dash. Our headstones have the year we were born and the year we die, with a dash between them. The – represents what we did in this life. My goal every day is to try to make a difference in the lives of others, to have a positive impact on someone, to be a blessing to someone and to leave a person with a smile. I pray that my – can just be half the size of Mama's, because hers was a mile-long.

Contact: 1rickjoyner@gmail.com
WWW.THERJE.COM
www.therickjoynerexperience.com
https://www.facebook.com/pages/The-Rick-Joyner-Experience/341752492508852?ref=hl

Russ Murphy

For I know the plans I have for you," declares the Lord, "plans to prosper you and not to harm you, plans to give you hope and a future. - Jeremiah 29:11

I was becoming suspicious of my mother's giddy laughter on that frosty Halloween night in Hubbard, TX. I later discovered while my sisters and I went house to house she was in the process of drinking a full pint of vodka. By the time we headed home her words were slurred and her eyes were barely open. I knew that the ride home would be the terrifying; maybe even deadly. From the back seat I tried to calmly instruct her where she needed to turn to get to our house. As we approached the street I prayed as I said, "Now, mom, here's our turn. You need to slow down mom. Here it is. You need to turn. You've got to turn. Now!!" As my words died out she slowly slumped over in the front seat with her foot jammed on the gas pedal as our car hurtled out into the darkness on the Waco highway. We frantically tried to wake her and pull her back up, but it was no use because she was unconscious. I didn't know what to do. From the back seat I couldn't reach the brakes, but I knew I had stop the car before we ran off the road or worse yet, hit another vehicle. Without thinking I lunged forward and rammed the gear shift into park. The car filled with the smoke of hot oil as grinding gears moaned and groaned before we came to a halt. The only problem was that we were on the left side of the road on a hill putting us in the direct path of an oncoming car. Thank God two young men drove up and pushed our car to the right shoulder and then one waited with us while the other went to get our dad. When we got home my mom and dad continued their nightly episodes of yelling and fighting which was even more frightening than the darkness of the Waco highway.

My mom and dad were madly in love, but alcohol robbed them and us of a loving, stable home. If this was what marriage was all about then I wanted nothing to do with it. However, my grandparents lived just 3 blocks away and I saw them every day and spent the night each Saturday so I could go to church with them on Sundays. Over the years I'm sure I spent the night with them hundreds of times and I observed the same ritual take place every morning. At 6 am my granddad would go to my grandmother's bedside, lean down and kiss her right on mouth. That was the grossest thing I had ever seen and thought there ought to be a law that prohibits any mouth kissing after the age of 70. Of course, I feel different about that now. After the kiss they would talk and even though I couldn't understand the words I could tell by the soft, gentle tones they were speaking kind, encouraging words to each other. I often wondered what my granddad said to my grandmother. Years later I found out.

My wife, Saralyn, was a school teacher and went to bed around 8:45 each night and I would always tuck her into bed. I would kneel by her bedside and put my hand on her shoulder and talk to her. I'd tell her how wonderful she was to me. How blessed I was that she was my best friend and wife. Then I'd pray for her. I was committed to being sure that the last words Saralyn heard every night would be the voice of her husband praising her and praying for her. One night, in the hallway after our "time" together I heard the Lord speak to my heart saying, "Russ, I know you've always wanted to know what your granddad said to your grandmother." I said, "I really have, Lord. I've always wondered about that." I could almost see Him smile as He told me, "Well, I'm going to tell you what he said." I stopped and held my breath because I knew I was about the learn something profound. That's when the Lord said, "Russ, the words your granddad said to your grandmother.......were the same words you just spoke to Saralyn. You've had the answer the entire time in your heart, you just didn't realize it."

After my parents divorced I made a promise to God. (Now, remember I was just a normal 15 year old boy who played in a rock band, was the starting right half back on our junior high football team, ran track and tormented my little sisters.) My promise to God was that if I ever married that I was going to be a great husband, not just a good husband, but the very best I could ever be. Several months later I met Saralyn who 7 years later would be my wife. I made the promise of "what" (being a great husband) before the Lord ever showed me the "who."

Saralyn and I started our relationship as friends. Jack and Jill rather than Romeo and Juliet. I was amazed by the fact she knew Jesus as Savior, Lord and Friend. I knew Him as Savior and Lord (Lord most of the time) but I didn't understand the friendship part. For 6 months our friendship grew deeper making our commitment to Christ and our friendship as the foundation of our relationship. Not long after becoming friends I asked the Lord if He would one day teach me about His friendship. He began answering that prayer immediately but on June 16th, 2014 He showed me what the friendship of Christ really meant.

On Sunday, June 15th, we were staying in the small garage apartment of some friends in Lubbock, TX. Saralyn was washing up for bed as I serenaded her. I was so filled with the joy of being married to my best friend for over 40 years and I asked, "Hey, Sweetheart, what time is it?" She came out of the bathroom, looked at her watch and said, "Its 10:15, why do you want to know?" I smiled and answered, "Mark it down; at 10:15 pm on June 15th is the happiest moment in my life. I have been so blessed by the Lord because He gave me you, my dearest one, to walk hand in hand together through this world." We both wiped a few tears away and as she hugged me she said, "I believe the same thing; I've never been so happy in my entire life." As we held each other we had no idea in less than 6 hours, our lives would be changed forever.

At 4 am that next morning Saralyn sat up in bed and said, "Russ, I think something is wrong." She indicated that there was some pain near her heart and upper back. I knew it was very unlikely that she was having a heart attack because she exercised every day, ate healthy, no bad habits or family background of heart disease. I called 911 and just a few minutes later we were on our way to the hospital to run tests to see if they could determine what was wrong. All the tests came back negative and Saralyn was released at 6 pm that afternoon. She was not in any great pain and told me that she'd like to have some soup. As she sat down at the dinner table her head tilted forward and she started to fall out of her chair. I thought she had just passed out and I caught her before she hit the kitchen floor telling my friend to call 911. The EMS ambulance arrived in just minutes. All the while I frantically tried to do CPR on my precious wife, but when I looked into her eyes I could see that she had just crossed over into heaven. And even though we tried so hard to bring her back she was gone from this world and is now safely resting in the arms of Jesus.

I wish I could tell you that I immediately started praising the Lord for bringing His daughter home, but I didn't. I was confused, shocked, in disbelief not knowing how or what to feel. In just minutes word got out and soon the house was filled with friends coming to pray for me and comfort me the best they could. By 10 pm Saralyn's body had been taken away and my friends had gone home. I quietly entered the apartment where just 24 hours earlier we had made our declaration that we had never been happier. I looked around the quiet room and could not

318

believe what had just happened. Was I dreaming? How could this be? What was I going to do?

As I sat on the bed and put my head in my hands I felt the Lord draw near to me and say, "Russ, I want you to know that Saralyn is with me and having the most wonderful time of her life. I also want you to know that you're going to be alright because I'm going to go on this journey with you; you will not be alone." He went on to say, "But there are some things that you MUST do as you walk on this journey called "Not Alone."

He continued, "The first thing is that you must make ME the 1) Foundation of Your Life - the JOY of your life. The DELIGHT of your heart. Because your world has just been rocked and you're going to feel like you're going through a hurricane and earthquake at the same time. Then He said that, "You need to put all of your 2) Focus on Me - keep your eyes on Me at all times. Just like Peter when he walked on water you'll see the flashes of lighting and hear the roar of thunder, but don't look at the storm, look at Me. In other words, keep reading your Bible, continue to pray, and stay active in the church. This is not a good time to pull away from Me, instead draw near to Me and I will draw near to you.

Then He said something else that is so important is that I must decide if I believe what I already know; if my 3) Faith was real. He asked me, "Russ, do you believe I can do ALL things through Christ, supply ALL of your needs, give you an ABUNDANT life even without Saralyn by your side?" Such hard questions for me to answer in that time of incredible grief. But I thought to myself and said, "I may not feel like it right now but I do believe Your word and I choose to believe Your word instead of my feelings."

There was one more thing He said would be revealed to me later. Surprisingly I did manage to get some sleep that night and begin a journey of Hideous Joy. So painful, yet so rewarding.

The last thing the Lord revealed to me was in August and that was His amazing 4) Friendship. The grief I suffered in July, August, and September was a sadness that I have never experienced before. The pain felt as sharp daggers that had been thrust into my heart. The sorrow was so heavy I even wondered if I'd survive. Each day I would walk a "trail of tears" in my home where I'd walk a path through the living room and weep so badly that I literally had to stop and times just to catch my breath. However as I walked I kept praising the Lord for Saralyn, our marriage, for sending Jesus to die for my sins. This is the place where I began to understand what Saralyn knew about the friendship of Christ. Each day as I grieved He never put me down, scolded, or said He was disappointed in me. Instead, my Friend, Jesus, cried with me.

One day, after a time of very hard tears, I went to the bathroom to wash my face. However, I was stunned when I looked in the mirror and saw bloodshot eyes still brimming with tears. My hair was matted to my forehead with sweat. There were little pieces of Kleenex stuck to my face from all of the tears and blowing my nose. I immediately apologized to Jesus for looking so dreadful and that I was embarrassed for Him to see me in that condition. But He said to me, "Russ, you've never looked more beautiful to Me because in spite of your tears and sorrow you have still praised My name. I am so proud of you." Then He helped me wash and dry my face before once again drawing close to walk with me on our journey. He mentioned something to me one day that I couldn't fully understand like I do now when He said, "The blessing is in the pain and one day you will look back on our time together as something that drew you closer to Me than ever before. Then you'll finally understand that I am not just your Lord and Savior; I am also your best Friend and the LOVE of your life.

Contact: russ@russmurphyministries.com
www.russmurphyministries.com.

Magnificent Man

Sean Guerrero

"But seek ye first the kingdom of God, and His righteousness; and all these things shall be added unto you." Matthew 6:33

In everything that we do in life, one of the most important things we will ever do after giving our lives to Jesus Christ (which is the most important) is to develop a relationship with Jesus. That is what Jesus told me in this vision in which I will share with you now to start.

Literally, in a matter of 1 – 2 days, I had a lot of things happen. My dog died, I lost my job, something happened to my sister, car got wrecked (while parked), etc. I mean it was just one of those "wow" moments. I remember I went outside of my friend's house, sat on the steps, and then I just cried and said

"Jesus, I need to hear something from You. It's cool if You want to speak through someone else, but I need to hear from You directly." So much happened that I needed to hear something directly from God himself. I went back inside and told my friend Raphael, who agreed to pray with me that Jesus would speak with me. Later that night, I had a visitation from Jesus Himself!

I remember being taken up to a place in the Heavens where I was in a big mansion type place. I walked over to a room and there was this dinner table with forks, plates, etc. set-up; I was reminded of the Marriage Supper of The Lamb. I then looked over at a window at the end of the table and saw this light/star come shining across and my heart immediately starting pumping as I said "It's Jesus" nervously. Then someone came to me and said "Come on, Come on, Jesus is coming!" So I made my way down towards the front and I looked over to my left and saw through a window that same light/star come floating across and I said again "It's Jesus" as I became even more nervous. Then, that same person came back to me with such excitement and said "Come on, Come on, Jesus is here!" Well, I then made my way to the front and saw all these people standing around this hill / green grassy area as this light/star came down from above in the heavens and landed softly on this hill...Low and behold – There Was Jesus! He had His knee up and His other leg stretched out and everyone just went running to Him! I stood there in shock, fear, and excitement all at the same time! I couldn't move! I said "It's Him, it's Jesus!" I couldn't go to Him because I was so afraid as I knew that He would know everything I've thought, said, done, felt, acted, and been in! I felt so dirty and ashamed, I just couldn't move.

All of a sudden, something inside of me just turned and my heart was tugged and said "No, you must go to Him, this is what you've waited for!" I was immediately pulled and then I just went running to Him! I plowed His neck and let me tell you, I tried and tried to cry and repent and repent of things I had already repented of and it was almost "Impossible" to cry as I hugged His

322

neck and was so overwhelmed with Love, Joy, and Peace…there was no room for tears.

Jesus then put His hands on both my front arm/shoulders and pulled me off and looked at me and said "Sean" with a smile and confidence I'll never forget! I said within myself "Holy smokes, He knows my name!"

It was like I knew Him and He knew me automatically! Ever seen the movie Ghost with Patrick Swayze? In the end he says "All the love inside, you take it with you." I tell you the truth; that is the truth! When I saw Jesus, it was like everything mattered! From the smallest things to the largest things, all matter to God! Whether you do the dishes for your mom, you tell someone Jesus loves you, you teach about Jesus, you think about God, you worship, you talk to God, you talk about God, you help someone cross the street – IT ALL MATTERS TO GOD and it's like it all is captured inside of your heart and when you see Jesus, it all comes pouring out!

The Word of God says, "Lay not up for yourselves treasures on earth, but rather treasures in Heaven, for where your heart is, there will you be also." Jesus is the Mediator between us and The Father. It's like everything we do is filtered through and stored in Heaven and when we see Jesus, it all comes pouring out, treasures are built into mansions, jewels on our crowns (which we'll lay back at Jesus' feet), etc. and etc. When we see Jesus, He knows our name and we'll know Him!

Jesus then told me, "Sean, when you tell this vision, tell them this…the most important thing you'll ever do next to salvation is building a relationship with Me" and then He crossed His first 2 fingers (to symbolize the closeness and importance of such). Everything we do matters to God for He cares for us so much and His love (as He Is Love) is greater than the universe could possibly try and contain (if it could). There's so much He desires to share, teach, give, fill, and just build with us - ah, Jesus is so amazing!

I also remember that as I sat next to Jesus, I asked Jesus "Jesus, where's your hair?" I asked this because when I looked, I saw Jesus' hair in a ponytail. Jesus then smiled and looked at me and said "Oh," He turned and then bam! His hair was officially out of the ponytail! I'll tell the meaning behind this in a moment.

So many things Jesus shared with me, but as Jesus told me, building a relationship with him is so important. How do we do it? Communication and worship. Jesus loves us so much that he cares for all that we do no matter how small or large – whether playing basketball, dancing, singing, acting, worship, driving, preaching, etc. – whatever the cause or desire is; God cares for you! He desires to be a part of our lives. God doesn't owe us anything, but He desires to give us everything because He loves us just that much!

Well, towards the end, Jesus put His hands on my shoulders (as we stood up back on the steps) and He said "Sean, you really do love me don't you" and I said "Yes Lord!"

I woke up and I got off my bed in tears from what had happened as Jesus himself gave me a physical healing through that visitation on an area in my life (during that visitation) and gave me an experience I'll never forget; I could never forget that smile He has towards me :)

As for the hair; I had asked Jesus what His hair in a ponytail symbolized - (what do you think?). Jesus told me this... Jesus said (in summary), if you go to a wedding, you dress in a certain way, if you go to fight, you dress in a certain way - "You dress for the occasion!" Jesus showed me that He is in preparation for His return!

This is a summary of the visitation - I pray that God keeps you in all that you do for His names sake and Glory. I pray that Jesus fills your life with Joy, Prosperity, Peace, and Laughter always in Jesus name!

In all things that we do, we are called to touch The Heart of Christ Jesus. Let us not grow weary in well doing, but rather grow strong in the boldness for and with Jesus Christ through The Holy Spirit to the edifying and glory of Abba Father. Everything we do in life matters...from the smallest to the greatest. We need not to wonder to the left or to the right. We only are to walk straight in Truth for Jesus is Truth.

Another dream Jesus gave me one day was along these same lines. I had a dream that I was on the front porch of my house and saw an empty parking lot as it was dark outside. I knew not to wander, yet I decided to go for a stroll not thinking there would be any harm or danger. As I began to wander into the empty parking lot, I turned around and looked at my home then realizing that I had made a mistake and found myself in an area that I should not have been. I was separated and alone in a strange area, a strange land. I had noticed a dark figure in the parking lot that was dressed in black with a ski-like mask on as if he was a thief. In John 10:10, God said..."The thief cometh not, but for to steal, and to kill, and to destroy: I am come that they might have life, and that they might have it more abundantly."

When I saw the thief – looking figure, I began to slowly walk back towards the safety of my home and noticed the thief began to walk towards me. Every move I made, the thief moved towards me. Then I sprinted back towards my home with the thief nearly catching me. A dog intercepted the thief then returned it back to its place of dark and emptiness. In Psalms 91:1, God says "He that dwelleth in the secret place of the most High shall abide under the shadow of the Almighty." God showed me that my home was representation of dwelling in God's perfect Will, in The Lord's presence, under The Shadow of the Almighty...I was in God's presence. When we leave, wonder or even fall...we step off of God's porch, covering, place of rest for a mere pleasure of thought for satisfaction which is dangerous for all ill intent and purposes that are not to edify and bring Glory to our Lord Jesus Christ.

The figure I saw in the parking lot was just that, a figure – the thief – that old serpent the devil who seeks to steal, kill and destroy God's Holy people. The enemy cannot come into your place of rest where you dwell under the shadow of the Almighty and pull you out, instead, the enemy looks to lure you out with temptations and fiery darts (which can be found in Ephesians 6:16 – "Above all, taking the shield of faith, wherewith ye shall be able to quench all the fiery darts of the wicked.").

If the enemy can draw you out from the dwelling of God's perfect will and have you go wandering astray, the enemy will look to secure you in his grip to steal that which God has given you whether that be Joy, Peace, Healing, Visionary or Dreams. Even if one finds themselves wandering, God keeps us and is able to restore and bring us back to him if we will just take the step in faith. Jesus said in Matthew 17:20…"And Jesus said unto them, Because of your unbelief: for verily I say unto you, If ye have faith as a grain of mustard seed, ye shall say unto this mountain, remove hence to yonder place; and it shall remove; and nothing shall be impossible unto you." God gives us innumerable amounts of Mercy and Grace to keep us and guard us from harm. God also said in his word…Psalms 91: 11-12 "For he shall give his angels charge over thee, to keep thee in all thy ways. They shall bear thee up in *their* hands, lest thou dash thy foot against a stone." Just like the dog that I had seen where the dog intercepted the thief…God has His Angels keeping us in all our ways and we should never take God's presence, Covering, Word and Guardianship for granted – for Jesus is Holy and Worthy to be praised!

Let us not leave the covering we are called to be under to get to know the heart of the one who keeps us safe, sound and filled with perfect peace, love and joy so that we may live abundantly to get to know The Heart of Jesus Christ our Lord and Savior through his Holy Spirit to the Glory of Abba Father.

We remember and are never to forget that we are loved and how much God desires for us to get to know Him in fellowship and Worship in Spirit and Truth. If we will take the time to wait and listen to The Heart of Jesus Christ, we can hear The Voice of God in the fashion He sees fit to speak with us under His terms that are able to receive to spread the good news of Jesus Christ and His ultimate sacrifice.

Contact: seanguerrero481@msn.com
www.sgmusic.us
www.twitter.com/seanguerrero777
www.facebook.com/sean.guerrero.777

Shawn R. Hutchinson

The steps of a good man are ordered by the LORD: and He is delighted in his way. Psalms 37:23

I would like to impress upon you how to activate **your inner power** and to totally transform your life. Not necessarily in motivation for the moment, that can serve as a "temporary high" or a quick "pick-me-up". But the kind of change that make your life count for what it's truly worth and leaves an indelible mark on the world.

I say "your inner power" because that's exactly what it is: *your* power. It is my belief that everything you need to make it from one stage to the transformation of reality is right within your reach. I've made it my mission to help you access it now.

Who is Shawn Hutcherson you ask? I'm American by pledge and Jamaican by birth and ALWAYS a Man of God first!

My God given passion for growth and a desire for a life that exceeds all expectations—even my own—has given me the power to excel in ways I could have only imagined. It has protected me as a young student athlete growing up in rough surroundings. How? In a snapshot ~ at this very moment, it is fueling my successful career in the banking industry, my first published book and bestseller "Real Men Can Wear Pink," my stage-play-turned movie titled: "Burning Bridges," and the international transformational coaching initiative, *"The Secret of the Ambitious Mind;" my second book to be released in 2015*, are just a few tangibles ways. I established "The Formula Group", a company on the quest to promote strong family values throughout various enterprising aspects. The most intriguing thing about this is that **this is all the same power presented through growth and change that lies within you**. In other words, "it's not all for (me) Shawn Hutchinson, you too may achieve and enjoy these principles and the ultimate level of success."

You and I are not alone in our personal desire to see things change for the better and to experience phenomenal growth. Whether it is pursuing our passion, the jobs which we choose to work, or to earn and to build a successful family that will carry on a legacy of greatness for generations to come. History is full of stories of people just like us who saw untapped potential and possibilities while everyone else went about life like horses with blinders on. There was once a time when society believed that the world was flat..... sailing beyond the horizon of the seas to the "ends of the earth" was insanity and suicide, all wrapped in one doomed mission.

It took the sweat equity and vision many brave, relentless pioneers to push the beyond boundaries of collective thought. Often even their own limitations as well, to discover that the "ends of the earth" were actually just the beginning. Their life-changing journeys altered the course of history, and **your journey has the same power to transform you, your family, your business, your community, and your world.** However the growth that changes any of these things must start with you.

I actually coined the term *"Ambitious Mind"* because like you, my vision for my path to success in any area of my life cannot be confined by glass ceilings or defined by superficial approaches to "making it big." Reality is the key and the best medicine for me and the rest of us. As someone who used difficulty as a catalyst for success, my life is tangible proof of the power of a relentless, ambitious spirit is trusting my God!

However, this is where I currently am, but my story began very differently without anyone planning for my life to be interesting as it is or very promising for that matter. I have learned now as I embarked up greater levels that sacrifice is a major requirement when you are ambitious about your desired success.

We are indeed a peculiar people to have been created by such an almighty God, and then to have "Him" delight in our ways for being obedient to Him, is just amazing. Well, of course we did not hop out of our mother's womb knowing such valuable information from the start. It took a process that would prepare us God fearing people for uncompromised, teaching of God's Word and the true commitment of ambitious faith. I was fortunate to have a few of those folks around for me when I was younger. To God be the glory!

Born on the beautiful Island of Jamaica where the grass is "literally" always green (not necessarily greener) and the sun is always smiling. Whereas Jamaica is considered a third world country, it definitely inhabits the beauty & grace of God's infinite creative abilities. Three months after I was born in Kingston, which is the capital of Jamaica, my mom had to hand me over to my grandparents who lived in the country, in order for her to work and provide for me. My dad was in the Jamaica Defense Force (Military) at the time and was sent off to study in England. So Mom made the best and one of the hardest decisions ever to give me to her parents. At my grandparents' home, love, care, and prayers were ever present. I was told that at the age of three months old that I was not born a healthy baby. I had very bad jaundice, in addition to a sunken soft spot on the top of my head. Doctors were extremely concerned that even with good home care, if someone's thumb pushed the spot too hard, it could possibly damage my skull. The country area of Jamaica where my grandparents lived was about an hour away from the hospital. The means of getting there was by traveling partially on foot for miles, before reaching access to public transportation. My health and the lack of access to health services caused me to spend more time in the hospital than I or anyone else wanted me to spend.

Indeed, I had a praying grandmother who would not miss church for anything, a loving care giver who ensured that my best interest was first in mind and who took everything to God in prayer. On the other hand there was my grandfather who was a vegetation farmer, an awesome provider who would never drink; but smoked and cussed like a sailor, and he would never go to church if his life depended on it. Yes! It was really the extreme sides of both worlds.

Nevertheless, growing up in an atmosphere where everyone around including neighbors, people in the community, teachers at school, and parents at home seemed to be on one accord when it came to discipline and good manners. It was almost a cliché that these next instructions were repeated to us youngster's day in and day out. "Good manners and ambition will take you very far in life". Can you imagine the consequences that would follow for us in the event that we disrespected an elder? (I can't and I'm now a blessed full grown man) Well let's just say I can still recall them like yesterday. For me it was not what I did, but what I did not do, that was considered rude.

Who hasn't heard the age old adage "It takes a village to raise a child?" For me it was definitely the idea of being raised by a village that I experienced growing up from a boy to adult. At the time it appeared more agonizing with everyone telling you what is right; now looking back they are the same golden rules that I now mentor my two beautiful kids and others by. Needless to say good mannerism is universal across the globe regardless of your ethnicity, culture, age or background.

At the age of about seven, still living with my grandparents on the vegetation (in the country), I would travel back and forth to the city to spend holidays with my mom. But on one particular Easter holiday I had to stay on the farm. I recall vividly sitting on the porch watching the crucifixion on our only black and white television, which was a privilege to have in the first place. When the scene where Jesus Christ was being whipped and then nailed to the cross, I remember angrily calling out, "I wish I was in his time, I would beat all those men up for him." I later noticed a change in my behavior and would do everything I could to avoid getting in trouble. By the time I was in my early teens I had a healthy zeal for God and the basis of a strong faith.

Around this time I moved back to the city to live with my mom where it became survival versus support from peers or any of the people around me. Again, I observed the same consistency from the women in my family; my mom would be up for hours in the morning praying just as my grandmother did. Things became even more difficult after my mother migrated to the United States in order to make a better life for us. Thus leaving me to be raised by my aunts and uncles. I found solace in praying because it was what I always saw my mother do. I also spent a lot of time reading the book of Psalms from the Bible, since it was much easier for me to understand. It was because of this I that I nurtured and developed a very intense prayer life.

I began noticing strange things happening to me; I would dream of various events only to witness them to occur just as I dreamt them. I had dreams of elderly people passing on, making their transition and days later it would actually happen. These events were frequent enough that I was afraid of wanting to go to sleep and to dream, even though I had no control over the process.. Now living in the city as a young man and trying to surrender my life to Christ was almost impossible. Especially where girls, Reggae and dancehall music was a key part of the lively hood of our culture. So I made God a promise that "if He reunited me with my mom in the United States of America, I would give my life over to Him totally."

Things were out of control around me as far as my stability. By the time I graduated high school I had attended three different schools. The atmosphere promoted an intense will to survive the horrors of the streets. Knife slashing, stabbing, stone and glass bottling throwing and more! If you were in a fight, you could expect retaliation at any time. "Talk about living in uncertainty and all things that could possibly be life threatening" that was just the mentality of my surroundings back then. Life really did not look very promising for me. However my parents had filed my papers with immigration and they seemed to be at a standstill. Even though I had financial support, life in the city was dim. You could cross the wrong person at any time; knowingly or unknowingly and that would create a very perilous situation.

Months before graduation, I prayed earnestly to the point where I began telling myself that I will be re-united with my mom in the United States after high school. What could have taken years actually took months with my papers to be approved and I was on a flight to the USA, only four days after graduating from high school in Jamaica. Oh boy was my life was about to change forever for the greater good. I would now have opportunities I once never dreamed could be possible. Not only was it a turning point for my personal development, I was about to find out that God was orchestrating my whole life. Six months after arriving in the states, I totally surrendered my life to Jesus Christ as I promised I would. "Well, at least that is what I thought at the time....." At a prayer meeting The Lord reminded me of my spoken words when I was about seven years old. Perhaps around the time I saw the movie where Jesus was being persecuted and put to death. His words to me were: "Son, I did not need you to fight for me then but represent me now". My heart was sowed back to God then and He knew I would be obedient to follow with some guidance. Wow! He told me I would be the Joseph in my life that will reach out and help the family. That quest is now raging forward in many ways and I am forever grateful to my God for making it real. So all of the near death experiences such as my falling from tree tops four and five buildings high, a truck accident that claimed the lives of friends in which I would have been on but wasn't. The escaping gun shots, and near drowning at the river where some of friends did not make it from, "I did!"

Today I celebrate God because I have answered the call to advocate for the family. Who would have thought that little "Shawnee" who used to run around without a shirt, barefoot in the mud with rips and tears in the bottom of his pants would be a first generation college graduate. Traveling between the United States and England, sowing seeds of hope and success through transformational speaking, leadership, prayer and evangelizing. A thriving banking career, a youth mentor for the last seventeen years. A restaurant owner at nineteen, married at twenty three to a "drop dead gorgeous" woman of God, (beautiful inside and out) with the same commitment. Who stood before God and the masses and vowed to only give herself to her husband; while having a passion to care for others. My lovely wife is currently in nursing school and still manages to take excellent care of her loving family. I'm now blessed with two wonderful kids who are being shown and taught the distinctive principles that we know God will honor. The platform of those principles are to honor God first and the rest is history.

If you are being led by the Lord each step of your life, then life can be really interesting, enjoyable, and fruitful. The scriptures say that the righteous person's steps, or the righteous person's decisions are given to them by God. You may place these thoughts within your own imagination. Now if you are aware that God is supposed to lead you, consider yourself more than halfway there.

You are already very aware that when the "Holy Spirit" directs you, it is time to take action. Expect God to reveal things from His heart to yours. He wants you to know of His ways from

His word. So while you are going through the Word of God, listen to the Holy Spirit for revelation from the word.

Write down the impressions and ideas which He gives to you. Let the truth that He reveals to you settle in and allow it to grow and to work in you. For there are NO COINCIDENCE in your life walk. Embrace your "Ambitious Mind" today and see the wonders of God's grace as your ideas become the world's next coming attraction.

Every step that you have taken so far, every event be it daunting or great; "just know you were selected to take them and no one else can take them in place of you. This is how I live and see myself as a Magnificent Man." ~ **SRH** ~

Contact: info.theformulagroup@gmail.com
shawnhutchinson.org

Magnificent Man

Shedrich Webster

"Do you not know that in a race all the runners run, but only one receives the prize? So run that you may obtain it. Every athlete exercises self-control in all things. They do it to receive a perishable wreath, but we an imperishable. So I do not run aimlessly; I do not box as one beating the air. But I discipline my body and keep it under control, lest after preaching to others I myself should be disqualified." 1 Corinthians 9:24-27

Shedrich Webster is a 37 year old husband and father of two. He was born in Clarksville, Tennessee; but traveled the world as a military dependent during his childhood. He is currently the Operations Manager for the Clarksville Montgomery County School System and co-founder/owner of Clarksville Basketball League. In 2013, Shedrich competed in and worked to become the champion of the inaugural season of a weight loss reality show, Clarksville Fat 2 Fit. He has used that platform and the principles learned while losing weight to help individuals, organizations and teams to figure out what their phenomenal is, then he works to move them towards achieving that phenomenal despite the challenges, fears and obstacles impeding their progress. Coach Shed speaks about using Hardwork, Hustle and Heart to overcome challenges and accomplish goals. He has taken his unique motivational style to weight loss interest groups, network marketing teams, youth groups and Division I college athletes.

Words of Sharing (Your Story or Inspiration):

I make mistakes, I have shortcomings and my actions hurt others. I can be forgetful, difficult and insensitive. I have been perceived as inconsiderate, dogmatic, arrogant and self-serving. I alienate myself from others at times and I overeat. I forget to tell my wife how much she means to me and I get short with my children too often. I am not good at follow-up and I procrastinate. I am the worst type of perfectionist; the one that will quit something if there is no immediate success. I start projects and leave them unfinished. One of my long distance mentors (Coach Michael Burt) would call that being "monkey-minded". At times I oversell my abilities and have to make up for my deficiencies by out working my lack of experience or knowledge. That typically feeds into my "workaholism". I am prideful.

So why in the world am I writing a book for others to read and what do I have to offer that is of value to you? I am writing this to inspire regular people with the fact that though it looks bleak, you have the upper hand. You just don't know it. You see, I am not extraordinary. I am not exceptional, unique or inimitable. In fact, I am no better than you at all. I feel ill-prepared and unworthy of having people to read my writings. I am a black man, born poor in a southern town that was skipped by the Civil Rights movement. My single mother began rearing her first born knucklehead son while sharing a public housing project apartment with her mother and four siblings. However, we weren't disadvantaged. Our circumstances better prepared me for the challenges that I have and will face. I learned lessons in Lincoln Homes that I use when presenting before politicians. I acquired skills while attending nine schools from kindergarten through obtaining a bachelor's degree that have helped me in corporate sales meetings. There was no better way to prepare me for the competitive nature of the workforce than playgrounds and school yards where being the new kid, the young kid, the little kid, the black kid, the Uncle Tom kid or the poor kid meant proving yourself to gain access. I got a head start and God knows I needed it, because I can mess up any blessing He gives me trying to do it my way.

God blesses all of us with a measure of health. He gives us everything we need for our body to function to its maximum potential. However, I treated the body He gave me with my own plan not His plan. Imagine how effective the ark would have been had Noah used his own plans. I worked my way well out of shape. I ballooned to over 300 lbs. I don't know my heaviest weight because I avoided the scale and the doctor's office. I estimate I was at least 325 lbs. I am not sure what health risks were prevalent with me.

Again, seeing the doctor was something that I was not eager to do. Like most men, I went when I was too sick to rest it off or take something over the counter. Heart disease, cancer, diabetes and other ailments run much more than people do in my family. I am Southern and black meaning that cooking and eating poorly is a point of pride. That's not a joke. Big Mamas, Memommas and Nanas get offended if the grandchildren don't eat everything on the plate piled full of fried delicacies, over seasoned vegetables, rich breads and chased by the sweetest of iced teas infused with fruit. The reward for over indulgence is decadent desserts such as banana pudding, pecan pie, peach cobbler, caramel cakes or cheesecake. Everybody's Uncle Bubba, Cousin Slim or Pop Pop serves the "World's Greatest" barbecue with a mean sauce, whether it be Carolina mustard based, Midwestern sweet and thick, Texas Dry or mid-south vinegar-based and hot. It's easy to overeat and downright rude not to in many situations.

So after 36 years of never consulting God about my eating habits, my weight and my body; I was less than fit. I found it difficult to do something that God had predestined for me to do. That is to impact the lives of young people and their families through coaching sports. I never set out for that as a goal, but God definitely set the plan in motion in His way. I grew up enjoying baseball and football. However, He blessed Carisa and me with a gym rat for a son. Bryce loves to hoop and even more so, loves to have his Dad around to try to coach. I also coached youth football and baseball. As the kids I coach have become more athletic and older, I could not challenge them physically without being a hypocrite. It still pangs me to admit that in asking them to do 10 pushups, I would be asking them to go beyond what Coach Shed could do. That's not a typo, at 36 I could not do the 10 pushups that I would ask of 10 year old ballplayers. Something had to change in a big way or I was destined to suffer an awful fate.

The opportunity to participate in a local weight loss reality show was available. I was fearful, reluctant and skeptical. However, I was also anxious and grateful that I had the public push that was necessary to hold me accountable. At the casting call they asked me why I should be selected for the show. Through heavy panting and sweat after a 30 minute boxing workout I said "I have taught kids for years the value of hard work, but I feel like I'm failing them because I don't work hard at getting fit." I had become the lovable large coach and funny fat guy in the room. I "carried it well" and was nice enough that business associates, church members and family didn't tell me that my weight was worrying them. As I look back on the videos of the show, I appreciate them sparing my feelings, but if any of you are reading this, y'all should have loved me enough to say something. I needed an intervention and a special called prayer meeting. Somebody should have pushed me away from the table and into a gym. I remember visiting a dear older gentleman in a medical rehab center a few months following the start of my fitness journey. Mr. Wilson Smith had been one of those gentlemen at church that mentored me as a young father and husband. He, like many others watched as I ballooned beyond just chubby to big and finally just plain fat. When I walked into his room his eyes lit up because we hadn't seen each other in a while. Mr. Smith didn't want to talk about his illness, the politics of the day or even the happenings at church. He wanted to tell me how proud he was of my weight loss, but more importantly how afraid he had become at my weight gain and my lack of health. He wasn't alone. Many others around me were worried about my health and could see the inevitable on the horizon. I could see the inevitable myself.

The journey was a difficult but rewarding one. It took much more of me than I had to give. So, I know without any doubt that God moved on me to accomplish the task. It is in His will that we have life and that more abundantly. I had replaced the abundance of health for an abundance of overeating and laziness. I am convinced that God increased in me a desire for hardwork, hustle and heart. Those principles applied created a level of fire and passion I was rarely able to tap into before this experience. Hardwork moved me to a place that I was willing to do the work in preparation that others aren't willing to do. Hustle is defined as finding a way to get to the goal before the competition. Heart can be described as having the ability to look at a bleak and hopeless situation and still fighting until God delivers success for His child.

Hardwork wouldn't allow me to sleep late, purchase the wrong foods at the grocery store or forget to pack both healthy meals and gym clothes each day. In order to change poor eating habits, I had to pack meals and snacks each night to get me through the pot lucks at work, Sunday dinners with family and even the basketball gyms and ballparks full of pizza, hot dogs or burgers. It takes a special kind of hardwork to pack raw almonds, raisins and carrot sticks to eat in a little league baseball dugout. Waking up at 5:30 AM is difficult, getting to the gym at 5:30 AM is a whole different level of difficult. Every child I've coached knows that we break huddles with the simple mantra "HARDWORK!" This took on a whole new meaning when it was apparent that I was applying the principle. The players could tell that I meant it and as I improved and displayed effort it seemed that they were catching on and working harder to improve. My words were no longer empty to them. I was getting better day by day. However, I knew that changing 30 years of bad habits would require God and a special effort on my part; a type of preparation uncommon and unique

Hustle meant different things in different stages of my life. I had heard coaches implore teammates and me to hustle for years. I also knew, growing up around "street entrepreneurs" and "resourceful characters" that one might need a side hustle or two to make ends meet. While the meanings were different, the goal was the same. Beat the competition to the goal. I was able to apply what I knew about hustle and the natural competitive spirit of a first born child to this competition. I began by thinking my competition was the four contestants on the show with me. I soon found out that God was standing with me in a battle against my inner man. (My pastor, Robert Harris, often says that our biggest enemy is the inner me.) That cat in the mirror who was willing to allow me to die a slow death from poor eating and inactivity.

Our selfish nature is what separates us from our destiny, separates us from God. One of my favorite songs spells it out eloquently. In *Another Chance* popularized by the DFW Mass Choir, the lead sings "Every time I try to do the right thing. I always end up doing the wrong thing. The only thing I seem to do is keep on messing up." When we allow the carnal man to lead us we fall into a level of weakness that will destroy us. Carnality will leave us addicted to power and porn, crack and snacks. The selfish man in all of us will indulge in whatever looks, tastes, smells, feels and sounds good. He will be content with leaving us entrapped in our failure. I had to beat him then and I continue to fight him daily on one front or another. With God, I win.

I come from a long line of fighters. My uncle Do Do is known for not just fighting guys as he grew up, but pummeling them until he had to be pulled off by several onlookers. I have a great aunt that literally battled world-class, Olympic legend Wilma Rudolph on the track and many a times came out on top. I am in the lineage of a great grandmother who birthed 11 children, adopted a 12th and lived to see them all through to adulthood. She fought with prayer. I have seen my grandmother fight poverty and hunger with a strong work ethic and humility. I watched a grandmother in her 70's fight cancer with a grace and poise that would confound most. She learned to rest in a peace that surpasses all understanding. This type of fight comes from having heart. Enough heart to look at a bleak situation and see the one glimmer of hope that inspires you to keep going. Heart is looking at all of the failed fitness plans of my past, all of the poor imbedded habits of my present and the darkness of a future full of the illnesses that come along with obesity; yet still holding on to the hope that if anyone could get healthier, it could be me.

See I don't have a false hope or faith. I had experienced God move in hopelessness before. I witnessed him transform my parents' broken marriage and my stepfather's hardened heart to show me how to fight through marital discourse. I have seen him provide for a family of four when I was abruptly fired from a management position making close to $60,000 year and benefits. He made a way for our family to survive on a sporadic income earned by my loving wife as a hairstylist for months. I have also seen Him open doors for a young boy who once received free and reduced lunch at a school he was bused to, get the opportunity to serve in leadership of the district and help make decisions that impact every child in the district. It's easy to be optimistic when you have had dark days turn into light. Once I conquered the fear of failing in this adventure, it was easy to remember to all the trials that God had brought me through. Having heart enough to compete against the odds, when the loss looks inevitable only comes from an experiential faith.

Closing:

After you prepare with hardwork, you hustle harder than anybody else in the room and dig deep with enough heart to push past your previous failure, you will realize the success that is already in you. You are already great; now let's let the rest of the world see it. Quit hiding behind mediocrity and average. Dare to be exceptional. Shine bright at home, at work and at school. Quit letting the fact that others around won't be successful keep you from being as great as you really are. There is a greatness in you that is undeniable and God-given. When we invest in self-doubt, destructive and unproductive behaviors we rob the world of one of God's gifts. I challenge you to unwrap the gift or your greatness and present it to the world.

Contact Info: To contact Coach Shed for speaking engagements for your organization, group or company, please email him. You can also follow him on social media for tidbits, tips and encouragement.

Contact: mr_sdwebster@yahoo.com
www.facebook.com/shedrichwebster
Twitter:@coachshed
Instagram:COACH_SHED

Magnificent Man

Steve W. Sanders

For God so loved the world, that he gave his only begotten Son, that whosoever believeth in him should not perish, but have everlasting life. John 3:16 (KJV).

INTRODUCTION

My name is Steve Wilbert Sanders and I was born February 26, 1945, at Burt Mercy Hospital on the east side of Detroit. The hospital is no longer there. I was born with the disease polio. My doctors never thought I would ever walk. I had this disease until the age of 4, and then God healed me. I am blessed. The doctors could not figure it out, but looking back, I know that it was God.

I am named after my father, the late Steve Wilbert and my mother was the late Odessa Sanders. I grew up in a two parent home and was raised by both parents. My parents never divorced.

They were married for 50 years. I grew up with one older brother and 7 sisters. My father was a strict man. He only wanted the best for his children. We always had several chores to perform. Living under my father's roof, we were taught to work hard, and the word 'lazy' was unheard of and prohibited within our family home.

My father was employed by the Ford Motor Company. He was a hard worker, and retired after 31 years of service. As kids, we were taught to work hard, go to school, and church. Because of my parents, these three things have stuck with me all of my life, and still do today.

Church

Soon after I was born, my family had moved to River Rouge, MI. As a young boy, I remember the importance of God in my life. I was raised with a religious background. My grandfather was a pastor and his church affiliation was with the Church of God in Christ on the east side of Detroit, and I remember my grandmother was a praying woman. She always prayed for us. We would love to visit their home.

My mother faithfully took us to the Church of God In Christ in the same city we lived. The church was a place where my family gathered together to worship and praise God. We never missed a service. Back then you had to go to church and to Sunday school. I remember when church would last for long hours, and I didn't understand why so much church. There were times I didn't want to go. But looking back, I am grateful my mother Odessa Sanders took us to church. My father would never go with us to church, but after years of praying for him, he finally started going to church every Sunday. After his retirement he gave his life to God.

Respect

In our community, we grew up respecting for our elders. We were not allowed to talk back or complain. I remember playing with friends before and after the church service, but whenever church service began, we were not allowed to talk or play. We had to sit still and listen to the preacher. We could not fall asleep or we would get pinched or spanked. My parents did not believe in sparing the rod. They both believed in discipline. It was not abuse, but love. Many children today experience a lack of love from their parents. I know that in today's times that things are different and many children are being raised by single parents. But respect is something that is taught and passed down. Our children need our support and guidance. I believe our country failed when we took God out of our homes and schools; also when we stopped taking our children to church.

HOME LIFE

My father was a proud man raising 9 children and we were not ashamed. I grew up poor, but there were plenty of good times, lots of laughter, and love. I remember having two or three pairs of shoes that we called Chuck Taylor's back in the day, and if you looked closely, you could see how the soles of our shoes were worn down from repeated wear. My mother would take us to the Shoe Fair. The Shoe Fair was place where parents took their kids because the shoes were cheap. We might have been poor, but my parents always made sure we were suited up nicely for church on Sunday mornings. Back then you dressed up for church, not like today where you come as you are. Back in my day, parents didn't believe in that. You had to wear nice clothes to church; period. We never had new clothes, but instead we wore hand me downs that came from others, or clothing from the goodwill. We were not afforded many of the luxurious comforts that our children have today. We would play outside with our friends until the street lights came on. We didn't have power lawn mowers back then, only push mowers, and we walked to school every day. Our family believed in sitting down at the

347

dinner table to eat where we would say grace. We would say please and thank you. We would demonstrate manners.

My father taught his children so much about life, work, and responsibility. He was such a hard worker. Growing up becoming a man, I watched what my dad went through and I respected him more as a man. I knew that in life I would have to earn my own way and provide for my family just as my dad did provide a home for his wife and his children. I looked up to my dad as my hero.

I attended the River Rouge Public School system. As a teen, I was a 6'4" star athlete who played basketball, football, baseball, and ran track all while maintaining a job in school along with my usual family chores and homework. My first real job was delivering the Jet Magazine and The Chronicle. I would deliver the papers after school each day and sometimes my sisters would help me if I had basketball practice. I had a very successful route. I learned early in life that I could make as much money as I wanted to if I worked hard.

ADULT LIFE & FAMILY

After graduating high school, I got a job working at Chrysler on August 13, 1964. I will never forget the day I got this job. My father was proud of me. By the age of 21, I would marry the love of my life; my wife Joan Sanders. I have 5 daughters all together named Tracy, Alesia, Treva, Melissa, and Melanie. I love all of my children the same and they make me proud to be their father.

Celebrating birthdays, family reunions, and especially the holidays are always great times with my family. When the kids were small, I enjoyed taking them to parades, telling them fun stories about Santa Claus, the Tooth Fairy, and more. I always told my girls that all things are possible through God, and that they could do or be anything in life they wanted to be as long as they put God first in their lives and remain humble. My job has been to help guide them in life. I taught them to work hard and to be on time. I believe in being on time. Their mother took great care of the girls. She always had their hair fixed pretty. She always took them to church.

Today, I have 12 grandchildren, 7 great grandchildren, and am having the best of time of my life. My grandchildren range in age from age 32 all the way down to 5 months. I have a grandson in the Navy. I am a dedicated grandparent, I spend time with them. Some of my grandchildren call me every day by phone to check up on me and to talk. I enjoy that.

When my children were young we did lots of things together. There were fishing trips, family vacations, playing basketball at the park, swimming in the pool and more. My wife and I would take long trips in the summer and would travel all around to different states in the U.S. and also to Canada. These were memorable and fun times.

During our drive, we'd listen to music, and sing silly songs, with lots of laughter in the car. Some places we had traveled to included Toronto, Montreal, Ontario, Canada, Atlanta, GA, Dayton, OH, Tennessee, Alabama, and more. Most memorable places we visited were Niagara Falls, Mammoth Cave, Ruby Falls, Cedar Point, Sea World, Boblo Island Amusement Park, The Guinness Book of World Records, Kings Island, Graceland, The Football Hall of Fame, and more. We did it all. I was able to be the father that my dad was to me. I was blessed to provide for my family.

In the mid 70's, I had to have open heart surgery that winter and knew that I couldn't shovel the snow. It was also one of the biggest snow storms to hit our area. That winter, I taught my oldest daughter who was around 11 years old at the time, how to shovel the snow without causing hurt or harm to her. She listened. I have always tried to pour fatherly advice and wisdom into my girls. God has truly been good to me. I have been blessed a father blessed to enjoy nice cars, new suits, and travel.

He blessed our family home.

During my employment at Chrysler, there were a few times I received company layoffs. One layoff I remember lasted for two years. My daughter Treva helped me to secure a job at a local restaurant. Her boss hired me as a dishwasher and busboy. I never complained. I went from making really good money to very little money. I thank God. I never complained. What I treasure most is the time that I was able to work with my daughter. We each worked the afternoon shift together and it was great spending that time with my daughter. She looked out for me and I looked out for her. I was eventually called back to Chrysler.

STILL BLESSED

In 1986 my sister Shirley passed away. This was a very sad time in my life; after she passed, my father passed in 1990, and then my mother in 1992. In 1993, after nearly 30 years of marriage, I lost my wife to cancer. I was now left to finish raising my two youngest daughters. These were difficult years, but God never left me.

In 1994, I retired from Chrysler with 30 years and 6 months. I eventually sold the family home. Today I live in Ecorse, MI. I am grateful for such great memories God. This year I am enjoying life as a 70 year old man. My hope for my children, grandchildren, and great grandchildren is that they will serve the Lord, take their children to church, and treat people right. This is my prayer.

I am so blessed by the love I receive from my family, friends, and also for my involvement into the community. I am a member of the Triumph Baptist Church where Reverend Kinloch is my pastor. The church is growing. I serve on the usher board and have for nearly 4 years. I assist people and families who come to the church.

For several years, I have traveled out of town and state to assist my daughters and their families. I have one grandson who I drove to school every day throughout his high school years. I now help take him to work every day. He is working to obtain his driver's license. For many years, I often traveled down to Tennessee to help my daughter Treva and her husband Robert with their children when they were younger. I would sometimes come and stay for a month at a time with my grandchildren. I have also flown to Texas to visit my daughter Melanie with her 3 children, assisted my daughters Tracy and Melissa with their children. I would help my daughter Alesia with her businesses by sitting with the elderly residents.

My greatest passion in life is for our young people. My job is to motivate them. It is important to obtain your education, whether applying for a trade or skill, or completing your degree. I tell young people to apply themselves in school because there aren't many good jobs out here. I motivate them to own their own businesses, and to start by putting God first. In order to get a good job, you need the skills, and education. Today we don't have a lot of jobs like we used to. When I was coming up there were lots of jobs like Chrysler, Ford, and General Motors. I encourage our young people to succeed.

Testify

One of my favorite passages of scripture that has stuck with me is Psalm 23 (KJV).

This passage of scripture has blessed me over the years. It is the power of your testimony. A few years ago, I was hospitalized at Wyandotte Hospital with pneumonia. My lungs were filled with fluid. I was on a respirator and could not breathe. I was placed in the ICU for two months. The nurses had taken great care of me. My life expectancy seemed dim. But God. He healed my body completely and made a way out of no way.

Then there was another time when one of my daughters was gravely ill after the birth of her child. Her life expectancy also seemed dim, but with prayer God came in and healed her body. I dropped everything I was doing to go and be with her.

Then yet another time while on vacation, my youngest daughter nearly drowned in the hotel swimming pool. I was able to jump in and save her.

Then another time, one of my daughters had suffered a major asthma attack. She could barely breathe. I saw the power of God move.

I can go on and on about how awesome God truly is. There is so much to tell that I just cannot tell it all in one chapter. But God. My prayer is that you will accept Him and allow Him to come inside your heart. All of our help comes from the Lord. All we have to do is trust Him (Prov. 3:5,6).

Last but not least, I am honored to be included inside the Magnificent Men book sharing my story of inspiration with such great men of faith. I know that there is something you can enjoy in every chapter. I would like to thank my daughter Treva for putting this book together, and my son-in-law Robert. In the early years of their business, I encouraged them always to keep going, and so that is what I am saying to you all today. I am telling you to "Keep Going. You can't give up. You must keep going." If it was always easy, you would never try.

Expressions of Love from My Daughters:

Melissa Sanders: "Thank you dad for always being there for me and for loving me. Thank you for helping me with my children and for the great memories shared. You have been a major role model to me. You taught me to work hard and the importance of being on time. I now teach this to my own children because of you."

Melanie Sanders: "Thank you dad for being a hard worker. This is what I learned from you. You made sure we had everything, and kept us in the nicest things. That is why I am a hard worker. I love basketball because of you. I am thankful for the times you would take me out to the restaurant every Friday to eat. Dad you have been a blessing."

Treva Gordon: "Dad I want to thank you for being my biggest inspiration on this earth. I think of you every day. Your favorite advice for me is be patient and slow down. You taught me to work hard in life. You were there after the birth of all of my children. Whenever I needed someone to talk to, you were there. You walked me down the aisle at my wedding more than 20 years ago, taught me to drive my first car, and how to ride my first bicycle. Love you forever and always."

Alesia Carter: "My dad has taught me many things, several of them have stayed with me as an adult. 1: Treat people the way you want to be treated. 2: Always believe in yourself and something that he still tells me today. LISTEN!"

Catherine Tracy: "My dad taught me to be strong and independent. I was the oldest out of 5 girls and didn't understand why he wanted me to be strong willed and to be able to stand on two feet and to be capable of taking care of myself."

Contact: ccshopper@bellsouth.net

Magnificent Man

Terry Boykin

For I know the thoughts that I think toward you, says the LORD,
thoughts of peace and not of evil, to give you a future and a hope.
Jeremiah 29:11-13

My name is Terry Boykin Jr. and I am a native Detroiter and have always been inspired to play hoop ball. I live and breathe basketball and I've never wanted to do anything else! I have a passion for the game and it's inherent in me. My parents told me that as early as a year old I actually had a basketball in my hands and could actually dribble the ball at 13 months old. My Dad was a high school basketball star at Northwestern High School in Detroit, Michigan so there's no doubt that the hoop game made a great impression on my life and my destiny because athleticism is a strong part of my core and foundation.

Very early on, my Dad taught me everything that he knew about basketball. I learned by his hands-on training but mostly by observing him out on the court, in practice and in competition. But I discovered that it's even deeper than that; the execution has deeper levels of training that always proves to be invaluable. This is where you develop your own unique style that sets you apart noticeably and prepares you to go into the heat of the most intense games and execute that style. Basketball is an art and it's displayed on the court with the ingenuity of the assist, the exact timing of the steal, the force and indignation of the rebound, the clever control of ball handling and the three-point connection which all require training and the desire to learn and commit to the game. The bottom line is, You Play Like You Practice! There is nothing like the relationship between a hooper and basketball, but the day you decide to cheat on basketball it will catch up to you. When you cheat on basketball, you do it behind closed doors. No one knows that you are cheating but the basketball. You cheat by not working on your game and doing those little things that got you on top. The thing is that basketball won't say anything to you about it, but come game day when you have hundreds or thousands of people watching you, basketball will put you on stage and let the world know that you've been cheating. Whether it's missed shots, poor defense, or turnovers your cheating is going to catch up with you.

Becoming a great player requires determination and hard work. If you love the game and have big dreams to succeed, you must do a better job of building the relationship with basketball. Just like any other relationship, it's not going to be easy. There are going to be some ups and downs and sometimes you are going to have to sacrifice some things you like to do to spend time with basketball, but in the end it will all be worth it. Love the game and it will love you back.

I attended and played for Detroit Catholic Central High School under the instruction of Michigan High School coaching legend and veteran five-star basketball camp counselor, Bernie Holowicki. I am still infected with the passion of the game that he passed on to me. I take what I do as a basketball skill developer very seriously because I understand and grasped the positive

356

influence that Coach Holowicki had on me not only as a basketball player, but also as a person. His style of coaching has impacted every area of my life and I use something he taught me each and every day. There were days when I didn't like him very much but grateful he held me accountable. His influence on me in Michigan is impacting kids all over Tennessee and Kentucky and surrounding states. As a member of the team, I shared in a city Catholic League championship and three district titles. As an individual player, I was named Detroit Free Press Catholic League Player of the Year, all area, all city, all metro and all state, as well as Honorable Mention McDonald's All American. After graduating from Detroit Catholic Central High School in 1989, I was awarded a scholarship to Austin Peay State University in Tennessee. I served as the point guard for the Governors and was a two-year captain. I've always been known as a smart, fundamentally sound player with a high basketball IQ.

During the middle of my junior season at Austin Peay, unfortunately, I suffered a severe ankle injury that almost ended my basketball career. I underwent two surgeries and had to sit out the entire next season. It was during this time that I absolutely learned the true meaning of HARD WORK as I underwent a vigorous rehabilitation program. I also had the opportunity to get my priorities in order and focus in on getting my college degree. The last year of my eight-year career in corporate America, I began training local high school and college players for fun and volunteering my basketball expertise at local high schools and middle schools in Clarksville, Tennessee. Being involved in the atmosphere of the game again gave me a renewed passion to teach young kids the fundamentals of the game and life skills through basketball. I began the Advanced Guard Camp in the summer of 2005. In a year's time, it grew to be one of the hottest camps on the summer circuit, touching three states: Tennessee, Kentucky, and Georgia.

I created Playmaker Basketball Academy to teach youth how to make plays on and off the court. I've always had a burning desire to help bring out the best in young student-athletes. In the lab, I teach young basketball players the importance of being balanced on the court but more importantly I try to express to them the importance of a balanced lifestyle. Playmaker Basketball Academy is a year round basketball skills development program designed to help players develop the skills necessary to reach their full potential as basketball players. As coach and mentor, I encourage a positive work ethic on the court and in the classroom. We offer encouragement and development of a player's self-confidence, which is a necessity for a successful player.

As coach, I've developed a comprehensive program that instills the basic foundations of dedication, concentration and hard work. Playmaker Basketball Academy is designed to train and develop champions! If the player has the desire to play the game and wants to advance, I will undoubtedly tap into their potential and take their game to the next level because I really do believe that there's a winner in every player that I train. Coaching and training players is my life. It is most important to me that Playmaker Basketball brings the very best out of players regardless of their age or the status of a player. For instance, some of my players have become popular locally or even celebrities in their own right but they receive the same attention and detail that I give each and every player. I don't have favorites, I have players that come in and have the heart to become a champion and with their hard work and the Playmaker development program there's nothing together we cannot achieve! However, it's entirely up to the player. You must bring a desire to work into the coaching session; anything else is a distraction and a waste of everybody's time. There's only one agenda in a session and that is to work and develop the skills to get better and better!

I am not a hard taskmaster but a trainer and teacher at heart and each and every little thing I see improved I am excited about! It makes me proud and proves over and over that my coaching style is effective. Every year Playmaker Basketball works with hundreds of kids to not just learn how to play basketball, but to learn teamwork, perseverance, alertness,

358

sharing, graciousness, and so much more. By hosting events for these kids, we are able to work with them on a more personal level to teach them strong values and opportunities that they may not have had or experienced elsewhere. Playmaker Academy recognizes that talent alone is not enough to be successful in life. We also encourage academic achievement, but most importantly we hope to serve as one of the means to connect the community to Christ. The "Beyond The Court" series consists of inspirational messages geared towards encouraging an intimate relationship with Christ.

I have been fortunate throughout my years playing basketball because I have always had coaches that were motivators. They always knew when I wasn't giving my best effort on the court and in the classroom, and they knew just what to say to get me back in line. Sometimes it was an arm around my shoulder with words of encouragement and other times it was them yelling at the top of their lungs because they were running out of patience with me. I appreciate those coaches for caring about me and trying to get the best out of me, but when I look back on those days, I realize that it really wasn't their job to have to motivate me ALL of the time. Don't get me wrong, all coaches should be able to motivate his or her players, but if I had really understood at the time how fortunate I was to be in the position that I was in being on the team, I should have been able to motivate myself. What I didn't realize was that when the buzzer sounded the last game of my senior year in college, it really wasn't the coaches' job to motivate me anymore. It was time for coach to use that energy on players that were still in his program.

When I look back at my old teammates and analyze each one, I found that the leaders on the team were the players that were self-motivated. They pushed themselves when they were tired. They were the first person to dive on the floor for a loose ball at the 7:30 am practice when everyone else was dreading being there. They didn't want to be at practice that early anymore than anyone else but they were mentally tough enough to make themselves work hard. The self-motivated person was also that person who studied on the team bus for a test that was scheduled for the day the team returned from a road trip instead of using being gone as an excuse to postpone taking the test at a later date. Again, a self-motivated person is a leader and a person that has learned how to take charge of their life: a person who can push him or herself to the limits even when they don't feel up to the task.

So if a self-motivated person is a leader, what does that make a person who's not self-motivated? A person that has to be constantly motivated in order to perform is a follower. These people have no control of their lives. They are like toys that need batteries to operate. They have to be forced to perform at a high level and they are never consistent in their efforts. What's sad is that a lot of times, the people that are not self-motivated usually are the most talented ones and don't realize how good they could be if they just took control of their lives in order to maximize their abilities and full potential. What scares me about these talented young players is the fact that if they don't learn how to work and push themselves at the high school or college levels, what's going to happen to them when they get into "the real world" and they have no one to depend on but themselves. Believe me, it's a lonely feeling knowing that you are on your own and you haven't developed the skills to take control of your own life. Seriously, no one is going to force you to go to class or look over your shoulders to make sure you are getting good grades. That's your job - It's all on you to motivate yourself.

If you don't believe what I am saying, pay attention to the classified ads for jobs. The ads will give a brief description of the duties of the job and then they will tell you the kind of employee they are looking for to represent their company. Ninety percent of companies say they are looking for a person who is self-motivated or a self-starter. Just like coaches, companies want people who choose to go the extra mile in order to get the job done. In addition, they look for people who can self-manage and don't require someone else to constantly monitor them to perform. Companies and coaches have a lot in common because they both want people who are self-motivated. Better yet they prefer leaders. Which one are you? Take a long look at yourself and determine whether or not you are a leader or a follower. Are you in control of your life or does someone else have to wind you up like a toy to get you to perform?

There are few people in the world that will love you unconditionally, your parents, your grandparents and maybe even your brothers and sisters. But, sometimes we all abuse these relationships and we might not even speak to these people for a while, but we really don't sweat it because we know that deep down our parents or grandparents will forgive us and love us, regardless of what we do or how we treat them. They don't want to see you fail and they hate to see you suffer so they may still buy you some expensive gear or give you some money to put in your pocket, even if you don't deserve it. We take these relationships for granted and often times we don't even spend quality time with these special people in our lives because we feel that no matter what, they are going to love us unconditionally. "One big mistake that I see young basketball players making nowadays is that they try to treat basketball like their close relatives. Love them one day and then don't come around for a week or so or until they need something. They really don't spend quality time with basketball, but they want basketball to get them into college or make them money one day. But they fail to realize one thing, unlike your parents and grandparents; basketball does not love you unconditionally. If you take a day off on basketball, it will take 2 days off on you. Basketball will only love you if you love it back. Trust me, if you love basketball and you put your heart and soul into it, it will reward you like you can't imagine."

I can have a typical training session, an average coaching session or an amazing exchange with one of my players. The latter is magical because this type of player will implement my drills and put their individual spin on it and this is where I get the most excited! It lets me know that they get it! Unfortunately some players will not get it because they don't come in with a

361

blank canvas but rather an agenda to impress or just do things their own way. In this case, I am not the right coach to teach them. I'm not saying that my way is the only way but rather in a session if you're that good, you should be able to switch it up and perform and handle the ball with flexibility, while comprehending the drills with the intention of raising the value of your game. I show you the drill, you execute it, plain and simple! But, this is exactly why some players have problems in competition. The coach sees the situation on the floor and strategically guides the player to get in and pass the ball for the score because at that time one of the forwards just happen to be in the zone, however because that player refuses to listen or follow through and attempts to shoot a three pointer, the team - the entire team loses the game because the player given the strategic direction had another agenda. It's difficult to train a player like this because they will never become a team player nor have a desire to put forth a team effort. You must be willing to take directives and apply them effectively on the court. A team player is an asset to the whole team. Team playing adds value to a player and let's the other team members know that in the clutch you always have their best interest at hand! A ball hog will always lose in the end.

God has always been a force in my life. Trust in the Lord with all your heart, and lean not on your own understanding; in all your ways acknowledge Him, and He shall direct your paths. Proverbs 3:5-6. This Bible verse exemplifies my heart and how I'm guided through life every day. God has always showed up consistently in my life and I live to praise Him in everything that I do. Whatever I do I always check myself and my intentions because I never want God to be disappointed in me and I teach my children that same principle.

One of my mentors is Pastor Harris, who has made a huge impact on my family's life and on me. I thank God for him and his continued support which is invaluable.

The Playmaker Basketball slogan is "Making plays on and off the court" and while we teach athletic skills, we also stress the importance of excellence in and throughout a player's educational journey. I cannot stress enough the importance to excel in academics. My wife is a schoolteacher and an expert in remedial reading techniques and this principle is very important in our home. We bring that same expectation into our Playmaker program. We have a foundational teaching platform with the goal to teach and train excellence in and outside of the gym. Recently we added a seminar to show high school, college and professionals how to conduct themselves while being interviewed. This is most important that a player knows how to communicate effectively on radio or before the camera. It's important for an athlete to be able to intellectually convey his/ her thoughts collectively.

One of my favorite Bible scriptures is Jeremiah 29:11-13 For I know the thoughts that I think toward you, says the LORD, thoughts of peace and not of evil, to give you a future and a hope. Then you will call upon Me and go and pray to Me, and I will listen to you. And you will seek Me and find *Me,* when you search for Me with all your heart. This scripture totally encompasses how I feel about my own personal goals, my goals for my family, my peers, the players that I train and the future goals of the Playmaker Basketball Academy.

Contact: tboykin7@gmail.org
playmakerbasketball.org

TN State Senator Mark Green

So that you may live a life worthy of the Lord and please him in every way: bearing fruit in every good work, growing in the knowledge of God, ~ Colossians 1:10

I grew up in rural southern Mississippi, along a dirt road near a small town, the son of larger-than-life father and a mother who loved to quote Bible verses. They instilled in me a work ethic, a drive to excel -- and, most important, they taught me to serve others.

While I was in first grade, my dad developed bone cancer as the result of his exposure to radiation while serving in the Air Force. I'll never forget my father coming back from the hospital with no right arm. I was so stunned that I can't remember the words I spoke, but I'm told I looked up and asked him, "Can we still go fishing?" My dad replied, "You'll have to bait daddy's hook" -- and we went fishing within the month.

There was no Americans with Disabilities Act in those days, and few protections for disabled workers like my dad. He'd been a machine operator before his amputation, but on his return he was treated as if he was half a man, his salary cut in half and he was placed in a desk job. The cut in pay caused significant hardship on our family. My dad, too proud to accept assistance or even to consider himself disabled, chose to take a series of odd jobs.

Soon, he was painting signs for the local car wash. He had been right-handed and had to quickly master the use of his left -- but he managed. The sign painting put a few dollars in his pocket, but not enough to make ends meet, so my one-armed father took a job roofing houses. The image of my dad going up a ladder, balancing a bundle of shingles on the stump of his arm, will never leave me. He would start the nails by slamming the nail into the shingle with the palm of his left hand, then retrieve the hammer and drive it in with his left.

Sharing this story with friends is somewhat of an "Ah Ha" moment for them understanding why I am a "workaholic." If I am, it's partly my mother's doing, too: she quoted scripture daily, and one of her favorites was Colossians 3:23: "whatever you do, work at it with all your heart, as if working for God." Both my mom and my dad taught me through words and deeds that all work has spiritual meaning and should never be taken lightly.

Mom also introduced me to the parable of the Ten Talents in Matthew 25. Here, Christ relates that his Father invests talents and resources in the lives of people -- and expects a return on the investment. As mom said, we bring credit to the God who made us when we use our gifts and abilities, much like a painting reflects the talents of its painter. Whether one's name is Michael Jordan or Yo Yo Ma, whether we are talented at medicine or farming, we each possess natural abilities that are gifts from God.

To fully realize those gifts, however, we require a disciplined work ethic -- and it is up to role models like parents to instill it. In my case, it was a combination: a father who never quit in the face of hardship and a mother who taught me to respect and utilize the gifts God gave me. Their combined influence is the source of my sense of duty, my determination to always do my very best and to strive for excellence. Needless to say, quitting was never an option.

As I grew older, dad and mom mentored me to serve people. I remember that during a rare ice storm, a neighbor had the flu and ran out of firewood to heat his home. Dad roused me out of bed to help him cut firewood (ice covered, I might add), so our neighbors would have heat. Although our neighbor had a case of the flu, it occurred to me that he had both arms and was in otherwise excellent health, and I'll admit now that I became angry at the sight of my one-armed father chopping and splitting wood for him. My dad never had any such misgivings. To him, the situation presented an opportunity to serve, to use his abilities on behalf of someone else.

They had imbued me with a real sense of duty, and so it seemed natural for me to apply to West Point. There I grew in my faith and, in my heart, a desire to serve the nation. Graduating from West Point with a degree in economics, I requested the Infantry and headed to Fort Benning, GA for Airborne, Ranger and Infantry Officer training. My first duty assignment was at Fort Knox, KY, where I led an infantry platoon, a scout reconnaissance platoon and served as a battalion personnel officer. Following the Infantry Officer's Commander's training back at Fort Benning and the Jump Masters Course, I reported to the 82nd Airborne Division at Fort Bragg, NC.

At Fort Knox I met and married the Chaplain's daughter. Best decision of my life. This year Camie and I celebrate our 27th wedding anniversary. No one has taught me more about communicating than my wife. She is my best friend and a terrific mother to our two beautiful children. The story of her service and sacrifice to the country as a soldier's spouse warrants its own entry in a book like this.

Being an infantry officer was a source of pride for me. The Army has several career fields, from armor troops, to aviation, to field artillery, but I was drawn to the infantry because of its mission: to "seize and hold terrain." No other career field in the Army had that mission. At least for those of us in the infantry, we felt the entire Army was there to support us. At Bragg I commanded an airborne infantry company. Each of us in the unit was aware of the legendary history of the 82nd Airborne's exploits in World Wars I and II; the reputation of the unit no doubt motivated each of us to push for excellence.

During my command, my father had a catastrophic medical emergency that should have killed him. Dad spent 37 days in the ICU. Each day we were told not to expect him to survive, yet he did. The physician who took care of my father had served as an Army physician and over the course of his care for dad, he spoke with me about the Army's path to medical school. Once dad recovered, I realized that this physician had essentially prevented a 180-degree course reversal in our entire family's life. I immediately requested that the Army send me to medical school.

While preparing for medical school, I served as a recruiting company commander, allowing me to take the prerequisites for medical school that were not a part of my economics undergraduate degree. As a recruiting company commander, I also attended meetings of the Chamber of Commerce in Dayton, Ohio. It was my first introduction to the business world. It was fascinating to watch senior executives and CEOs of companies like AT&T Global Information Systems brief their strategic plans. This experience foreshadowed my own work as CEO of a large healthcare company many years later.

While I was in command of the recruiting company, in October of 1993, I remember watching the horrific scenes of our elite special operations soldiers' dead bodies being dragged through the streets of Mogadishu -- the incident later known as "Black Hawk Down." It was difficult to watch, and I never

368

would have imagined that exactly ten years from then, I would make my second trip to war as the doctor assigned to that very unit.

After four years of medical school and three more in an emergency medicine residency, I reported to the 160th, Special Operations Aviation Regiment, or SOAR for short. As it happened, I signed into my new unit on the first anniversary of 9/11. As I reported to the commander, the unit was hosting a memorial service for the soldiers who had died in the first year of the war. At that point, the 160th SOAR had more killed in action than any other unit in the Army. Watching the ceremony was a sobering way to begin a new Army assignment.

In March of 2003, I deployed for combat to Iraq and served with the special operations task force assigned to find weapons of mass destruction and to capture Saddam Hussein. During my time with SOAR, I would make two trips to Iraq and another to Afghanistan. The combat experience gave me a new appreciation for our soldiers. The bravery and self-sacrifice I witnessed on the battlefield is forever a part of my memories. Taking care of a wounded soldier in combat was a responsibility I cannot describe and don't think I will ever be able to replicate. I owe a great deal to the medics who together served the special operators.

As the task force surgeon, my job was to plan the casualty management for each battle, fly with the men to the targets, pull the wounded into my helicopter and then treat them en route to a medical facility. Even now, my mind flashes with images of the men, the missions, the wounded, the celebrations of battlefield success and the tears shed as flag-draped coffins were carried to the return flight home. I suppose those images will be with me forever.

One of those missions made a big change in my life.

In December of 2003, we were getting closer in our hunt for Saddam Hussein. Only a few weeks before, we had captured

369

his personal secretary; then we seized his personal physician. We knew we were getting close. Around the early part of December, my father, who was by now a pastor in South Mississippi, sent a letter to several of his fellow pastors inviting them to fast and pray, that our troops would capture Saddam Hussein. When the appointed day for fasting and prayer came, mom added to her prayers that I would be allowed to be a part of the mission.

While my parents do not know who all fasted and prayed, within a few days of the letter being sent, we were getting intelligence on Saddam's location. Later on the night of December 13th, we captured Saddam Hussein. I planned the medical portion of the mission and flew with the soldiers in the event there were any casualties; thank God there were none. As I stood outside the cell that held the Butcher of Bagdad, the task force commander came out and asked me if I would spend the night with Hussein. My answer was a resounding, "Yes, sir!" During the course of the night, Saddam could not sleep and would not stop talking. Through an interpreter, I conducted a historical interview, avoiding questions that might disrupt the investigation of his criminal behavior or the status of the weapons of mass destruction.

Seems mom's, and so many other prayers were answered.

I left special operations in 2004 to become director of the emergency department at Fort Campbell, KY, and in June of 2006, I signed out of the Army. Twenty years before, I had stood on the plain at West Point taking the oath to defend the nation. As they handed me my flag for service I'll admit a few tears came to my eyes. The camaraderie forged in battle has no rival. The commitment to serve our nation and one another runs deep when you have to grapple with the thought that death might be the price you pay. It is especially profound when you were able to come home and some friends were not.

Shortly after getting out of the Army I started my own emergency medicine staffing and management company. In just

5 years, our company has grown from serving one hospital to now providing emergency room staffing at hospitals in five southeastern states. We are a family of nearly 500 medical providers. Shortly after starting the company, we founded a non-profit foundation that sends doctors to third-world countries to provide health care to the neediest of God's children.

Having studied leadership all my life, I realized it was critical that our company make it a priority to develop leaders within our ranks. That decision has contributed greatly to our success -- the company's, the foundations, and the success of the individuals on our team. The company hosts leadership development conferences throughout the year and we put significant resources into developing our people to lead during times of crisis. After all, that's what happens in emergency departments every day.

Despite a lifetime of study at West Point, the battlefields of Afghanistan and Iraq and in the boardroom of our company, probably the best lesson on leadership I ever received was from my mom and dad. In Luke chapter 22, Jesus overhears his followers arguing among themselves about who will be the greatest, and who will succeed him as the leader of their group. Luke, a physician, records Jesus' response. Essentially in today's language Christ says, "The leaders of today, CEOs and politicians, too often see their position as one of benefactor, happy for the perks of the job. But that is not how the best leader views the role. No, a true leader is one who views the job as the servant of all; who places him or herself as last and all others as first." It was my mom and dad who pointed that out to me, and I'll always be grateful.

In the fall of 2011, Lieutenant Governor Ron Ramsey asked me to consider running for the Tennessee State Senate. After giving it much thought and prayer, I prepared to tell Lieutenant Governor Ramsey no; at that point, I thought the foundation would be my life's work.

Before calling Lt. Governor Ramsey to give him my answer, I took my son to my 25th reunion at West Point. In a briefing room, the Commandant of Cadets described to us alumni the many changes to the academy since we had graduated. One thing that had not changed -- and I hope never will -- is the mission of West Point: "To Create Lifelong Leaders for Service to the Nation."

On our way from the meeting hall, my son and I stepped onto the "plain." The "plain" at West Point is where our nation's earliest battles for freedom were fought; it is where men like MacArthur, Eisenhower, Grant and Patton had once paraded as cadets, and it holds a special place in the hearts of the "Long Grey Line" of West Point graduates.

On that particular afternoon, the sun was setting a brilliant orange and the trees were in their fall beauty. As I walked up to the statue of General Douglas MacArthur, the inscription hit me like a ton of bricks: it was the quote I and every other Plebe had memorized and recited countless times: "Duty, Honor, and Country. Those three hallowed words reverently dictate what you can be, what you ought to be, what you will be." "Duty." The word would not leave my mind. I had taken a spot at a school whose purpose was to train leaders for service. I owed back a duty. I phoned our Lieutenant Governor and told him that yes, I would run.

Having seen my father and mother go through the hardship of losing half their income despite working multiple jobs, I feel a profound duty to help those who cannot find a good job. Just like my father, we Americans are a hard-working people who want to contribute and would do anything to avoid taking a handout. They are being squeezed in an economy where -- no matter how hard they look -- there are just not enough jobs for everyone who wants to work.

Our ability to meet the needs of those who are unable to help themselves requires a prosperous nation with a growing economy. With the bounty that comes through thrift, hard work, innovation and risk, we are better able to care for those less fortunate. Policies that make it harder for people to use their God-given talents decrease the freedom of man, diminish prosperity and frustrate the expression of the Creator who gave each person his or her abilities. To unleash the abilities of our people, we must get government out of the way of the very people and businesses who will use their resources to create opportunities for all of us.

Serving in the Tennessee State Senate has been a great opportunity to do that. Tennessee has the lowest debt in the country and the sixth-lowest combined tax burden. With fewer taxes and less debt, our state has created 190,000 jobs in the last four years and we are the 4th highest per capita job creator in the nation.

Taxes (and fear of taxes) keep businesses from investing, individuals from spending, and the economy from growing. In other words, taxes keep the unemployed from finding a job. Further, as Tennessee businesses hire more people, the demand for workers increases and wages and benefits go up for Tennesseans. Bringing increasing prosperity to people is the duty that directs my work in the legislature. By helping people find rewarding work, they are able to use the gifts God gave them, revealing His artistry to the created.

From my roots as the son of a man who toiled all his life and a woman who loved scripture, I've been fortunate in my life and my heart's desire now is to help others achieve the American Dream. In the end, it is freedom that brings prosperity, and it is prosperity that enables each of us to live up to His expectations: realizing our full individual and collective potential and helping those who cannot help themselves.

Contact: sen.mark.green@capitol.tn.gov
www.markgreenfortennessee.com

Magnificent Man

Tony Curtis Carter

*For I was hungry and you gave meat, I was thirsty and you gave
me drink, I was a stranger and you took me in, naked and you
clothed me, I was sick and you visited me, I was in prison and you
came unto me.*   *Matthew 25:35*

I always knew that I was somewhat different, because
when all the other children were out playing sports, riding their
bikes, and playing ball, I was out rescuing stray animals, and
helping the elderly with work around their houses. My elderly
aunt, when I was sixteen, told me that I was going to be a
preacher. I told her, "I can't be a preacher, because I'm a D.J"
Unbeknown to me, I was being prepared for something at the
time that was going to be the same passion, but it was going to be
on a much larger scale.

Born in Stuttgart, Germany February 19, 1961, I was the
youngest of four siblings. Growing up in a military family, I was
no stranger to structure and discipline. My parents instilled in me
at an early age what it meant to be honest and truthful in life, my
father used to say, if you're right you're right and if you're wrong
you're wrong. I accepted Christ at an early age, and was baptized

in the chilling waters of a spring creek. My family wasn't rich or wealthy, but I lacked for nothing as far as necessities of life. It is stated in Proverbs Chapter 22: Train up a child in the way he should go: and when he is old, he will not depart from it.

I was raised in Clarksville, TN, where I attended elementary, middle and high school. After graduating, I went straight into the entertainment field, which led me into radio on our local radio station WABD 1370. Then after four years on radio in Clarksville, TN. I moved to Nashville, TN. Where I worked at Meharry Medical College as an audiovisual technician for four years. I also took a part-time job as an on air personality at radio station WQQK 92-Q. Being in entertainment in my early 20s was quite exciting and glamorous. I rubbed elbows with superstars, MC'd concerts and was known throughout the city.

After meeting a young lady and dating for a year, she graduated and took a job in Silver Springs Maryland at NIH. We were in love with each other and made the move together. Her thing was baby you don't have to work; I make enough money for us to live. I was always told "God bless the child that has his own" so I found a job and went to work. After about six months, the relationship ended, and we both went our separate ways, but we remained friends. During that time, I lost my brother to a tragic car wreck, and then my father passed away. Those were my first brushes with death that I had ever experienced in my immediate family. After about a month, I decided to return to the line of work that I knew all so well, entertainment. I found a job in a nightclub that was a franchise and had clubs throughout the country.

While in entertainment I got so wrapped up in living the high life, I forgot about who was watching over me. At one point, I was introduced to drugs and then came alcohol. That could have led to destruction of most people, but it's obvious now that God had other plans for me. Although I was brought up in church and taught right from wrong, when I got out on my own things changed. As we know, when you become part of the world, the world becomes a part of you and that's a recipe for disaster. Drugs and alcohol became a part of everyday life for me for years. I thought it was the norm and that it came with the territory, when in fact it was the enemy trying to take me out early. I had lost focus, self-respect, and could have lost my life. But because of God's grace and mercy like the song says, "I'm still here."

After about 8 years of working in the club and all the foolishness that I allowed to happen, I was burnt out and needed a new start. I can remember praying and crying to GOD please help me to change. I called my friend in Atlanta and shared what was happening, and he said, "Why don't you move down to Atlanta?" Since I had lost everything, except my mind and belief in God, I moved. I got a job two weeks after I arrived there, but not in entertainment, thank you Jesus for a new start. It was like GOD reached in and snatched me out the fire. Things went well after the move to Atlanta. I worked as an audiovisual technician for four years. Then, I moved up into the lead technician and after that, I became the assistant manager in five years. Did I mention, I had repented and returned back to church? Well, I did!

After ten years in Atlanta, the company that I worked for asked me if I would go to Nashville and help for three weeks to set up the company at the Opryland hotel where we were taking over the production contract. I agreed to undertake that task, because I was going to be able to spend time with my surviving family. After getting the company set up and returning to Atlanta, I was offered a position as a coordinator, which was going to increase my pay by 40%. It was really a no brainer; I got to move back home to be closer to my family and made more money. God worked the situation out for my good. So, I took the new position and moved back to Nashville in 2005. Little did I know that it was going to be a bittersweet move? I found out after I returned home to Nashville, that my oldest brother had stage four cancer and my mother had suffered several mini strokes. But they were taking care of each other the best they could. Being the youngest in the family, they didn't want to tell me any of this, because they thought it would disrupt my life. So, I worked in Nashville for a couple of years and went back in fourth to Clarksville quite often. It was in 2006, on the streets of Nashville, TN. I was called into the ministry to spread the word and to tell how good God is. It started with the first bottle of water that I handed to someone who was living on the street. The person had nowhere to go and nothing to eat or drink. At that time, I was working a job that the Lord had blessed me with, and I was using those finances to buy water and food to give out to those individuals that found themselves living on the streets.

I found that a kind word, something to eat or drink, some scripture and prayer could help change lives or at least give someone hope. During my research on the street, I've found that there are some people that would rather be homeless than to get a job and be responsible. But there are those that have lost their job or a loved one and other situations that fell victim of the streets, and they wanted to get back on their feet, but they did not know how or where to get help. I have experienced firsthand, and I know the pain and mental stress it can cause in one's life. After hearing about a young black woman, who I had met, while ministering on the streets of Nashville, had been killed by two white men, while she slept by the river in the park. The call on my life became stronger and the mission became greater.

I joined one of Nashville's oldest black churches, where I got baptized and also played drums. Something started happened after that experience. It seemed that I would stand out on the corner by the church, and someone would come by needing some type of help, but they didn't know where to go. I started doing research on different agencies to find out what services they offered, and what people would need do to get help from the agencies. It became clear that there needed to be someone on the streets to be an advocate for those that had no clue what to do or where to go. I had already been blessed with the physical needs to go out and share information, a van, RV and the Spirit from God of helping. Little did I know; I was going to need much more than that.

"Jesus said, "My people are destroyed for lack of knowledge.""

In 2007 after praying about it, I left my well-paying job with benefits to do ministry full time on the streets of Nashville, and I never looked back. I gave away all my furniture, moved out of my apartment, and I lived in my RV in a RV park. Not long after that, I awoke one morning in tears, realizing I no longer had a paying job. What was I going to do? How was I going to make it? I knew this was what I was supposed to be doing. So, why was I worried? But as certain calmness came over me that morning, and my tears dried up, God said, "I will provide all of your needs." Then, he gave me the name of the organization, Homeless Task Force. I would wake up every morning and thank God for another day and guidance. After that, I headed to the streets of Nashville.

Soon, I returned to Clarksville to live with my family. I helped to take care of them. I took my brother to his chemotherapy and radiation appointments. My mother, although in her eighties, was a strong and virtuous woman, although she needed help going places and doing some things. In November, my brother's health took a turn for the worse, and he had to be rushed to the VA hospital in Nashville and put into CCU. I stayed by his side in a bed next to him for a week. On November 30th 2009, my brother lost his battle with cancer, and he went home to be with the Lord. Six months later, my mother had a massive stroke that took her speech and mobility at the same time. I stayed by her side until the end, and although my mother was a strong woman, this proved to be more than she could take. My sister and I had to admit her into a rehab, so she could receive the care that she couldn't get at home. My mother never recovered, and on November 7, 2010 she also went home to be with the Lord.

After losing my brother and then my mother within a year of each other, I felt that it was best for me to take some time off from the streets, and I hung up the uniform. I let God heal my pain and put me back together, because I was certainly broken. It was undoubtedly the hardest time of my life. I know GOD won't put more on you than you can handle. Although it was an emotional rollercoaster for about a year, it became clear to me that the uniform needed to be put back on, and I had to continue the mission. I knew that my mother and my brother, as well as my brother and father that preceded them, were proud of what I had accomplish through this ministry and that's what they would have expected of me. I know GOD doesn't make mistakes, and He will heal a broken heart. Today the Homeless Task Force in a strong and vibrant organization bridging the gap between the streets and the agencies of Clarksville, TN. The people get the help they need to get back on their feet by collaborating with all the local agencies here in the city. God has restored everything that the enemy had taken from me and multiplied it, which has made me become a stronger God-fearing man. I will stand up, be an advocate, and a voice for those whose voices would not be heard.

The Homeless Task Force has received several awards and letters for its contribution to the communities both in Nashville, TN. and Clarksville, TN. Although we are not a national organization like some outreach groups; our job and mission is just as important, to be able to extend the Kingdom is truly a blessing. To God be the glory for the things He has done.

Contact: tonycarter271@yahoo.com

Magnificent Man

Tre' Corley

In the day of prosperity be joyful, but in the day of adversity consider: God also hath set the one over against the other, to the end that man should find nothing after him. Ecclesiastes 7:14

I was only five years old when I stepped into the Oak Ridge Boy's studio for the first time with my family. I was not the least bit nervous because my brothers Bill, Sam and Paul along with my sister Hope, always encouraged. I remember being so excited to sing on my first single, "Smile", a song written by my late brother Sam Corley III and produced by Kenny Hinson, a friend of our family. The lyrics were written specifically for a little kid to sing, "even if you have false teeth, smile cause they look so neat! Smile, smile your frown away." It's crazy to think that my first and "only" single would actually get airplay in the Nashville area. After the single I went on to record my first full record, "To All My Friends". It was on this record I played the drums and sang, coached by my older brothers, Paul and Sam.

It was very rewarding growing up in a Southern Gospel family group, as it would pave the way to the future I would one day be blown away to have. I realized more as I got older that being on the road was never easy. My parents, Sam and Linda Corley, worked very hard to provide for our family and to keep a ministry going. They taught me how to never give up and that anything is possible with God. My Mom would always quote scriptures like Psalms 91, and my Father would always tell me to "Seek ye first the Kingdom of God..." I was blessed to always be surrounded by positive influences. I remember watching my Dad give his last $200 to a family in need knowing that it would keep us from having some of the things we wanted. My dad was a giver, which has heavily impacted my life.

At the age of nine God lead my parents to start a church in Joplin, MO. called Church On The Rock. It was there where my family set up our first "real" recording studio. No more makeshift vocal booths and singing out of bathrooms for us! My brother Paul was a genius at cutting two inch tape and fixing anything that was broken. At this time ADATs had just came out and we had our first two machines. It was Heaven! At this point in my life I really wasn't involved in the studio yet, but I was always watching as my brothers would play and my sister would sing background vocals to create albums for other artists. I was constantly surrounded by music because of my siblings and parents. Paul taught me drums, Sam taught me piano, Hope taught me how to deal with Sam and Paul... and my Mom prayed that we wouldn't all kill each other. We were a very close family.

By the age of sixteen I was the music director and played the piano at my parent's church. My brother Sam had moved to Arkansas to fulfill his calling, leaving some big shoes to fill. My brother Paul was left to run the studio by himself. I'll never forget when Paul entrusted me with a key to the studio and a set of my own ADAT tapes. I would play and record for hours upon hours, writing and arranging my own music from musical influences passed down from my family. I can't say that any of them were necessarily any good, but let's just say that I was the best producer in the room. Oh yeah... I was the ONLY producer in the room! This was the beginning of my producing career alongside Paul. We would work on projects together and if something got too hard Sam was just a few hours away and would always come help us finish.

One day I got a phone call from my brother Sam telling me he was packing up his family and moving to Nashville to start a record label. A few months later I found myself loading up my Toyota 4x4 pickup truck and moving too. Paul felt it was a good time to relocate Rock Solid Studio and his family as well. The year was 1998, and it was official, the Corley Brothers were reunited and ready to take on the Nashville scene together. I didn't start doing session work right off the bat, I still had to work on my chart reading and the ability to play in a high stress studio environment without mentally breaking down. I didn't want to fail as I had heard many stories of other musicians relocating only to plummet. You see in my home town I was a "Big Deal", but here.... HA! I found out the first day I had a lot of learning to do. In fact, one of my first studio session experiences didn't go so well. I found myself trying to play and sound like some of the other drummers I had looked up to in the studio. One of the players, Mike Douchette, came up to me and asked me what was wrong. I began to tell him that I was trying so hard to sound like Brewster, Bears, Porcaro and Phillips and I wasn't stacking up. He folded his arms and said, "If they want Brewster, they will hire Brewster, if they want Bears they will hire Bears, but they hired Tre' Corley, they want your style." I will never forget that moment. A light kicked on for me and I began to stop comparing myself to everyone else. Even the Bible teaches us that it isn't wise to compare yourself to one another. Sometimes we see what people have but we don't know what it took for them to get there. I also remember on a record Sam was producing where he was very irritated at me! He felt like I wasn't playing to the best of my abilities that day. He walked into the drum booth and yelled

"What in the world are you doing?!" I raised up a little off of my drum stool and sarcastically replied, "Well, I'm sitting on a drum throne... I've got drumsticks... I think I'm playing the drums!" He did not think that was very funny but laughed about it a lot later. Imagine having three very strong willed men with opinions, we butted heads all the time! It's a surprise somebody didn't get murdered! Only by the grace of God, my sister's refereeing and my Mother's prayers did we all survive.

At the age of nineteen I married my childhood sweetheart, Shawnel Davis, whom my brother Sam introduced me to when I was only fourteen. Yes, our first date was to the movie, "Water World", with my parents. Shawnel grew up in a very musical home as well and was willing to take on the lifestyle of a producer/musician. I've never asked her, but I don't know if she would be willing to do it a second time! The Bible says if you have found a good wife you've found a good thing. I am very grateful that God allowed us to meet at such a young age. Our history together is irreplaceable. Unfortunately, nobody explained to me that after you got married and moved into an apartment that you would not have enough money to do anything. We both had jobs working at Sam Ash Music struggling to make ends meet while trying to be an aspiring producer. At the time our studio, now called Oak Tree Studio, was in a small storefront building that Paul and I were running together. There wasn't enough money to take salaries so we both had full time jobs as well. Tired of struggling and wondering if I would ever make it I was offered a higher position at Sam Ash that paid more money. The only catch was it would take me away from the studio work I loved so much. I was already working tireless hours at my job during the day and programming and arranging all night long. Now I wouldn't even have time to do that. I sat with my wife and told her I really needed to take this position because I didn't feel like I was cut out to be a producer here, plus I needed to provide for my family. She took a stack of sticky notes and put all through the house, the mirrors, the doors, the hallways, "You are a producer, you can do it, I believe in you!" Try brushing your teeth or walking down a hallway seeing those notes everywhere! Needless to say I didn't take the position. As I said earlier, when you find a good wife you find a good thing.

The next decade of my life came with a lot of tests that I didn't know how to deal with. My oldest brother Bill, passed away, soon to follow him my Mother, and not to long after her my brother Sam. Family who I needed in my life to encourage me had all been taken from me by cancer.... Why did God allow this to happen to me? These were people who served God and loved God their whole life. My Mother was only 54 years old when she died, my brother Sam only 43, and here I am doing Christian music, trying to make a difference, and I felt He took the pieces that I needed to succeed. Not to mention my marriage was failing.

I kept searching for ways to change people and to make them what I wanted them to be. If it had not been for Joseph and Yolanda Morgan, my Pastors during this time, I would have lost my home. Pastor Morgan once told me you can have a house but that doesn't mean you have a home. I remember as I talked to both of them about why God was letting all of this happen to me. I was a good guy, I had made mistakes and wasn't perfect, but I didn't feel like I deserved all of this. Pastor Yolanda told me something I will never forget. She said, "Tre', when you were in high school what did the teacher do during a test?" I arrogantly said "I don't know"... I was so frustrated because God wasn't speaking to me through all of this. She said it again, "When you were in high school what did your teacher do during a test?" I said, "I don't know what you mean..." She said, "Did the teacher talk to you during the test?" My heart dropped, as I looked at her and said, "No ma'am... they didn't." She told me that the teacher is always silent during a test. "Don't fail this test Tre'!". I learned from this conversation and many others that I had some things internally to fix. Ecclesiastes 7:14 "In the day of prosperity be joyful, but in the day of adversity consider: God also hath set the one over against the other, to the end that man should find nothing after him." The Message Bible says "On a good day give thanks, on a bad day evaluate yourself..." I began to evaluate myself. I learned that God would never take away what I needed to fulfill His purpose for my life. That was the problem, I was trying to fulfill my purpose and not His. My focus changed from music, family, God to God, family, music.

My wife and I became the youth pastors of Celebration of Life Church. We began to pour into teenagers and in return we were fulfilled. I wasn't driven by music anymore, I was seeking God's purpose for my family. I had been nominated for several small awards, but nothing to really brag about. On a Wednesday night in 2006 I received a phone call after church from Jason Crabb asking me if I would like to attend the Grammys with him that year for a project we had worked on together, "Live at Brooklyn Tabernacle - The Crabb Family". I was blown away, I was not even trying to get that nomination. It was as if God gave me the desires of my heart and all I had to do was seek Him first. Oh wait that's what my Dad had been telling me since I was 5! Now I'm finally listening... They have a saying in the music business, "It's not what you know, it's who you know". I totally believe that now. It's not what you know, it's not how good you are, it's about being connected to God. If you don't know God you're not going to know His voice, if you don't have a relationship with Him how would you know what He sounds like? I began to have a prayer life with God daily, and it changed my life. Can you imagine never speaking to the person you love most and only speaking to them when you need something? That was my relationship with God. God wants to hear from us on a daily basis. He wants to be involved with your decision making, not just the decisions that don't matter.

I had several nominations for Dove awards, along with a few wins, and in 2009 I won my first Grammy after several nominations. I believe one of the keys to my success alongside seeking after God was discerning when He was testing me. If you don't realize that God is testing you and perfecting you then you can make very bad decisions based on what you feel instead of what you know. There's a lot to this story, this is just a small excerpt of mine. I remember my Mother lying in her bed before she passed away. It was just her and I in the room when she asked me what I was working on. I told her that Paul and I were working on a show for "Dino" but we had canceled so we could be with her. She was very upset because my Mother was adamant about her children succeeding. Despite her weakness she still managed the strength to lean up and say, "Get your butt back to work!"

We sometimes make decisions based on feelings, not realizing that life just happens. How many opportunities have we missed out on because we assumed we needed to quit? I'm not saying I shouldn't have postponed the job, but I am saying why was it in my head to quit? Remember I said earlier, God will never take away from you what you need to fulfill His purpose. So why should I be concerned about who and what God lets me keep and have? Yes, I'm very sad I lost my Mother and brothers, but through that I learned to never give up. In fact, it fueled my fire for success. The Bible says that weapons would be formed against us but none would prosper, and many have been formed to try and take my family out.

I am blessed to say that at 35 years old I have accomplished more in the music business than some people have in their whole life. I have had several interns and aspiring producers ask me what I did to get to where I am today. I always answer, "I learned to seek after God and His will." I also live by the philosophy that everything I have is really God's, so if He takes something away that means one of three things; He is testing me, it was a distraction, or He has something better! I don't look at loss anymore as a negative... I remind myself to look inwardly and either I truly believe that God has control of everything or He doesn't. Our company's tagline is "Taking over the world with positive music". How can I expect God to trust me with taking over the world if I can't trust Him with my money, my family, my job, etc?

My Pastor taught me to tie my gift to God's purpose for my life. If I can allow what I love to do which is "music", to be used with God's purpose He has for me then He will touch and multiply what I have. I am working now with clients and artists I would have never dreamed I would. My family now owns a studio and we now produce our own TV show. We didn't go in search of these things, God made them happen, and only He can shut the doors that He has opened for you. I want to encourage you today "Never Give Up!" God is in charge of everything no matter the situation and most of the time He is just waiting on you to let Him have full control. Thank you God for everything you have given me. I am forever grateful...

Contact: tre@oaktreestudio.com
www.oaktreestudio.com

Magnificent Man

Tyrone "Hollywood" Brown

God gave all of us 2 ends, one to think with and one to sit on. The amount of success that each and every one of us achieves in life depends on which end we use the most. It's just a mere decision of heads you win and tails you lose. – Tex Harrison

Background

I was born in Savannah, GA; the fourth of five siblings. My memories of childhood are happy and adventurous. I was fortunate to live in a neighborhood that was filled with athletes. We occupied ourselves playing collective games of football, basketball, and other sports. My neighborhood ties are very important to me. There was violence all around, but it didn't affect me. My love of sports kept me occupied. My memories are filled with fun and happy times. We believed that it took a village to raise a child; and a village is what we were.

I had my first experience with the Harlem Globetrotters at the age of nine watching ABC's Wide World of Sports. Mesmerized after seeing them, I told my mother I wanted to be one. She told me at the tender age of 9 that if I stay in school and take care of my body I could do anything. So I wrote down on a piece of paper these words, "I WANT TO BE A HARLEM GLOBETROTTER!" I hung it where I could see it and looked at it every day before I went to school. When I came home in the afternoons, I practiced from three o'clock, until my mother made me come inside.

So many children talk about what they want to be when they grow up, but so many do not put the time and work into it. They expect something to just happen for them over night. You not only have to work towards your goal, but you have to write it down! Eventually something will happen. Words have power.

Words Become Life

I have had the great fortune and privilege of knowing Coach Gator Rivers of the Harlem Globetrotters from a small child. Gator would come to our community center and teach me and other children about basketball. He would come to Savannah, GA during the Harlem Globetrotters off season to teach the Globetrotters show and tricks to kids at the center. I caught his attention by learning all of his tricks and then coming up with some of my own. He assured me a Globetrotter try-out after I completed college. I attended 2 years at Savannah State and also another junior college a few years later

After college I was excited to begin my basketball career. It did not turn out to be the journey that I had anticipated. I was cut 14 times from several different teams including the 76ers, the Hawks, and 11 continental basketball teams. I was not one to be discouraged, and Gator came through on his promise to get me the try-out for the Harlem Globetrotters.

I was excited and ready on try-out day to be a Harlem Globetrotter. I went into that gym and showed them everything I had. I worked hard and knew that this was definitely about to be the moment I had been waiting for since I was nine years old. I was cut from the Globetrotter team 2 weeks into the camp. I was not willing to let go at the point either. During this time, I tried out for the opposing rival team of the Harlem Globetrotters, the Washington Generals. They were the main rivals of the Globetrotters. I made Washington's team and after three months of playing for the Generals, our first game against the Globetrotters, I was given a chance by the owner of the Globetrotters to play for their team then was recruited and offered a contract. The rest is now history.

Life as a Harlem Globetrotter

Playing ball was just one of the amazing benefits of being a Harlem Globetrotter. I was able to see the world. People will ask me what are some places I've been and I tell them, it would be easier to tell you some places I have not been. I have been to the Great Wall of China. I saw the Berlin Wall before AND after it was taken down. I've been inside the Rome Coliseum and floated in the Dead Sea. I have met so many people and have had fabulous opportunities to participate in productions such as Michael Jackson's Smooth Criminal video and other music videos as well. I had a spot on LA Law and in the Hank Aaron story. I have been able to do some screenwriting and wrote a children's book.

I have never taken this experience for granted. I am thankful for the many blessings I have received. I was able to pay it all forward by going back to my community and getting two of my childhood friends to try-out for the Globetrotters team, and they both made the team as well.

Life Now

I am often asked do I miss playing for the Globetrotters. I can answer with an easy no. I still have a platform and get to entertain and encourage children. Every year I get to speak to more than 150 schools and motivate their students. I teach them to make great choices in life, set goals, work hard and be determined to achieve those goals. I am truly honored and inspired by the reception I get from them. My prayer each day is that God allows me to reach at least one child; and He certainly goes farther beyond just the one. I can also see the difference it makes in the teachers and administrators as well.

A PIECE OF PAPER

TYRONE "HOLLYWOOD" BROWN

Fan Support

I have been so blessed by the great support and reviews about my book **A Piece of Paper.** My mother was my biggest inspiration who believed in me along with so many others. I am humbled, blessed, and grateful. I am very inspired to continue writing and supporting our youth. With so many children in our world today going astray, they need more role models from local communities that they can see. People who will inspire them to succeed. Because I wrote it down on a piece of paper, as my mother instructed me, I am thankful for where God has taken me. My fans from throughout the globe mean the world to me. I am encouraged by their words daily and want to thank them all for encouraging me to keep pushing ahead. Here are some comments I'd like to share from readers who have taken out the time to read my first book. This is my way of saying 'Thank You' to them as well. Their feedback about the book has only encouraged me more in my writing and in profession. Again, I am thankful and inspired by your words. Humbly blessed.

"This was an interesting inside look into the career path of a former Harlem Globetrotter. I enjoyed Mr. Brown's book A Piece of Paper and would especially recommend this work to young men who are struggling to set goals for their life and stay on track, in school and aimed at the target. Tyrone shares how thankful he is to all of the people in his life who gave him encouragement, a hand up and help along the way to get to where he wanted to go. He tells of meeting famous folks, performing for huge crowds and small classrooms and finally being able to meet his idols, the Globetrotters themselves. I was shocked to learn how training intensive the HG team is and how busy their travel schedule is. Good little read here, especially for young men close to being launched from home into the world."   **-Paul D.**

"This book is more than just the life story of a basketball player. It is also a good example of setting a goal and striving to achieve it. It is about having a passion for something and going for it. However, the book teaches another lesson to youngsters. It

tells them having a goal and the passion for it is not enough. You must be prepared and determined to get back on track if you happen to get side-tracked for any reason. You may fail after several attempts but you must have the strength and the determination to get back up and try until you succeed. Having a mentor is a huge plus. A useful book for anyone setting out on a path in search of success." **-S. Roystone Neverstone**

"Does writing to a paper make you successful? Does thinking make you a man of time? Does hard work alone take you to the top? Does it happen the next day? 1001 questions and this answers it all. Its NOT just one of those, but all of those. Tyrone "Hollywood" Brown had positive attitude, perseverance and determination to become a Harlem Globetrotter. He did not work for 1 year or 2 years, but for 16 years, he worked hard to improve his game, along with a great attitude. Colors, illustrations, etc make this book even better.

"I did not read this to understand success, but to get more energy to persist longer, stronger and better! I recommend this book to anyone who needs to succeed, who is yet to start in the path of success, who is confused, who is about to quit, who is in doubt on your success, and anyone whose lives are marked with words goals, aim, success, failure or at least an urge to do something." **-Karnika E. Y.**

"The autobiographical story of Tyrone 'Hollywood' Brown makes fascinating reading for kids who have a dream and want it to come true. It shows how a wish, simply written on a piece of paper at the age of nine, combined with hard training, has turned a little kid with a dream into a Harlem Globetrotter superstar. Well written and entertaining to read. I can recommend this book to children between the age of nine to twelve." **-E. N. Heenk**

"A Piece of Paper" is a great inspirational story, not just for kids, but also preteens, teens, and even young adults. The story is perfect for teaching you to never lose hope on your

394

dreams, don't give up because you've been shot down a couple of times, and also the importance of exercise. If you have any dream whatsoever, you should never give up. What I like about this book is that, besides the fact of it being a lesson, it's also Tyrone "Hollywood" Brown's memoir. Most memoirs are, honestly, self-centered, talking about how great they are at whatever it is they do. Brown wants to inform his readers, give them advice, and help them be healthy.' - **Carey S.**

"For the past 40 years I have had a calling to inspire youth. From leading the "children's" service at my church to teaching in the public school system, I have always been on the lookout for that one at-risk boy or girl that needs some direction. When I was a child my mother couldn't afford to feed my brothers and sisters, so instead of ending up living on the street, she placed me in a children's home. I grew up with a bad attitude until a teacher got a hold of me and turned my life around. Because of that teacher who showed me how to dedicate myself, I ended up playing football, became a star in high school back in the 60's, and was even known city wide for my prowess. I used my story to inspire youth that have had the wrong attitude or were simply misguided. Tragically, after my wife passed away last year, I lost much of my inspiration. I am now a substitute teacher and found myself avoiding the troubled youth, something I would have taken head on prior to my wife passing away. Yet today is a different day. This book has re-inspired me to keep working with children and youth. "Hollywood" Brown's story is one that youth and adults should read. The youth need to see what they can accomplish with dedication and hard work, and adults to remind them that we do make a difference in the lives of this young generation. I plan on recommending this book to every student I can reach and so should you.

I give this book my highest recommendation. It is well worth the purchase price and should be read and shared with everyone you come into contact with." - **Bobby H.**

"I loved this inspirational story that warmed my heart! Tyrone Brown is an inspiration who shows that with hard work and persistence, humongous goals can be achieved! This is a book I plan on saving and sharing with my children." - **Tamara**

Conclusion

I do currently have a book out entitled, <u>A Piece of Paper</u>. When you read it, I don't want you to just think about sports. Being a professional athlete does not last forever. There are so many choices out there; doctor, lawyer, radio dj, talk show hosts, CEOs and the list continues. You can take my story and apply it to any career choice that you have.

It doesn't matter what goals you set in life, make sure that they are positive. If you are determined, and you are persistent and you work hard, there's the strong possibility that you can achieve any goal that you set out to achieve.

Contact: tybro2000@yahoo.com
https://www.linkedin.com/in/tyronehollywoodbrown

Sponsored Remarks

Where there is no vision, the people perish
Black History Month is Not Dead
Sponsored Chapter by Magnificent Man Pastor Jimmy Terry

Waiting for possibility thinkers to emerge.
If we work for Black History Month, Black History Month will work for us.

An open letter to the more than 42 million African Americans in these United States. Am I the only African American in this county whose eyes are open to the vast possibilities and opportunities locked up in Black History Month? My name is Jimmy Terry, Sr., I was born in Tuscaloosa, AL. I am seventy-six years old. I love my God, my country, and my people. The intent of this open letter is to glorify my God, strengthen my country and uplift my people.

The Opening of My Eyes
Learn the song "Lift Ev'ry Voice and Sing"

Where there is no vision, the people perish. As a lad growing up, I periodically overheard the elders say in my little community with mild frustration, *"Just think if every colored person would give just one dollar. Just think what we would have."* Leaving Tuscaloosa at the age of seventeen to live in Dayton, OH, I heard the same sentiments. Joining the United States Navy on the U.S.S. Saratoga (Plank Owner), the same words were uttered. Upon getting settled in at Clarksville, Tennessee (the home of Wilma Rudolph, three-time Olympic Gold Medal Winner) you guessed it, "Just think if every African American just gave one dollar, look what we would have." Even today, these words are being expressed in our barber shops, beauty shops, on the job, in sermons, in bars, social clubs, fraternities, sororities, family reunions, etc. – ENOUGH TALK!!!

My brothers and sisters I have carried many of these thoughts within me since childhood. Now I am sharing them with you, praying that Almighty God will open your eyes, as He has mine, so that you may be able to see the vast possibilities and opportunities locked up in Black History Month as I see them. Ask yourself this question, what is 'the national vision for African Americans in this country" To my knowledge there is none. The Bible says, "Where there is no vision, the people perish." Proverbs 29:18a KJV. As I see it, we are slowly perishing. But I say unto you, we can and must correct his slow demise.

The Vision
Learn the song, "Lift Ev'ry Voice ad Sing

Dr. Carter G. Woodson, the father of Black History Month, declared prophetically in 1922 "Liberty is to come to the Negro, not as a bequest, but as a conquest. When I speak of it as a conquest, I mean that the Negro must contribute something to the good of his race, something to the good of his county and something to the honor and glory of God. Economic independence is the first step in that direction.

Where there is no vision, the people perish. I want to put before you the vision God has given me in conjunction with Dr. Woodson's statement of economic independence for 2015 and beyond. We have entered another Black History Month another the twenty-eight days- African Americas – another twenty-eight days, 28 DAYS! What will we do with them? 1) Blame others for our shortcomings 2) Reminisce about the good old days; 3) Talk about your 40 acres and your mule; 4) Fret, because February is the shortest month of the year 5) Glory in the accomplishments of Booker T. Washington, Harriet Tubman, etc. Would you agree with me that we should: 1. Reflect on our past history. We learn from that; 2. Evaluate the Present. See where we are now; 3. Plan and project for the future. That we may build on it year after year! I truly believe that Black History Month should indeed be a time for reflection on the past, but not for twenty-eight days!

African Americans you know as well as I that money is a significant driving force in this country and as a people we must accumulate and control a portion of the financial resources for the betterment of our people and America as a whole. For too long we have waited, pleased, begged and protested for others to do for us what we can do for ourselves.

1. **IF ONE MILLION AFRICAN AMERICANS GAVE $1000 THAT WOULD BE ONE BILLION DOLLARS - $1,000,000,000**
2. **IF ONE MILLION GAVE $500 THAT WOULD BE FIVE HUNDRED MILLION DOLLARS - $500,000,000**
3. **IF ONE MILLION GAVE $100 THAT WOULD BE ONE HUNDRED MILLION DOLLARS - $100,000,000**
4. **IF ONE MILLION GAVE JUST $25 THAT WOULD BE TWENTY-FIVE MILLION DOLLARS. $25,000,000. TOTALLING: ONE BILLION SIX HUNDRED AND TWENTY-FIVE MILLION DOLLARS - $1,625,000,000**

Stay with me now…Did you notice that this only reflects four categories of the 24 million African Americans in this country. African Americans, WE CAN DO THIS!

What I am suggesting is being done successfully every year by the United Way and other worthwhile causes to accomplish their goals. Over the years we have faithfully helped the United Way reach its goal. African Americans can do this for ourselves as well and even better if we choose to do so. By the way, continue to support the United Way and these organizations. We can do this, we must do this. With God's help we will do this.

African Americans for fear you have not noticed this is 2015 and we are living in a million, billion, trillion dollar society. Keep in mind we are speaking of repeating this consolidated effort every – February – Black History Month – every year – We can Do This!!! WE must redefine Black History Month.

THE CHALLENGE
Learn the song, "Lift Ev'ry Voice and Sing"

Where there is no vision, the people perish.
Now you are asking what steps must we take? Well, the first thing we must do is PRAY Jesus said, *"Without me you can do nothing."* John 15:5

THE CHALLENGE
Learn the song, "Lift Ev'ry Voice and Sing"
Where there is no vision, the people perish.

Now you are asking what steps must we take? Well, the first thing we must do is PRAY Jesus said, "Without me you can do nothing." John 15:5, PRAY, The second thing is to seek national African American leaders that will catch the vision such as:

Presidents of the National Religion Conventions, Harry Belafonte, Bill Cosby, Oprah Winfrey, George Curry, Congressman John Lewis, General Colin Powell, Ervin Magic Johnson, Condoleezza Rice, Tom Joyner, Tony Brown, Steve Harvey, Earl Graves, Sr. or Jr. or both and other people of such influence. As well as Historically Black College Presidents, who I think should take the lead, Historically Black College Alumni Presidents, presidents of fraternities and sororities, the chairman of the National Black Caucus, Masonic Lodges, and Eastern Stars.

Persons such as these along with the black press would convene at a historical Black College for this purpose and this one purpose ONLY and use their expertise and influence to bring together a group of people and staff to make this vision a reality. I see financial empowerment as the last great frontier for us as a people to conquer. We cannot wait for anyone else to do it for us. We must do it ourselves. I applaud our brothers and sisters of other races the Jews, Cubans, Koreans, Vietnamese, Hispanics, Germans, Irish, Italians, Hungarians and other ethnic groups who have come to this country and accomplished great things. Let's not criticize them but learn from them and move ahead with possibility thinking as well.

Brothers and Sisters we have been in this country since 1619. Considering the hardships we've come through, to put it mildly, we've done well. As a preacher/pastor visionary, again I say, I truly believe that this is the final frontier for African Americans to CONQUER – and we should strive with every ounce of blood, sweat and tears to make it a reality for this present and future generations.

EXPRESSING LONG OVERDUE GRATITUDE
Learn the song, "Lift Ev'ry Voice and Sing"

Where there is no vision, the people perish.

Let us make Dr. W.E.B. DuBois proud for he said *"The Negro race, like all races, is going to be saved by its exceptional men. The problem of education, then, among Negroes must first of all deal with the Talented Tenth; It is the problem of developing the Best of this race that they may guide the Mass away from the contamination and death of the Worst, in their own and other races"*

Let us do it in honor of the many both living and dead such as Dr. Martin Luther King, Jr., John Brown, The Little Rock Nine Congressman John Lewis, Fannie Lou Hamer, Megar Evers, Ron Brown, Jackie Robinson, Thurgood Marshall, Thaddeus Stevens, The Greensboro Four, Julie Rosenwald, Al Sharpton, Jessie Lewis Jackson, Frederick Douglas and so many more, especially our white brothers and sisters who risked and even lost their lives to help us secure our freedom. Roy Wilkins, Nat Turner, Diane Nash, Louis Farrakhan, Tony Brown, James Earl Chaney, Andrew Goodman, and Michael Schwerner, the 16th Street Baptist Church Sunday School Girls of Birmingham, AL, Sept.

401

15, 1963 and the list goes on.

Let us remember the challenging words of Senator Robert Kennedy –

"The future does not belong to those who are content with today, apathetic toward common problems and their fellowman alike, timid and fearful in the face of new ideas and bold projects. Rather it will belong to those who can blend vision, reason and courage in a personal commitment to the ideals and great enterprises of American society." -1966 South Africa on their Day of Affirmation.

President Barack Obama

As our illustrious President Barack Obama stated on January 8, 2008, *"For when we have faced down impossible odds; when we have been told that we are not ready, or that we should not try or that we are not ready, or that we should not try or that we can't, generations of Americans have responded with a simple creed that sums up the spirit of a people: YES WE CAN."*

It worked once, it will work again. YES WE CAN!

Let's make this the last year we utter these worn out platitudes and clichés of "Where do we go from here?" or "Yes, we have come a long way, but we have a long way to go." Working hand-in-hand we can shorten this journey. My brothers and sisters, we can do this only by moving ahead with great vision and great possibility thinking. You know as well as I, it will take an unrelenting dedication and totally embracing this vision to make it a reality and to make America a better place to live. We can do this!

This is not a "Somebody need to do something" article, it is a suggestive, workable plan that God has given me for approximately 42 million African Americans in this country to come together and dream big dreams with the vision presented

402

here.

As Grace Malone, a seven year old first grader at Tabernacle Christian School in Clarksville, Tennessee, wrote after sitting in her solitary space to finish writing Joshua 1:8.9 from memory with all of her grammatical errors she wrote: "I did my Best." So I say to you, Lord, "I've done my best. Now brothers and sisters we must together step forward and collectively take it from here.

If anything I've said in this open letter offends anyone, please forgive me that was never my intents. Philemon 1:21 KJV (look it up).

Learn the song, "Lift Ev'ry Voice and Sing"
James Weldon Johnson & J. Rosamond Johnson

1. Lift every voice and sing, till earth and Heaven ring,
   Ring with the harmonies of liberty;
   Let our rejoicing rise, high as the listening skies,
   Let it resound loud as the rolling sea.
   Sing a song full of the faith that the dark past has taught us,
   Sing a song full of the hope that the present has brought us;
   Facing the rising sun of our new day begun,
   Let us march on till victory is won.

2. Stony the road we trod, bitter the chastening rod,
   Felt in the days when hope unborn had died;
   Yet with a steady beat, have not our weary feet,
   Come to the place for which our fathers sighed?
   We have come over a way that with tears has been watered,
   We have come, treading our path through the blood of the slaughtered;
   Out from the gloomy past, till now we stand at last
   Where the white gleam of our bright star is cast.

403

3. God of our weary years, God of our silent tears,
Thou Who hast brought us thus far on the way;
Thou Who hast by Thy might, led us into the light,
Keep us forever in the path, we pray.
Lest our feet stray from the places, our God, where we
met Thee.
Lest our hearts, drunk with the wine of the world, we
forget Thee.
Shadowed beneath Thy hand, may we forever stand,
True to our God, true to our native land.

Contact: VisonTB@Bellsouth.net

The above written article is a sponsored piece by Pastor Jimmy Terry. It does not belong to the Magnificent Men Book or to Treva R. Gordon or to its authors. It is a sponsored article.

A Special Note of Thanks from Treva R. Gordon

I want to thank God for all things made possible. Thanking God for my husband, Robert, for his support and for our children, Robert Jr, Tevin, and Robyn Gordon.

Special thanks to the following angels for their assistance. I thank you all so much for your support:

Jamie Lynn
Tara Eckwood
Marie Lewis
Melissa Schaffner
Edward Eick
Carol Berry
Deborah A. Culp
Yolonda Williams
Richard "Reason" Garrett

Don't Quit

When Things go wrong, as they sometimes will,
When the road you're trudging seems all uphill,
When the funds are low and debts are high,
And you want to Smile but have to sigh.
When care is pressing you down a bit,
Rest, if you must, but don't you quit.

Life is queer with its twists and turns,
As every one of us sometimes learns,
And many a failure turns about,
When he might have won if he'd stuck it out,
Don't give up though the pace seems slow,
You might succeed with another blow.

Often the struggler has given up,
When he might captured the victor's cup.
And he learned too late, when the night slipped down,
How close he was to the golden crown,

Success is failure turned inside out,
The silver tint of clouds of doubt,
And you never can tell how close you are,
It may be near when it seems afar,
So stick to the fight when you're hardest hit,
It's when things seem worst that you mustn't quit.

About the Author and Visionary

Evangelist Treva R. Gordon is an author, publisher, motivational speaker, and founding visionary of the books Magnificent Men and Leading Ladies. She is responsible for spearheading the collection of more than 100 authors to date. In 2013, she published her first book through Xlibris Publishing called Leading Ladies - Sharing Our Stories of Inspiration and Faith. After much prayer and consideration, she released her second book in 2015 under Liberated Publishing called Magnificent Men - Telling Our Stories, and Sharing Our Faith with 50 authors. These books are very inspiring.

Mrs. Gordon is a native of Detroit, Michigan, now living Tennessee with her husband Robert of 22 years, and together they have 3 children (Robert Jr. 19- serving in the U.S. Navy, Tevin 14- Sports Analyst for the Treva Radio Show, and Robyn 11- USA National Miss Preteen Tennessee).

Treva also works in the media as a TV/Radio Show Host, Producer, and Personality. She is the Publisher and CEO of Convenient Shopper Magazine for a decade. Treva holds a B.S. in

Corporate Communications and Marketing from Austin Peay State University. Throughout the years she has spearheaded conferences, workshops, luncheons, plays, business networking events, and more to include sharing major platforms with men and women such as Wess Morgan, Dr. Bobby Jones, Elbernita "Twinkie" Clark, Dr. Dorinda Clark Cole, Tye Tribbett, Pastors Joseph and Yolanda Morgan, and others. She has covered major award shows and red carpets to include the Stellars, Dove, Gospel Music City Awards, and the Inspirational Country Music Awards.

She has appeared on national TV networks to include The WORD Channel, TBN, CBN, and other affiliates. In 2010, she founded Clarksville Unity Day, a community day set aside to honor local hometown heroes. She also serves as Vice President of Gordon Publishing, alongside her husband Robert Gordon, who established the company in 2002. In 2011, her ministry gave birth to Team Purpose; a ministry that goes behind the prison walls to share God's love with staff and inmates. In 2014, Treva's medical miracle testimony aired worldwide on the CBN 700 Club Network. It was through God's healing power that she is alive today after a near death experience after the birth of her daughter Robyn in 2004.

Treva gives all praise, glory, and honor to God, who allows her faith in Christ to triumph. For more information about Treva Gordon, Leading Ladies, Magnificent Men, or more, visit: www.TrevaGordon.com or www.TrevaGordonSpeaks.com

Order the book
Leading Ladies Sharing Our Stories of Inspiration and Faith
by Treva R. Gordon

Featuring 50 Women sharing their personal stories of faith. It is
an inspiration to all who will read. The foreword is written by
Tennessee State Senator Thelma Harper and also includes
Grammy Award Winning Recording Artist Dr. Dorinda Clark
Cole, Pastor Yolanda Morgan, Tennessee Speaker of the House
of Representatives Beth Harwell, Clarksville, TN Mayor Kim
McMillan and more. The book was first published in 2013.

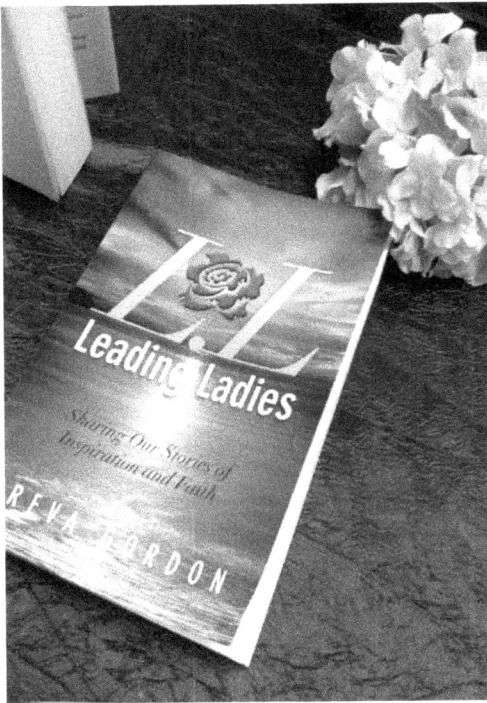

Soft $19.99
Hard $29.99
www.TrevaGordon.com

Photo Billboard Shoot for Leading Ladies and Magnificent Men 2015 (stay tuned)

Makeup Artist: Kennie Hall, Nashville, TN
Salon: Salon Ice - Tanya Davis of Nashville, TN
Photography: Jonathan Snorten
Chris Bond of Symmetry Media Group

From Left to Right:
Celestine McNeal, Katobwa Stallworth, Jacqueline Lisenby,
Laura Payne, Treva R. Gordon, Chris Bond,
Tanya Davis, Sandra Vega-Jones, Ebony Rivers.

Look for great events, productions, and more coming:
www.TrevaGordon.com
www.TrevaGordonSpeaks.com
www.GodsMagnificentMen.com
www.LeadingLadiesWin.com
www.CshopperMagazine.com

MAGNIFICENT MMEN.

One Moment in Time
Photo by: Kelvin Braxton of Braxton
Photography
Makeup Artist: Tomeka Jones
Location site: Nashville, TN at Centennial Park

Photo feature from left to right:
Tre' Corley
Wess Morgan
Maurice Johnson
Kevin C. Kennedy
Ralph Payne
Pastor Franklin Jackson
Elder, Dr. Shawn A. Jenkins Sr.

About the Publisher

City Councilman Richard Garrett has gained extensive business knowledge and negotiating skills as the Executive Director of the LEAP Organization. LEAP provides youth development services. As a licensed realtor for Keller Williams Realty, he is known for his tenacity, perseverance, honesty, and fairness. A proud APSU alum, Richard graduated with Honors with a Bachelors in Public Management.

Richard is a former active duty Marine, father of 4, and a husband with strong ties to the community. He is a graduate of Leadership Clarksville and Leadership CMCSS and is a member of Clarksville Rotary, Clarksville Area Ministerial Association, Chamber of Commerce, Clarksville Association of Realtors Public Relations & Charity Relations Committees, and Clarksville Community Partners Group.

In his spare time, Richard is also the CEO of Liberated Publishing Inc., which he started in March of 2007 after publishing his first novel "Sensual Delights Fantasies of a Poet." His 2nd novel "Reality Check" was published in 2010.

Personal Notes

"Be Inspired to LIVE, LIVE to be INSPIRED"
– Treva R. Gordon

Personal Notes

"A Magnificent Man is a Man who Loves God, Family, and Community. He is a man of Faith and of Courage. He will work to pursue peace. He is a man of action and integrity." – Treva R. Gordon

---

Inspirational Quotes from Treva R. Gordon

"The more you GO, the more you KNOW, therefore you GROW. Step out on Faith. Now is your time."

"God will reward the man who at least tries, versus the man who does nothing at all. Don't be afraid of challenges. Get up and Get it Done."

"Be who God has called you to be. You are not a duplicate of someone else. You may be often imitated but never duplicated."

"Love stretches far and wide, so bask in it. Now Feel It, then Give it, for others to Share It."

"Give every situation over to God, because He can handle all things. Not only is He a burden lifter, but He is a delight who brings great joy."

"Be committed to your cause; quitting isn't or shouldn't be your option. God is with you every step that you take."

"You are better with God, than without Him. Take God everyone you go."

Liberated Publishing Inc.
1860 Wilma Rudolph Blvd
Clarksville, TN 37040
info@liberatedpublishing.com
931-378-0500

www.LiberatedPublishing.com

www.ingramcontent.com/pod-product-compliance
Lightning Source LLC
Chambersburg PA
CBHW062356090426
42740CB00010B/1298